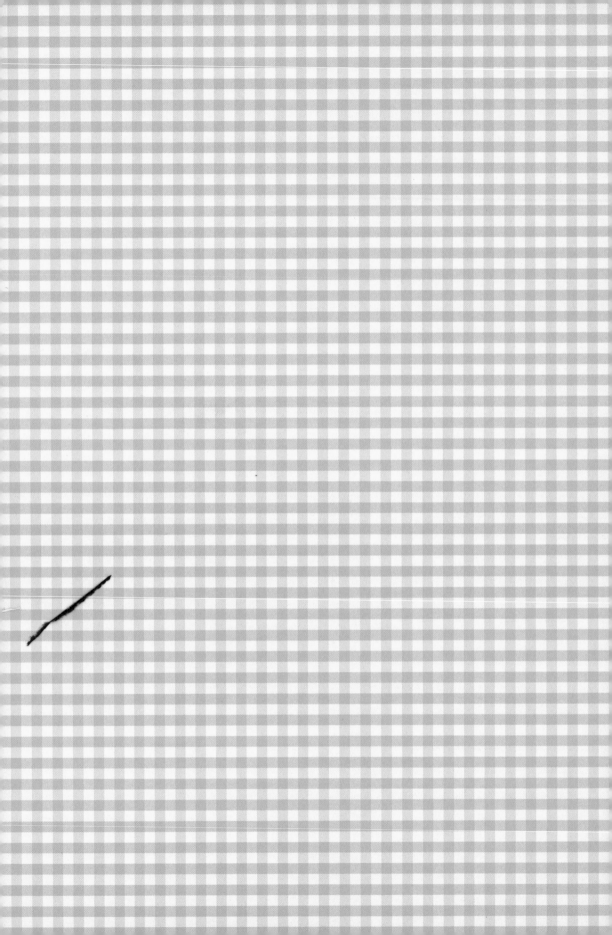

This book belongs to:

_____

_____

OVERNIGHT MARINATED SHRIMP

Also known as pickled shrimp, this appetizer is showstopping party fare. Serve this in a lovely glass bowl, large jar, or one of those enormous shell-shaped serving bowls. The tempting ingredients are too pretty to hide.

Makes 12 to 15 servings

1   Tbsp. plus ½ tsp. salt, divided
3   lb. unpeeled, large fresh shrimp
2   small red onions, cut into strips
1   yellow bell pepper, cut into strips
1   cup vegetable oil
1   cup red wine vinegar
3   Tbsp. sugar
1   Tbsp. finely grated fresh lemon zest

3   Tbsp. fresh lemon juice
1   Tbsp. Worcestershire sauce
1   Tbsp. hot sauce
1   Tbsp. Dijon mustard
½   tsp. salt
2   garlic cloves, finely chopped
½   cup chopped fresh basil
Garnish: basil leaves

1. Bring 7½ cups water and 1 Tbsp. salt to a boil. Remove from heat. Add shrimp, and let stand 2 to 3 minutes or only until shrimp turn pink, stirring once. Drain and rinse with cold water. Peel shrimp, and, if desired, devein.
2. Layer shrimp, onion, and bell pepper in an airtight container.
3. Whisk together vegetable oil, vinegar, sugar, lemon zest, lemon juice, Worcestershire, hot sauce, Dijon, salt, and garlic; pour over shrimp. Cover and chill 24 hours, stirring occasionally.
4. Stir in basil just before serving.

From the kitchen of Ursula Ann Mazzolini
Santa Rosa Beach, Florida

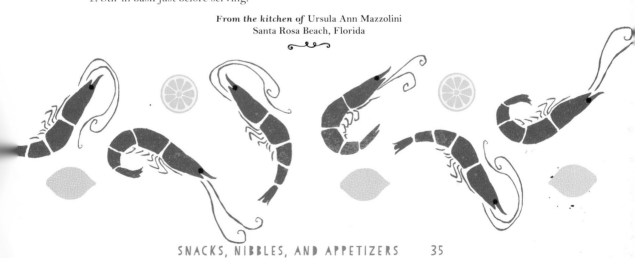

BROILED OYSTERS ON THE HALF SHELL

For many of us, few treats feel more luxurious than a platter of oysters. Because of our long coastline, there are few places in the South where we can't get great fresh oysters. Lucky us. If you are looking for good advice on selecting, shucking, and serving oysters, talk to an oyster fisherman or trusted fishmonger. They will never steer you wrong when giving advice on how to best enjoy their wares. By the way, "oyster liquor" is the delicious liquid that surrounds the oyster in the shell, not some sort of experimental distillation gone horribly wrong. Shucked oysters are sold in their liquor.

Makes 8 to 10 servings

Rock salt
2 dozen medium-size fresh oysters in the shell
2 Tbsp. butter, divided
2 Tbsp. olive oil, divided
1½ cups day-old breadcrumbs from French bread
¾ cup finely chopped green onions
¼ cup (1 oz.) freshly grated Parmigiano-Reggiano cheese

4 garlic cloves, finely chopped
4 Tbsp. finely chopped fresh flat-leaf parsley
2 tsp. finely chopped fresh thyme
2 tsp. finely chopped fresh oregano
½ tsp. kosher salt
½ tsp. freshly ground black pepper
Pinch of ground red pepper

1. Spread rock salt in a ⅛-inch layer in a roasting pan or other very large shallow baking pan.
2. Shuck oysters, reserving bottom shells; discard top shells. Reserve 1 Tbsp. oyster liquor. Gently loosen oyster from shell, using an oyster knife. Place oysters, in shells, on rock salt.
3. Preheat broiler with oven rack 6 inches from heat.
4. Melt 1 Tbsp. butter with 1 Tbsp. olive oil in a large skillet over low heat. Stir in bread-crumbs, green onions, Parmigiano-Reggiano, garlic, parsley, thyme, oregano, salt, black pepper, and ground red pepper. Remove from heat.
5. Melt remaining 1 Tbsp. butter and 1 Tbsp. olive oil in a small microwave-safe bowl at HIGH for 20 seconds or in a small saucepan over low heat. Stir in reserved oyster liquor.
6. Spoon breadcrumb mixture over oysters; drizzle with butter mixture.
7. Broil 5 to 6 minutes or until tops are crisp and browned. Serve immediately.

BROILED OYSTERS:

Preshucked oysters work well for this. Reserve 2 Tbsp. oyster liquor. Omit rock salt. Prepare recipe as directed, doubling ingredient amounts. Shuck oysters, discarding shells, and place oysters in a single layer in a 13- x 9-inch pan. Top with breadcrumb mixture; broil until tops are crisp and browned.

From the kitchen of Jim Gossen
Grand Isle, Louisiana

FRESH BLUEBERRY SALSA

Fresh blueberries provide the sweet while crunchy peppers and cilantro provide the savory in this fresh, colorful salsa. This recipe is equally delicious made with fresh strawberries, mango, or pineapple. Fruit salsa can be served with chips, of course, but also makes a great relish for grilled chicken or fish.

Makes about 3½ cups

- 2   cups coarsely chopped fresh blueberries
- 1   cup whole fresh blueberries
- ¼   cup fresh lemon juice
- 3   Tbsp. chopped fresh cilantro
- 2   jalapeño peppers, seeded and finely chopped
- ⅓   cup diced red bell pepper
- ½   tsp. kosher salt
- ½   tsp. packed brown sugar (optional)

Serve with: flour tortilla chips or cinnamon-sugar pita crisps

1. Toss together chopped blueberries, whole blueberries, lemon juice, cilantro, jalapeños, bell pepper, and salt in a large bowl. Stir in brown sugar, if desired. Let stand 5 minutes, stirring occasionally.

2. Serve immediately, or cover and chill up to 8 hours. Serve with chips or crisps.

From the kitchen of Julie Foster
Norcross, Georgia

CANDIED BACON BITES

Salty, sweet, and smoky—this is what some people call pig candy. Think bacon doesn't sound like a party food? Put out a bowl of bite-sized pieces (perhaps mixed with candied pecans) and see how quickly people empty the bowl, if you don't eat it all by yourself before they get a chance. Candied bacon makes a wonderful bar snack to accompany bourbon or Champagne.

Makes 1 lb.

1   lb. thick-cut bacon slices
½   cup firmly packed dark brown sugar

1   Tbsp. freshly cracked black pepper

1. Preheat oven to 325°. Line a rimmed baking sheet with parchment paper or aluminum foil.
2. Separate bacon into slices, and let stand at room temperature 5 minutes.
3. Stir together sugar and pepper. Lightly and evenly coat bacon slices in brown sugar mixture.
4. Arrange slices on baking sheet in single layer. Sprinkle any remaining sugar mixture over bacon.
5. Bake at 325° in center of oven for 35 minutes or until golden brown and firm. Let stand 1 minute; transfer to plate in single layer to cool. (Do not let bacon cool on baking sheet or it will stick fast.) Bacon continues to crisp as it cools.
6. Cut slices into bite-sized pieces, if desired.

From the kitchen of Jackie Sineath
Safety Harbor, Florida

DEVILED HAM

A survey of Southern cookbooks from the 1950s and 1960s would suggest that canned deviled ham was a pantry staple. Cooks put it in everything, from appetizers to soups to entrées. Perhaps we overdid it. Time has passed, and homemade deviled ham deserves a second chance. It's also a great way to use up the last of a baked holiday ham.

Makes about 4 cups

4	cups (1½ lb.) coarsely chopped smoked ham
½	cup finely chopped fresh parsley
½	cup mayonnaise
6	Tbsp. butter, softened
¼	cup whole-grain Dijon mustard
3	Tbsp. dry white wine

1	celery rib, finely chopped
2	green onions, finely chopped
1	tsp. finely grated fresh lemon zest
¾	tsp. freshly ground black pepper
¼	tsp. ground red pepper

Serve with: crackers and Quick-Pickled Winter Vegetables

1. Pulse ham, in batches, in a food processor 4 to 6 times or until shredded. (Do not over-process.) Stir together parsley, mayonnaise, butter, mustard, wine, celery, green onions, lemon zest, black pepper, and red pepper in a large bowl. Stir in ham.
2. Spoon into a terrine or other serving dish. Cover and chill 8 hours. Store refrigerated up to 3 days. Let stand at room temperature 30 minutes before serving.
3. Serve with crackers and Quick-Pickled Winter Vegetables.

QUICK-PICKLED WINTER VEGETABLES

We often think of pickling as a summertime endeavor, but these delightfully crunchy quick pickles are a great way to showcase winter fare.

Makes about 4 cups

1	cup cider vinegar
1½	cups water
⅓	cup sugar
2	Tbsp. kosher salt
2	garlic cloves, crushed
½	tsp. mustard seed

½	tsp. fennel seed
½	tsp. black peppercorns
¼	tsp. dried crushed red pepper
4	cups assorted raw vegetables, cut into bite-sized pieces

1. Bring vinegar, water, sugar, salt, garlic, mustard seed, fennel seed, peppercorns, and dried pepper to a boil in a large nonaluminum saucepan over medium-high heat, stirring until sugar dissolves; boil 1 minute. Let stand 30 minutes.
2. Meanwhile, cook vegetables, one variety at a time, in boiling water 1 to 3 minutes or until crisp-tender. Remove with a slotted spoon and immediately transfer into a large bowl of ice water to stop the cooking process; drain. Transfer vegetables to a 2½-qt. container.
3. Pour vinegar mixture over vegetables. Let stand 1 hour.
4. Cover and chill 1 day before serving. Store refrigerated up to 2 weeks.

From the kitchen of Meredith Boswell
Fayetteville, Arkansas

ARTICHOKE-STUFFED MUSHROOMS

This appetizer combines two perennial favorites: stuffed mushrooms and hot artichoke dip. For best results, select mushrooms with caps that are tightly closed around the stems. Mushroom caps open as they age, so closed caps are a sign of freshness.

Makes 2 dozen

24 large fresh button or crimini mushrooms (about 1½ lb.)
1 Tbsp. olive oil
¼ cup chopped onion
2 garlic cloves, chopped
¼ cup dry white wine
¼ cup soft, fresh breadcrumbs
1 (14-oz.) can artichoke hearts, drained and chopped

3 green onions, chopped
½ cup (2 oz.) freshly grated Parmesan cheese
½ cup mayonnaise
¼ tsp. salt
¼ tsp. black pepper

1. Preheat oven to 350°. Lightly grease a wire rack. Place rack in rimmed baking sheet.
2. Brush any debris off mushrooms. Remove and chop stems. Place mushroom caps upright on wire rack.
3. Heat oil in large skillet over medium-high heat. Add chopped mushroom stems, onion, and garlic; cook 5 minutes or until tender.
4. Add wine, and cook 2 minutes or until liquid evaporates. Remove from heat, and let cool. Stir in breadcrumbs.
5. Combine breadcrumb mixture, artichoke hearts, green onions, Parmesan, mayonnaise, salt, and pepper. Spoon into mushroom caps.
6. Bake at 350° for 12 to 15 minutes or until golden. Serve warm.

From the kitchen of Robin Jean Davis
Charleston, West Virginia

HINT:

When a recipe calls for soft, fresh breadcrumbs, it means
that you should start with fresh or day-old bread, such as sandwich
slices, buns, rolls, or a piece of baguette. Tear the crumbs
by hand or pulse the bread in a food processor into small
pieces, but not pulverized.

MARGARITA OLIVES

Bathing them in a delicious marinade is a great way to perk up a bowl of olives. This marinade contains many of the flavors found in a delicious margarita. This time, the cocktail goes in the olives rather than the other way around.

Makes about 3 cups

1	lb. pitted kalamata olives, drained	¼	cup tequila
3	oz. pimento-stuffed green olives, drained	¼	cup fresh lime juice
3	oz. pickled serrano or jalapeno peppers, drained	2	Tbsp. orange liqueur
		¼	cup finely chopped fresh cilantro
		2	tsp. finely grated fresh orange zest

Stir together all ingredients in a large bowl or glass jar. Cover and chill 8 hours. Return to room temperature for serving.

From the kitchen of Park Kerr
El Paso, Texas

CANDIED POPCORN and PEANUTS

This is a wonderful treat for children, not to mention those of us who want to feel like a kid again. There are some good brands of candied popcorn out there, but none can compare to homemade. This is so easy, and so worth it.

Makes about 3 qt.

12 cups freshly popped popcorn
1 cup roasted, salted peanuts
1 cup packed dark brown sugar
½ cup light-colored corn syrup
⅓ cup butter

1 Tbsp. light molasses or sorghum syrup
1½ tsp. vanilla extract
½ tsp. baking soda
½ tsp. salt

1. Preheat oven to 250°. Lightly grease a large rimmed baking sheet.
2. Place popcorn and peanuts in a very large bowl.
3. Stir together sugar, corn syrup, butter, and molasses in a medium saucepan. Bring to a boil over medium heat. Cook 5 minutes, stirring once.
4. Remove from heat; stir in vanilla, baking soda, and salt. Pour sugar mixture over popcorn in a steady stream, stirring to coat. Spread popcorn mixture evenly on pan.
5. Bake at 250° 1 hour, stirring every 15 minutes. Cool 15 minutes, stirring to break up any large clumps. Store cooled mixture in an airtight container up to 1 week.

***From the kitchen of** Deanne Anthony*
Poteau, Oklahoma

Taste of THE SOUTH

peanuts

Southerners love these tasty and versatile legumes. Peanuts started as a garden item in the colonies but grew into a comercial crop in Virginia by the early 1800s. Peanuts became a popular snack when vendors started hawking them at the first traveling circuses and carnivals. Sporting events and tailgates today wouldn't be complete without a sack of salty or boiled, roasted peanuts for munching.

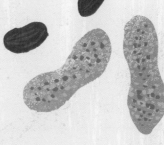
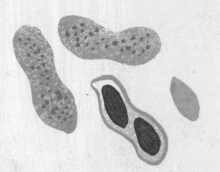

CORN and CRAB FRITTERS WITH CRIOLLA RÉMOULADE SAUCE

Part crab cake and part corn fritter, corn and fresh crab are a match made in heaven, made all the better when folded into tasty batter and quickly pan-fried until crisp. Don't be surprised if people hover near the skillet waiting for these to be ready!

Makes about 2 dozen

Rémoulade Sauce
- 1 cup mayonnaise
- ¼ cup Creole mustard
- ¼ cup chopped sweet pickles
- 2 Tbsp. capers, drained
- 2 tsp. Worcestershire sauce
- 2 tsp. prepared horseradish
- 2 tsp. anchovy paste
- 1 tsp. Old Bay seasoning
- 1 Tbsp. finely chopped fresh parsley
- 1 tsp. paprika

Fritters
- 3 Tbsp. butter
- 1½ cups thawed whole corn kernels
- ⅓ cup finely chopped red bell pepper

- 3 green onions, finely chopped
- 1 cup plain yellow cornmeal
- ½ cup all-purpose flour
- 1 tsp. baking powder
- 1 tsp. baking soda
- 1 tsp. salt
- 1 tsp. freshly ground black pepper
- 2 large eggs, lightly beaten
- 1 cup ricotta cheese
- ½ cup buttermilk
- 1 Tbsp. fresh lime juice
- 1 lb. fresh lump crabmeat, drained and picked through

Vegetable oil

Lemon wedges (optional)

1. To prepare sauce, stir together all ingredients in a medium bowl. Cover and chill at least 1 hour. Store in an airtight container up to 1 week.

2. To prepare fritters, preheat oven to 225°.

3. Melt butter in a large skillet. Stir in corn, bell pepper, and onions; cook, stirring often, 5 minutes or until tender. Remove from heat.

4. Whisk together cornmeal, flour, baking powder, baking soda, salt, and pepper in a large bowl. Make a well in the center.

5. Whisk together eggs, ricotta, buttermilk, and lime juice in medium bowl. Pour into cornmeal mixture. Stir only until blended.

6. Stir in corn mixture. Fold in crab. Shape ¼ cupful into patties.

7. Pour oil to depth of ¼ inch in a heavy skillet. Heat until shimmering over medium-high heat. Working in batches, cook fritters 2 to 3 minutes on each side or until golden, turning once. Drain on paper towels. (Keep fried fritters warm in oven up to 15 minutes.) Serve hot with rémoulade and lemon wedges, if desired.

CITRUS RÉMOULADE

Prepare Rémoulade Sauce as directed, omitting capers and parsley. Stir in 1 Tbsp. chopped cilantro, ½ tsp. finely grated fresh lemon zest, 1 Tbsp. fresh lemon juice, and 1 tsp. finely grated orange zest. Cover and chill as directed.

From the kitchen of Johnny Earles
Grayton Beach, Florida

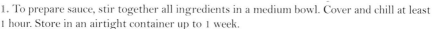

CHAMPIONSHIP COOKBOOK

Tea-Time at the Masters
(Copyright 1977; 1986; The Junior League of Augusta, Georgia)

When most people hear Augusta, they think of the Masters, the annual golf championship played on the dream course of Bobby Jones where The Masters was first held in 1934. Each spring Mother Nature ensures that the course is bursting with azaleas in full bloom by the time the first player steps up to the first tee. The golf is nice, and the winners sure love to don that green blazer, but I can't help but think that the higher purpose of The Masters is to provide a back-drop for a swell garden party.

When it came time for The Junior League of Augusta to create their cookbook, golf had to be part of their inspiration. The book's

forward tells us that, "In 1974 a membership of 426 voted to undertake the publication of a cookbook which would not only do honor to culinary skills, but at the same time pay tribute to the area's most famous annual event. Scattered through the book are recipes submitted by well-known golf clubs. Also included are numerous recipes from wives of Masters' participants, past and present. Each recipe in *Tea-Time* has been prepared over and over on the practice range and is therefore suitable for the big course under any playing conditions! There are no bogies, so 'tea' it up and fire away; not only will you make the cut, but you will be right there with the leaders in the club house after the last bite is down."

EASY SAUSAGE SWIRLS

Makes 20

1   (8-oz.) can refrigerated crescent rolls
1   Tbsp. spicy mustard

8   oz. bulk hot pork sausage
Parchment paper

1. Separate crescent roll dough along perforations into 2 rectangles.
2. Spread mustard evenly over dough. Scatter bits of sausage evenly over mustard.
3. Starting with a long edge, roll each rectangle of dough into a log. Wrap in plastic wrap, and chill until firm (about 1 hour).
4. Preheat oven to 400°. Line a baking sheet with parchment paper.
5. Cut each log crosswise into 10 equal rounds. Place rounds, cut-side down, on baking sheet. Press gently to flatten slightly. Bake at 400° for 18 to 20 minutes or until golden brown.

Tea-Time at the Masters
Junior League of Augusta, Georgia

POTATO-SKIN NESTS

Get a jump start on hot, crisp potato skins by starting with frozen hash browns.
These clever little cups emerge hot from a muffin pan, ready to fill with your favorite
toppings. Turn on the big game or press play on a good movie, and then dig in.

Makes 1 dozen

3   cups frozen shredded hash browns,
    thawed
2   large egg whites, lightly beaten
¾   cup (3 oz.) freshly shredded Parmesan
    cheese
1   tsp. onion powder
¾   tsp. salt

½   tsp. garlic powder
¼   tsp. freshly ground black pepper
Vegetable cooking spray
Toppings: shredded Colby-Jack cheese,
    sour cream, cooked and crumbled
    bacon, chopped fresh chives

1. Preheat oven to 450°. Lightly grease a 12-cup muffin pan or 24-cup miniature muffin pan.
2. Stir together hash browns, egg whites, Parmesan cheese, onion powder, salt, garlic powder,
and pepper.
3. Press about ¼ cup potato mixture into each cup of a lightly greased 12-cup muffin pan
(2 Tbsp. for mini muffins). Coat with vegetable cooking spray.
4. Bake at 450° 25 minutes or until golden. (Bake miniature muffin pan 20 minutes.) Cool in
pan on a wire rack 5 minutes. Gently run a knife around nests to loosen edges and remove
from pan to a serving platter.
5. Top nests with desired toppings.

From the kitchen of Melissa Sperka
Greensboro, North Carolina

CHILES RELLENOS SQUARES

These tender squares deliver the flavor of their namesake, the popular cheese-stuffed and deep-fried poblano chiles, but are lighter, quicker, and easier. Great unadorned, they are also tasty when topped with a dab of salsa and sour cream. To bump up their heat, use pepper Jack cheese and replace some of the mild green chiles with canned jalapeño peppers.

Makes 16

2 cups (8 oz.) shredded Monterey Jack cheese
2 cups (8 oz.) shredded Cheddar cheese
2 (4-oz.) cans chopped green chiles, drained

4 large eggs
¼ cup milk
2 Tbsp. all-purpose flour
Garnish: Pico de Gallo, sour cream, cilantro sprigs

1. Preheat oven to 375°. Lightly grease an 8-inch square baking dish.
2. Stir together cheeses. Place half of the cheese in dish. Sprinkle chiles over cheese. Top with remaining cheese.
3. Whisk together eggs, milk, and flour. Pour over cheese mixture.
4. Bake at 375° for 30 minutes or until set. Let stand 5 minutes. Cut into 2-inch squares, and serve warm.

From the kitchen of Mrs. William Huffert
Maxwell Air Force Base, Alabama

MAIN DISHES: MEAT, FOWL, FISH, and OTHERWISE

SUMMER PASTA

This entrée is like summer in a bowl, perfect for hot days when you want something light and inventive, yet satisfying. Wide ribbons of pappardelle pasta and delicate strands of fresh vegetables are lightly sauced with an herbed vegetable puree enriched with a touch of creamy mascarpone cheese. Crisp shards of prosciutto go on top, although those can be omitted for meatless fare.

Makes 4 to 6 servings

2   medium-size yellow squash (about 1 lb.), divided
2   medium zucchini (about 1 lb.), divided
2   medium carrots, divided
1   small onion, chopped
1   garlic clove, minced
¾   cup vegetable broth, divided
5   Tbsp. olive oil, divided
1   tsp. salt, divided
½   cup chopped fresh basil, divided
4   oz. prosciutto, torn into strips
1   Tbsp. butter
3   green onions, chopped
1   lb. pappardelle pasta
½   cup mascarpone cheese
¾   cup (3 oz.) freshly grated Parmesan cheese

1. Chop 1 squash, 1 zucchini, and 1 carrot. Place in a medium saucepan. Add onion, garlic, ½ cup vegetable broth, 3 Tbsp. olive oil, and ½ tsp. salt. Cover and cook over medium-low heat, stirring occasionally, 20 minutes or until vegetables are very tender. Stir in ¼ cup basil. Cool 10 minutes. Process cooked squash mixture and remaining ¼ cup broth in a blender or food processor until smooth. Pour puree into saucepan.

2. Cook prosciutto in a large nonstick skillet over medium heat 6 to 8 minutes or until browned and crisp; remove from skillet.

3. Cut remaining squash, zucchini, and carrot lengthwise into very thin, ribbon-like strips using a vegetable slicer or Y-shaped vegetable peeler. Stack ribbons, and cut in half lengthwise.

4. Melt butter with 1 Tbsp. olive oil in skillet over medium heat. Add vegetable ribbons, green onions, and remaining ½ tsp. salt, and cook 5 minutes or only until tender. Transfer to a plate, and cover.

5. Cook pasta in a large pot according to package directions; drain, reserving 1 cup hot pasta water. Return hot cooked pasta to pot.

6. Stir mascarpone cheese and ¼ cup Parmesan cheese into squash puree. Cook over medium-low heat 3 to 4 minutes or only until cheese melts and sauce is hot.

7. Pour sauce over pasta; toss to coat, adding desired amount of reserved hot pasta water to thin sauce, if necessary.

8. Top with vegetable ribbons, prosciutto, and remaining ½ cup Parmesan cheese and ¼ cup basil. Drizzle with remaining 1 Tbsp. olive oil.

From the kitchen of James Lewis
Birmingham, Alabama

RAVIOLI with TOMATO-BASIL CREAM SAUCE

All of us have busy days when we are in a rush to get dinner on the table without resorting to takeout. By combining a few fresh ingredients with high-quality convenience items, you can prepare this elegant pasta dish in minutes.

Makes 4 to 6 servings

1 (20-oz.) package refrigerated four-cheese ravioli
1 (16-oz.) jar sun-dried tomato Alfredo sauce
2 Tbsp. white wine
2 cups finely diced fresh tomato or 1 (14.5-oz.) can petite diced tomatoes, drained
½ cup chopped fresh basil
⅓ cup (3 oz.) shredded Parmesan cheese
Garnish: thinly sliced fresh basil leaves

1. Prepare ravioli according to package directions.
2. Meanwhile, pour Alfredo sauce into a large saucepan.
3. Pour wine into sauce jar; cover tightly, shake well, and stir into sauce.
4. Stir in tomatoes and chopped basil. Cook over medium-low heat 5 minutes or until thoroughly heated.
5. Drain pasta, add to sauce mixture, and stir gently to coat.
6. Sprinkle with Parmesan.

From the kitchen of Marguerite Cleveland
Fort Leavenworth, Kansas

LEXINGTON-STYLE GRILLED CHICKEN

It's hard to believe that a delicious six-ingredient marinade is the secret behind this flavorful dish. It's perfect for backyard cookouts or weeknight suppers.

Makes 8 to 10 servings

2   cups cider vinegar
¼   cup firmly packed dark brown sugar
¼   cup vegetable oil
3   Tbsp. dried crushed red pepper
4   tsp. salt
2   tsp. freshly ground black pepper
2   (2½- to 3-lb.) whole chickens, cut into serving
     pieces

1. Stir together vinegar, brown sugar, oil, dried pepper, salt, and pepper. Divide vinegar mixture between 2 large bowls or zip-top plastic freezer bags. Add 1 chicken to each; cover or seal. Chill chicken at least 2 hours or up to 8 hours, turning occasionally. Remove chicken, and discard marinade.
2. Grill chicken, covered with grill lid, over 350° to 400° (medium-high) heat 35 to 40 minutes or until done, turning occasionally.

BONELESS GRILLED CHICKEN:

Substitute 8 skinned and boned chicken breast halves and 8 skinned and boned chicken thighs for whole chickens. Chill in marinade 1 to 2 hours, turning occasionally. Grill chicken, covered with grill lid, over 350° to 400° (medium-high) heat 4 to 5 minutes on each side or until done.

From the kitchen of Larry Elder
Charlotte, North Carolina

SIT and CHAT

This grilled chicken is marinated with a bracing vinegar sauce inspired by the type of pork barbecue that is near and dear to Lexington, North Carolina. You can identify the origins of a Southern barbecue eater by figuring out what they call barbecue, much less what they eat and enjoy. Barbecue is a strident example of the intensely local preferences and loyalties that persist in the South.

SKILLET-FRIED CHICKEN
with GRAVY

If any simple dish truly deserves to be called sublime, this is it. For many people across the country, fried chicken is the first thing that comes to mind when they hear the words "Southern food." The chicken soaks in brine overnight, so plan ahead.

Makes 4 servings

Chicken
1   Tbsp. plus 1 tsp. salt
1   (2- to 2½-lb.) broiler-fryer, cut into
    serving pieces
1   tsp. freshly ground black pepper
1   cup all-purpose flour
2   cups vegetable oil
¼   cup bacon drippings

Gravy
¼   cup all-purpose flour
2   cups milk, chicken broth, or water,
    warmed
½   tsp. salt
¼   tsp. freshly ground black pepper

1. To prepare chicken, combine 3 qt. water and 1 Tbsp. salt in a large bowl. Add chicken, making sure it is submerged. Cover and chill 8 hours. Drain chicken; rinse with cold water, and pat dry.

2. Combine 1 tsp. salt and pepper; sprinkle half of pepper mixture evenly over chicken. Combine remaining pepper mixture and flour in a large freezer bag. Working with 2 pieces of chicken at a time, place chicken in bag. Seal and shake to coat evenly. Remove chicken, and set aside in single layer on a plate.

3. Combine vegetable oil and bacon drippings in a deep, 12-inch cast-iron skillet or chicken fryer; heat to 360°. Add chicken, a few pieces at a time, skin side down. Cover and cook 6 minutes; uncover and cook 9 minutes. For best results, keep the oil temperature between 300° and 325° as you fry the chicken.

4. Turn chicken pieces; cover and cook 6 minutes. Uncover and cook 5 to 9 minutes, turning pieces during the last 3 minutes for even browning, if necessary. Drain on paper towels.

5. To prepare gravy, pour off all but ¼ cup pan drippings, taking care to not dislodge browned bits from bottom of skillet.

6. Sprinkle flour over drippings, and whisk to blend. Cook over medium heat, whisking constantly, 2 to 3 minutes or until lightly browned.

7. Gradually whisk in milk. Stir constantly with a heat-proof spatula until gravy is thick and bubbly (3 to 5 minutes). Season with salt and pepper. Serve immediately.

BUTTERMILK FRIED CHICKEN:

Substitute 2 cups buttermilk for the saltwater solution used to soak the chicken pieces. Proceed as directed.

From the kitchen of John Egerton
Nashville, Tennessee

COMFORT AND JOY

Casseroles are evocative. Memories of great casseroles remind us that they can be an appealing, versatile, comforting one-pot meal. Recollections of mishmash casseroles that miss the mark cause us to snicker, if not shudder. Making a casserole is easy. You just toss everything into a dish and pop it into the oven. But making a great casserole requires thought about whether those ingredients will play well together. Consider an excellent casserole, full of fresh ingredients bound with a creamy, comforting sauce and topped with crisp, buttery crumbs—that's good stuff.

A casserole is an icon of Southern hospitality that can rise to any occasion, high or low, with grace and aplomb. Casseroles are what we take to friends who need more than a meal. This is my ode to casseroles that appeared in the January 2014 issue:

A new baby is born. A loved one passes on. A family is forever reshaped. It is possible to take comfort. You can carry it in your hands, in a casserole dish.

When welcoming a new baby, a casserole gives the joyous, exhausted parents a glimpse of family meals yet to come. During bereavement, a casserole offers a moment of respite. In times of upheaval, a casserole is reassuringly familiar. This meal asks no more of the beleaguered than to peel back the foil.

The day of my adored grandmother Madge Marie Reece Castle's funeral was filled with equal parts immeasurable love and unspeakable loss. The family returned home to find the kitchen brimming with homemade food brought by friends and neighbors. I found my favorite chicken-and-dressing casserole, spooned some up, and picked a quiet spot where I could sit with my toddler in my lap. One bowl and one spoon for the two of us. It was the only moment all day that made any sense. When words don't come easy, a casserole says plenty: "I understand that your normal life has come to a complete stop for a few days, so I'm going to pause mine long enough to make you something good to eat."

Homemade conveys heartfelt. A reliable casserole can deliver comfort and joy, but it's not the food so much as the gesture of genuine compassion. Casserole unto others as you would have them casserole unto you.

POPPY SEED CHICKEN CASSEROLE

Makes 6 servings

1 (10¾-oz.) can cream of chicken soup, undiluted

1 (16-oz.) container sour cream

¾ cup fresh peas

¾ cup chopped carrots

3 tsp. poppy seeds

3 cups chopped cooked chicken

31 round buttery crackers, crushed

¼ cup butter, melted

1. Preheat oven to 350°. Lightly grease an 11- x 7-inch baking dish.

2. Stir together first 5 ingredients in a large bowl. Stir in chicken. Pour into baking dish.

3. Toss together cracker crumbs and butter. Sprinkle over chicken mixture.

4. Bake at 350° for 35 to 40 minutes or until hot and bubbly. Let stand 5 minutes before serving.

From the kitchen of Kelly Skinner
Alpharetta, Georgia

CREAMY CHICKEN ENCHILADAS

This popular Tex-Mex dish has become a suppertime staple in many homes. It's easy to see why. Cooked chicken rolled up in tortillas and baked under a blanket of creamy, cheesy sauce simply has to be good. Use the toppings to add fresh vegetables and color to the plate.

Makes 4 servings

- 1 Tbsp. butter
- 1 medium onion, chopped
- 1 (4.5-oz.) can chopped green chiles, drained
- 8 oz. cream cheese, softened
- 3½ cups chopped cooked chicken
- 8 (8-inch) flour tortillas
- 1 cup Mexican crema, sour cream, or whipping cream
- 1 cup green taco sauce
- 4 cups (16 oz.) freshly shredded Monterey Jack cheese

Toppings: diced tomato, chopped avocado, chopped green onions, sliced ripe olives, chopped cilantro

1. Preheat oven to 350°. Lightly grease a 13- x 9-inch baking dish.
2. Melt butter in a large skillet over medium heat. Add onion and cook 5 minutes. Add green chiles; cook 1 minute.
3. Stir in cream cheese and chicken; cook, stirring constantly, until cream cheese melts.
4. Spoon 2 to 3 Tbsp. chicken mixture down center of each tortilla. Roll up tortillas, and place seam-side down in baking dish.
5. Stir together crema and taco sauce in a small bowl. Drizzle over tortillas. Sprinkle cheese over top.
6. Bake at 350° for 45 minutes. Serve with desired toppings.

From the kitchen of Becky Good
Dallas, Texas

SWEET and SOUR CHICKEN

This type of oven-barbecued chicken dish was all the rage in the '50s and '60s, when it was often called Asian or Oriental chicken. The flavors have remained popular over the years, and the technique couldn't be easier.

Makes 4 servings

2 Tbsp. vegetable oil	3 Tbsp. cider vinegar
8 bone-in chicken thighs, skinned (about 2 lb.)	3 Tbsp. ketchup
½ cup orange juice	½ tsp. dried crushed red pepper
½ cup pineapple juice	2 garlic cloves, minced
⅓ cup soy sauce	1 Tbsp. cornstarch
⅓ cup firmly packed light brown sugar	Serve with: 4 cups hot, cooked rice
2 Tbsp. minced fresh ginger	Garnish: ¼ cup chopped green onions

1. Heat oil in a large skillet over medium-high heat. Add chicken, and cook 6 minutes or until browned on both sides, turning once.

2. Combine juices in a medium bowl. Spoon 1 Tbsp. juice mixture into a small bowl; set aside.

3. Stir soy sauce, brown sugar, ginger, vinegar, ketchup, dried pepper, and garlic into remaining juice mixture; pour over chicken. Bring mixture to a boil. Reduce heat, cover, and simmer 35 minutes, turning chicken after 20 minutes.

4. Whisk cornstarch into reserved 1 Tbsp. juice mixture. Uncover chicken, and pour in cornstarch mixture. Cook, stirring constantly, 5 minutes or until sauce thickens.

5. Spoon rice onto a serving platter; top with chicken and sauce.

From the kitchen of Carol Daggers
Wilmington, Delaware

GRILLED QUAIL with RED WINE-BLACKBERRY SAUCE

In some communities, the first day of the annual quail hunting season is welcomed like a holiday. Happy hunters gather at camps, plantations, and lodges, and head into the grassy fields with gusto. Some hunters also take pride in their cooking skills, seeking to showcase what they bag.

This easy recipe pairs quail with blackberries, a classic combination. It works equally well with quail purchased at your neighborhood grocery store.

Makes 4 servings

4	(3.5-oz.) semiboneless quail	2	tsp. country-style Dijon mustard
1	cup bottled Italian dressing	½	tsp. coarsely ground black pepper
½	cup dry red wine		
1	cup seedless all-fruit blackberry spread or preserves		

1. Rinse quail, and pat dry. Place in a large bowl or zip-top freezer bag. Add Italian dressing. Cover or seal. Chill 8 hours, turning occasionally. Remove quail, and discard marinade.
2. Cook wine in a small saucepan over medium heat 5 minutes or until reduced by half. Whisk in blackberry spread, mustard, and pepper. Reserve ¾ cup.
3. Grill quail over 300° to 350° (medium) heat 15 minutes, turning once. Baste with remaining ¼ cup blackberry sauce.
4. Serve with reserved sauce.

From the kitchen of Philip Palmer
Athens, Georgia

HINT:

Semi-boneless quail have had the breast bones removed, leaving only the bones in the wings and leg-thigh sections. Some butchers insert a wire frame pin inside the quail's cavity to hold it open. The wire can be removed before or after cooking, so let the recipe be your guide.

KENTUCKY HOT BROWNS

In the 1920s, dinner dances at Louisville's Brown Hotel drew more than 1,000 guests. During band breaks, hungry revelers refueled on Chef Fred Schmidt's late-night suppers, including his signature Kentucky Hot Browns. This classic knife-and-fork sandwich consists of toast topped with sliced turkey and an avalanche of Mornay sauce. The whole thing is broiled until golden and bubbly. Toppings can vary, but in this version, the hot sandwiches are crowned with crisp bacon and slices of fresh tomato.

Makes 4 servings

Mornay Sauce
½   cup butter
⅓   cup all-purpose flour
3½ cups milk
½   cup (2 oz.) shredded Parmesan cheese
¼   tsp. salt
¼   tsp. freshly ground black pepper

Sandwiches
4   thick white bread slices
¾   lb. sliced roasted turkey
1   cup (4 oz.) shredded Parmesan cheese
3   plum tomatoes, sliced
8   bacon slices, cooked

1. To prepare sauce, melt butter in a medium saucepan over medium-high heat. Whisk in flour; cook, whisking constantly, 2 minutes. Gradually whisk in milk. Bring to a boil, and cook, whisking constantly, 1 to 2 minutes or until thickened. Whisk in Parmesan cheese, salt, and pepper. Keep warm over low heat.
2. To prepare sandwiches, preheat broiler with oven rack 6 inches from heat. Place bread slices on a baking sheet and broil 1 to 2 minutes on each side or until toasted.
3. Arrange bread slices in 4 lightly greased broiler-safe individual baking dishes. Top bread with turkey slices. Pour hot Mornay Sauce over turkey. Sprinkle with Parmesan cheese.
4. Broil 3 to 4 minutes or until bubbly and lightly browned.
5. Top sandwiches with tomatoes and bacon. Serve immediately.

From the kitchen of John and Joe Castro
Louisville, Kentucky

BOARDING HOUSE MEAT LOAF

Makes 6 servings

Loaf

1½	lb. lean ground beef
½	green bell pepper, finely chopped
½	small onion, finely chopped
2	large eggs, beaten
¾	cup uncooked regular oats
¼	cup ketchup
1½	tsp. salt

Sauce

2	Tbsp. butter
½	small onion, chopped
½	green bell pepper, chopped
¾	cup ketchup or chili sauce
1	Tbsp. cider vinegar

1. To prepare meatloaf, preheat oven to 350°. Lightly grease a 9- x 5-inch loaf pan.

2. Stir together beef, bell pepper, onion, eggs, oats, ketchup, and salt in a large bowl. Shape into a loaf, and place in pan.

3. Bake at 350° for 45 minutes. Meanwhile, make sauce.

4. To prepare sauce, melt butter in a large skillet over medium-high heat Add onion and bell pepper; cook 5 minutes or until vegetables are tender. Stir in ketchup and vinegar; simmer, stirring constantly, for 5 minutes or until sauce thickens slightly.

5. Remove loaf from oven and pour off pan juices. Spread half of sauce evenly over meatloaf; bake 25 more minutes.

6. Serve hot with remaining sauce.

From the kitchen of Barbara Ruth McGowan
Lynchburg, Tennessee

SIT and CHAT

Just off the village square in Lynchburg, not far from the Jack Daniel Distillery, is the famed Miss Mary Bobo's Boarding House. Since 1908, this historic home has served great meals with hospitality. Although they no longer host boarders, the restaurant offers up a midday feast of home-cooked comfort foods served family style. As the lazy Susan spins in the center of the table, a congenial docent spins yarns about the history of the distillery, the community, and "the product." This delightfully old-fashioned meatloaf is sometimes among the fare.

GRILLADES and GRITS

The inexpensive cut of meat is pounded until very thin and then braised in a well-seasoned tomato sauce until it turns spoon-tender.

Makes 8 to 10 servings

4 lb. boneless round steak, cut ½ inch thick	2 (14½-oz.) cans stewed tomatoes, undrained
½ cup bacon drippings, divided	1 cup dry red wine
½ cup all-purpose flour	1 Tbsp. salt
2 cups chopped green onions	1 tsp. freshly ground black pepper
1 cup chopped onion	2 bay leaves
¾ cup chopped green bell pepper	2 Tbsp. Worcestershire sauce
2 garlic cloves, minced	1 tsp. hot sauce
1 tsp. dried thyme	3 Tbsp. chopped parsley
½ tsp. dried tarragon	Serve with: hot buttered grits

1. Cut meat into 3-inch squares. Pound meat to ¼-inch thickness using a meat mallet. Heat ¼ cup drippings in a Dutch oven. Working in batches, brown meat on both sides. Transfer to a plate, and set aside.

2. Add remaining ¼ cup drippings to the pot. Whisk in flour; cook over low heat, stirring constantly, 10 minutes or until mixture is dark brown.

3. Add green onions, onion, and bell pepper. Cook 8 minutes or until tender, stirring often.

4. Add garlic, thyme, and tarragon, and cook 1 minute.

5. Stir in tomatoes, ½ cup water, wine, salt, pepper, bay leaves, Worcestershire, and hot sauce. Bring to a boil, reduce heat, and simmer 3 minutes. Return meat and any accumulated juices to the pot, submerging meat in the tomato mixture.

6. Cover and simmer gently 2 to 3 hours or until meat is very tender, stirring occasionally.

7. Cool, cover, and refrigerate overnight.

8. Reheat over medium heat, adding a little water if needed. Discard bay leaves. Stir in parsley. Serve hot over grits.

From the kitchen of Marcelle Bienvenue
St. Martinville, Louisiana

Taste of THE SOUTH

grillades and grits

Grillades and grits, like salt and pepper or bread and butter, are an assumed pair in New Orleans. This beef dish (which can also be made with veal or pork) sounds like dinner, and sometimes it is, but this Creole dish is more often found on the brunch menu. For best results, make it the night before you plan to serve it.

SALISBURY STEAK with MUSHROOM GRAVY

Makes 6 servings

3   Tbsp. vegetable oil, divided
1   large onion, chopped and divided (about 2 cups)
1   garlic clove, minced
2   lb. ground beef
2   large eggs, lightly beaten
¼   cup fine, dry breadcrumbs
2   tsp. yellow mustard
2   tsp. Worcestershire sauce
1   tsp. salt, divided
1   tsp. freshly ground black pepper, divided
8   oz. sliced fresh mushrooms
3   Tbsp. all-purpose flour
½   cup dry red wine
1½ cups low-sodium beef broth

1. Preheat oven to 350°. Lightly grease a shallow baking dish.
2. Heat 1 Tbsp. oil in a large skillet over medium-high heat. Add 1 cup onion, and cook 5 minutes or until tender. Add garlic, and cook 30 seconds. Pour into large bowl, and let cool.
3. Add beef, eggs, breadcrumbs, mustard, Worcestershire, ¼ tsp. salt, and ½ tsp. pepper. Mix well. Shape into 6 patties.
4. Cook patties in remaining 2 Tbsp. hot oil over medium-high heat 3 minutes on each side or until browned. (Do not cook until done.) Remove patties to baking dish.
5. Add remaining 1 cup onion to drippings in skillet, and cook over medium heat 5 minutes or until tender. Add mushrooms, and cook 3 minutes.
6. Whisk in flour, and cook, stirring constantly, 1 minute.
7. Whisk in wine, broth, and remaining ¾ tsp. salt and ½ tsp. pepper. Bring to a boil; reduce heat to low, and simmer, stirring occasionally, 5 minutes. Pour evenly over meat patties.
8. Bake, covered, at 350° for 25 minutes or until done.

From the kitchen of Vivian Waters
Thomasville, Georgia

SIT and CHAT

Not all hamburger steaks are this elegant. This dish was invented during the Civil War by a physician named James Salisbury, who prescribed minced beef for convalescing soldiers. It was popularized during World War II when economizing cooks sought tasty ways to use rationed beef. Now we eat it because it's nostalgic, and plenty good. This really hits the spot when we crave something homey and filling.

HOLIDAY BEEF TENDERLOIN

Beef tenderloin is the centerpiece of many special-occasion and holiday meals.

Makes 8 servings

1 (5-lb.) beef tenderloin, trimmed and tied
¼ cup olive oil
1 Tbsp. kosher salt
1½ tsp. onion powder

1½ tsp. garlic powder
1½ tsp. freshly ground black pepper
1 tsp. ground red pepper
½ tsp. ground cumin
½ tsp. ground nutmeg

1. Let tenderloin come to room temperature (about 30 minutes). Preheat oven to 500°.
2. Pat tenderloin dry with paper towels. Rub with oil.
3. Mix together salt, onion powder, garlic powder, pepper, ground red pepper, cumin, and nutmeg in a small bowl. Sprinkle evenly over meat.
4. Place tenderloin on a wire rack set inside a rimmed baking sheet.
5. Roast 10 minutes. Lower over temperature to 425°. Continue roasting until an instant-read thermometer inserted into center of the tenderloin registers 130° for medium-rare (about 15 to 20 minutes).
6. Tent loosely with aluminum foil, and let stand 15 minutes. The internal temperature will rise another 5 degrees while the meat rests. Discard kitchen string before slicing.

NOTE: For rare meat, cook tenderloin to 120°. For medium-rare meat, cook to 135°. For medium meat, cook to 140°. For medium-well meat, cook to 150°.

From the kitchen of Scott Segal
Charleston, West Virginia

HINT

Beef tenderloins are incredibly simple to prepare, so long as you use an instant-read thermometer to take the guesswork out of doneness. Be sure to let the roast come up to room temperature before roasting. Likewise, be sure to let it rest before carving. Those steps are as important as the roasting time to ensure the success of this recipe.

MOM'S SIGNATURE POT ROAST

Pot roast is a wonderful way to feed a large group, or to feed a small group for several delicious meals. There are two secrets to great pot roast. First, use the right cut of meat. A well-marbled chuck roast is ideal because it turns out very tender and full of flavor. Cuts that are too lean simply dry out. Second, pot roast must be deliberately overcooked. The meat will look done after about 1 hour of cooking, but it needs at least 4 hours to become fully tender. Most cooks who are unhappy with their pot roast didn't give the process enough time.

Makes 8 servings

1 (12-oz.) bottle dark beer
1 medium onion, chopped
8 garlic cloves, minced
1 lemon, thinly sliced
1 cup soy sauce
3 Tbsp. vegetable oil, divided
1 (3- to 4-lb.) boneless chuck roast, trimmed

2 tsp. fresh coarsely ground black pepper
8 carrots (about 1½ lb.), diagonally sliced
8 Yukon gold potatoes (about 3 lb.), peeled and cut into eighths
2 large onions, cut into eighths
2 Tbsp. cornstarch

1. Combine beer, onion, garlic, lemon, soy sauce, and 2 Tbsp. oil in a large bowl or zip-top plastic freezer bag. Add roast, cover or seal, and chill at least 8 hours or up to 24 hours, turning occasionally. Remove roast from marinade, reserving marinade.
2. Preheat oven to 300°. Sprinkle roast evenly with pepper.
3. Heat remaining 1 Tbsp. oil in a large Dutch oven (preferably enameled cast-iron) over medium-high heat. Sear roast until well-browned on all sides (about 4 minutes per side).
4. Add reserved marinade, stirring to loosen browned bits from bottom of pan. Bring to a boil. Cover with tight-fitting lid or with heavy-duty aluminum foil. Transfer to oven.
5. Bake at 300° for 2½ hours. Turn roast and stir in carrots, potatoes, and onions. Bake 2 more hours or until roast and vegetables are tender.
6. Transfer roast and vegetables to a serving platter. Skim fat from juices in pot.
7. Whisk together cornstarch and ¼ cup water in a small bowl until smooth. Whisk cornstarch mixture into juices in pot. Cook over medium-high heat 5 minutes or until thickened, whisking to loosen browned bits from bottom of pot.
8. Drizzle ½ cup gravy over roast. Serve remaining gravy with meat and vegetables.

COLA POT ROAST:

Substitute 1 (12-oz.) can cola soft drink (not diet) for beer. Proceed with recipe as directed.

From the kitchen of Carmen Lagarelli
Elkton, Maryland

✦

RICE PAPER ROLLS *with* VIETNAMESE GRILLED FLANK STEAK

There are several steps in this recipe, but none is difficult. Forming the rolls is easy. If you can roll up a burrito, you can make a rice paper roll. Rice paper wrappers can be found on the ethnic foods aisle of most grocery stores, along with the fish sauce and rice wine vinegar.

Makes 4 to 6 servings

Steak
- 1 lb. flank steak
- 2 Tbsp. sugar
- 1 Tbsp. chopped fresh lemon grass
- 1 Tbsp. minced garlic
- 1 Tbsp. soy sauce
- 1 Tbsp. vegetable oil
- ¾ tsp. cornstarch
- 1 tsp. salt
- ½ tsp. freshly ground black pepper

Sauce
- 1¼ cups hot water
- ½ cup fish sauce
- ⅓ cup sugar
- 2 tsp. rice wine vinegar
- ⅓ cup grated carrot

Rolls
- 16 (6-inch) rice paper spring roll wrappers (bánh tráng)
- ½ cup bean sprouts
- ⅓ cup grated carrot
- ½ cucumber, peeled, seeded, and cut into matchsticks
- ½ cup fresh pineapple slices, cut into matchsticks
- ¼ cup chopped fresh mint
- ¼ cup chopped fresh cilantro
- ½ head iceberg lettuce or green leaf lettuce, shredded

1. To prepare steak, cut meat diagonally across the grain into 16 (⅛- to ¼-inch-thick) slices.

2. Stir together sugar, lemon grass, garlic, soy sauce, oil, and cornstarch in a large bowl or zip-top plastic freezer bag. Add meat, stirring to coat. Cover or seal, and chill 30 minutes. Remove meat, and discard marinade. Sprinkle steak evenly with salt and pepper.

3. Grill flank steak slices over 350° to 400° (medium-high) heat, uncovered, 2 minutes on each side or until done. Cover with aluminum foil to keep warm.

4. To prepare sauce, stir together hot water, fish sauce, sugar, and vinegar until sugar dissolves. Stir in carrot. Set aside.

5. To prepare rolls, pour hot water to a depth of 1 inch in a large shallow dish. Working with 1 wrapper at a time, dip wrappers in hot water briefly to soften. Pat dry with paper towels. Set aside in a single layer.

6. Toss together bean sprouts, carrot, cucumber, pineapple, mint, and cilantro in a large bowl.

7. Place 1 slice of beef on wrapper; top with ⅛ cup lettuce. Place about ⅛ cup bean sprout mixture on lettuce on wrapper. Fold sides of wrapper over filling, and roll up, burrito style.

8. Serve rolls with fish sauce mixture for dipping.

NOTE: Prepare fresh lemon grass as you would a green onion: Peel off the outer layer, remove the root end, and use the white portion.

From the kitchen of Tri La
Houston, Texas

THREADGILL'S CHICKEN-FRIED STEAK and CREAM GRAVY

Makes 8 servings

Steaks

2	large eggs
2	cups milk
1½	cups all-purpose flour
1	tsp. salt
1	tsp. garlic powder
¼	tsp. freshly ground black pepper
¼	tsp. ground white pepper
⅛	tsp. ground red pepper
⅛	tsp. ground cumin
8	(6-oz.) cubed sirloin steaks

Vegetable oil

Gravy

2	Tbsp. all-purpose flour
2	cups milk, warmed
½	tsp. salt
½	tsp. freshly ground black pepper
2	tsp. Worcestershire sauce
1	tsp. hot sauce

SIT and CHAT

We don't know who first fried a cubed steak, much less fried it like one might fry chicken. The dish likely traces back to Germans who settled in Texas, bringing their expertise with wiener schnitzel with them. It was a fine idea, and over time, chicken-fried steak became a classic dish in cattle ranch country.

1. To prepare steaks, whisk together eggs and milk in a shallow bowl. Whisk together flour, salt, garlic powder, black pepper, white pepper, ground red pepper, and cumin in another shallow bowl.
2. Dip steaks in egg mixture. Coat in flour mixture. Dip again in egg mixture. Set aside in a single layer. Pour oil to depth of ¾ inch in a large heavy skillet. Heat until shimmering over high heat.
3. Working in batches, fry steaks 1½ to 2½ minutes on each side or until golden. Drain steaks on paper towels. Tent loosely with aluminum foil to keep warm. Pour off all but 2 Tbsp. drippings from skillet, taking care to not dislodge browned bits from bottom.
4. To prepare gravy, heat drippings in skillet over medium heat. Whisk in flour, and cook, whisking constantly, 2 minutes or until golden. Gradually whisk in milk. Cook, whisking constantly, until gravy is thick and bubbly. Stir in salt, pepper, Worcestershire, and hot sauce. Serve gravy over steaks.

From the kitchen of Eddie Wilson
Austin, Texas

ADAMS' RIBS

Some people take ribs very seriously. They gnaw the bones, sop the sauce, smack their lips, and lick their fingers. To that, others add the pursuit of preparing perfect ribs. Adams' Ribs are the hot and spicy product of a marriage. Anne-Marie's Cajun background inspired the spicy seasoning, while her husband Oscar's commitment to the best equipment and a perfectly built fire ensured the smoky tenderness. Two sauces plus one rub plus 8 pounds of ribs adds up to a great meal for about 10 people.

Makes 10 to 12 servings

Grill Basting Sauce

3   cups red wine vinegar
1   cup dry white wine
¾   cup ketchup
¼   cup firmly packed light brown sugar
¼   cup Worcestershire sauce
¼   cup yellow mustard
2   Tbsp. freshly ground black pepper
1   to 2 Tbsp. dried crushed red pepper
1   cup water

Serving Sauce

1   Tbsp. butter
1   medium-sized onion, finely chopped
1½ tsp. minced garlic

1   cup ketchup
½   cup white vinegar
¼   cup fresh lemon juice
¼   cup liquid steak seasoning
2   Tbsp. light brown sugar
1   Tbsp. Cajun seasoning
2   Tbsp. hickory liquid smoke

Ribs and Rub

1   Tbsp. garlic powder
1   Tbsp. Creole seasoning
2   Tbsp. freshly ground black pepper
1   Tbsp. Worcestershire sauce
8   lb. pork spareribs
Hickory wood chunks

1. To prepare basting sauce, stir together first 8 ingredients and 1 cup water in a large saucepan. Bring to a boil over medium-high heat. Reduce the heat to medium and simmer for 1 hour. Keep warm.

2. To prepare serving sauce, melt the butter in a large skillet over medium heat. Add the onion and garlic; cook 5 minutes or until tender. Add the ketchup, vinegar, lemon juice, steak seasoning, brown sugar, Cajun seasoning, and liquid smoke. Simmer 15 minutes. Cool completely (about 1 hour).

3. To prepare ribs, stir together the garlic powder, Creole seasoning, pepper, and Worcestershire sauce. Rub on all sides of the ribs.

4. Soak wood chunks, in water to cover for 30 minutes. Prepare charcoal fire in grill. Drain wood chunks and place on coals. Cook ribs, covered with grill lid, over medium coals (300° to 350°) about 3 hours, turning ribs after 1 hour and basting with Grill Basting Sauce after 2 hours. Turn once more after basting.

5. Serve ribs with Serving Sauce.

NOTE. To prepare ribs on a gas grill, light one side of the grill, heating to 300° to 350° (medium) heat; leave the other side unlit. Arrange the ribs over the unlit side, and grill, covered with the grill lid, for 2 to 3 hours, turning and basting with the basting sauce every hour. (The longer the ribs cook, the more tender they will be.) Increase the heat to 350° to 400° (medium-high) heat. Grill, covered with the grill lid, 1 hour more, basting with Grill Basting Sauce every 10 minutes.

From the kitchen of Oscar and Anne-Marie Adams
Birmingham, Alabama

Asian Turkey Lettuce wraps

This is, hands down, a fun and delicious hands-on meal. Ground turkey and shiitake mushrooms are seasoned with a flavorful mixture of teriyaki, peanut butter, and hoisin sauces. Many of us keep these staples in our pantries, ready for quick meals with Asian flair. Lettuce wraps are a welcome weeknight family meal, and are also great for casual entertaining.

1 tsp vegetable oil

1/2 cup finely chopped carrots

1 1/4 lb ground turkey

1 x can water chesnuts (8-oz)

1 cup chopped shiitake mushrooms

1/4 cup Peanut Butter

2 tbsp minced fresh ginger

1 tbsp toasted Sesame oil

1 tbsp Asian chili paste (optional)

3 garlic cloves minced

1/3 cup teriyaki Sauce

1 tbsp rice vinegar

12 large Boston lettuce leaves

1/2 cup sliced green onions

1/4 cup hoisin Sauce

1 Heat oil in a large skillet over medium-high heat. Add turkey and carrots; cook, stirring, about 5 minutes or until turkey crumbles and is no longer pink.

5 mins

2 Add mushrooms, water chestnuts, garlic, ginger, teriyaki sauce, peanut butter, sesame oil, vinegar, hoisin sauce, and, if desired, chili paste.

Increase heat to medium-high and cook, stirring constantly, 4 minutes.

4 mins

3 Add green onions and cook stirring constantly, 1 minute.

4 Spoon mixture evenly down center of lettuce leaves; roll up. Serve immediately with more hoisin sauce, if desired.

From the Kitchen of Susan Riley Allen, Texas

MAKES 4 SERVINGS

FROGMORE STEW

Frogmore Stew, otherwise known as Lowcountry boil, isn't really a stew, nor does it contain frogs. Instead, it is a simple and easy one-pot seafood and vegetable dinner, similar to a shrimp or crawfish boil. Although it can be prepared indoors, many people like to tackle a boil outdoors, perhaps in a huge pot set on a propane burner ring, served on a newspaper-covered picnic table, eaten with the fingers, and shared with family and friends.

Makes 12 servings

¼   cup Old Bay seasoning
4   lb. small red potatoes
2   lb. kielbasa or hot smoked link sausage, cut into 1½-inch pieces

6   ears fresh corn, halved crosswise
4   lb. unpeeled, large fresh shrimp
Serve with: Old Bay seasoning and cocktail sauce

1. Bring 5 qt. water and ¼ cup Old Bay to a rolling boil in a large covered stockpot.
2. Add potatoes. Return to a boil and cook, uncovered, 10 minutes.
3. Add sausage and corn. Return to a boil and cook 10 minutes or until potatoes are tender.
4. Add shrimp. Cook 3 to 4 minutes or until shrimp turn pink. Drain.
5. Sprinkle generously with more Old Bay, and serve with cocktail sauce.

From the kitchen of Richard Gay
St. Helena Island, South Carolina

CHICKEN, SHRIMP and HAM JAMBALAYA

Makes 6 to 8 servings

SIT and CHAT

Jambalaya is a rice-based, one-pot dish that benefits from multicultural roots and influences. There are countless variations of the dish, but experts explain that Creole jambalaya is red from tomato, while Cajun jambalaya is brown from meat drippings. If that's true, then this is a great example of red jambalaya from Eula Mae Doré, who for 57 years cooked for the McIlhenny family, makers of Tabasco, on Avery Island, Louisiana.

2   lb. unpeeled, medium-size fresh shrimp
1½   lb. skinned and boned chicken thighs, cut into 1-inch cubes
1   tsp. salt
⅛   tsp. freshly ground black pepper
⅛   tsp. ground red pepper
2   Tbsp. vegetable oil
8   oz. cooked ham, cut into ½-inch cubes
4   garlic cloves, chopped
2   medium-size yellow onions, chopped (2 cups)
2   celery ribs, chopped (1 cup)
1   medium-size green bell pepper, chopped (1 cup)
3   cups chicken broth
1   (14½-oz.) can diced tomatoes
3   green onions, chopped (½ cup)
2   Tbsp. chopped fresh parsley
2   cups uncooked long-grain rice
1   tsp. Tabasco sauce

1. Peel shrimp; devein, if desired.
2. Sprinkle chicken evenly with salt, black pepper, and ground red pepper.
3. Heat oil in a Dutch oven over medium heat. Add chicken and cook, stirring constantly, 8 to 10 minutes or until browned on all sides. Remove chicken using a slotted spoon.
4. Add ham to Dutch oven and cook, stirring constantly, 5 minutes or until lightly browned. Remove ham using a slotted spoon.
5. Add garlic, onions, celery, and bell pepper to Dutch oven. Stir to loosen browned bits from bottom. Stir in ham and chicken. Reduce heat to low, cover, and cook, stirring occasionally, 20 minutes.
6. Add chicken broth. Bring to a boil over medium-high heat; reduce heat to low, cover, and simmer 35 minutes.
7. Add tomatoes, green onions, parsley, and rice. Bring to a boil over medium-high heat, reduce heat to medium-low, cover, and simmer 20 minutes.
8. Stir in shrimp and hot sauce; cook, covered, 10 more minutes or until liquid is absorbed and rice is tender.

From the kitchen of Eula Mae Doré
Avery Island, Louisiana

CROOK'S CORNER SHRIMP and GRITS

Makes 4 servings

Cheese Grits

- 1¾ cups chicken broth
- ¾ cup half-and-half
- ¾ tsp. salt
- 1 cup regular grits
- ¾ cup (3 oz.) shredded Cheddar cheese
- ¼ cup (1 oz.) grated Parmesan cheese
- 2 Tbsp. butter
- ½ tsp. hot sauce
- ¼ tsp. ground white pepper

Shrimp Topping

- 3 bacon slices
- 1 lb. medium-size fresh shrimp, peeled and deveined
- ⅛ tsp. salt
- ¼ tsp. freshly ground black pepper
- ¼ cup all-purpose flour
- 1 cup sliced mushrooms
- ½ cup chopped green onions
- 2 garlic cloves, minced
- ½ cup low-sodium, fat-free chicken broth
- 2 Tbsp. fresh lemon juice
- ⅛ tsp. hot sauce
- Lemon wedges

1. To prepare grits, bring 2 cups water, broth, half-and-half, and ¾ tsp. salt to a boil in a medium saucepan. Gradually whisk in grits. Reduce heat and simmer, stirring occasionally, 10 minutes or until thickened. Add Cheddar, Parmesan, butter, hot sauce, and white pepper. Keep warm over very low heat, stirring occasionally.

2. To prepare shrimp topping, cook bacon in a large skillet until crisp; remove bacon, and drain on paper towels, reserving 1 Tbsp. drippings in skillet. Crumble bacon, and set aside.

3. Sprinkle shrimp with ⅛ tsp. salt and pepper. Coat shrimp lightly and evenly in flour. Set aside in a single layer on a plate.

4. Cook mushrooms in hot drippings in skillet 5 minutes or until tender.

5. Add green onions, and cook 2 minutes.

6. Add shrimp and garlic; cook 2 minutes or until shrimp are lightly browned.

7. Stir in chicken broth, lemon juice, and hot sauce, and cook 2 more minutes, stirring to loosen browned bits from bottom of skillet.

8. Spoon shrimp mixture over hot cheese grits. Top with crumbled bacon. Serve with lemon wedges.

From the kitchen of Bill Smith
Chapel Hill, North Carolina

BIG EASY BARBECUE SHRIMP

Southerners are very precise about how we use the word barbecue, carefully reserving the term to refer to meat cooked low-and-slow over hardwood—unless we aren't talking about that at all. For example, barbecue shrimp are cooked quickly in the oven. That doesn't mean they get short shrift. The results are fantastic. Created in 1954 at Pascal's Manale Italian restaurant in New Orleans, barbecue shrimp soon became a classic. The seasonings may vary, but it's always served with a loaf of crusty French bread for soaking up the spicy butter sauce. Cooking the shrimp in their shells is not only traditional, it's important—the shells contribute great flavor.

Makes 6 servings

3 lb. unpeeled large fresh shrimp	2 Tbsp. Old Bay seasoning
¾ cup butter	1 Tbsp. dried Italian seasoning
¼ cup Worcestershire sauce	2 Tbsp. Asian garlic-chili pepper sauce
¼ cup ketchup	2 tsp. hot sauce
3 bay leaves	Serve with: baguette slices
2 lemons, sliced	

1. Preheat oven to 325°.

2. Place shrimp in a shallow aluminum foil-lined broiler pan or roasting pan.

3. Stir together butter, Worcestershire, ketchup, bay leaves, lemons, Old Bay, Italian season-ing, pepper sauce, and hot sauce in a medium saucepan. Cook over low heat, stirring until butter melts; pour over shrimp.

4. Bake at 325° for 25 minutes, stirring and turning shrimp after 10 minutes. Discard bay leaves. Serve hot with baguette slices.

From the kitchen of Elizabeth Ross
Dallas, Texas

FISH CAKES with GARLIC-LEMON MAYONNAISE

Makes 6 servings

Garlic-Lemon Mayonnaise
- ¾ cup mayonnaise
- 2 garlic cloves, minced
- 1 tsp. lemon zest
- 1 Tbsp. fresh lemon juice
- ¼ tsp. salt
- ¼ tsp. freshly ground black pepper

Fish Cakes
- 2 Tbsp. mayonnaise
- 3 green onions, thinly sliced
- 3 large eggs, lightly beaten
- 2 Tbsp. chopped fresh parsley
- 1 tsp. Old Bay seasoning
- 1 tsp. Worcestershire sauce
- 2 cups crumbled cornbread
- 2 (5-oz.) pouches herb-and-garlic-flavored light tuna chunks
- 3 Tbsp. butter
- 3 Tbsp. vegetable oil
- Lemon wedges
- Garnish: fresh parsley

1. To prepare Garlic-Lemon Mayonnaise, stir together mayonnaise, garlic, lemon zest, lemon juice, salt, and pepper in a small bowl. Cover and chill until needed.
2. To prepare cakes, stir together mayonnaise, green onions, eggs, parsley, Old Bay, and Worcestershire in a large bowl.
3. Fold cornbread crumbs and tuna chunks into mayonnaise mixture until well blended. Shape tuna mixture into 8 patties, each about ½ inch thick.
4. Melt butter with vegetable oil in a large skillet over medium-high heat.
5. Working in batches, cook tuna patties 2 to 3 minutes on each side or until golden brown. Drain on paper towels. Serve cakes with Garlic-Lemon Mayonnaise and lemon wedges.

From the kitchen of Sherry Little
Sherwood, Arkansas

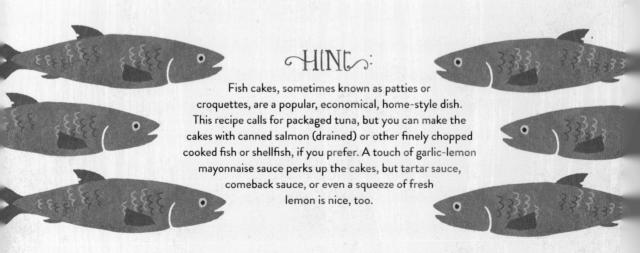

HINT:

Fish cakes, sometimes known as patties or croquettes, are a popular, economical, home-style dish. This recipe calls for packaged tuna, but you can make the cakes with canned salmon (drained) or other finely chopped cooked fish or shellfish, if you prefer. A touch of garlic-lemon mayonnaise sauce perks up the cakes, but tartar sauce, comeback sauce, or even a squeeze of fresh lemon is nice, too.

FIRECRACKER GRILLED SALMON

Salmon is a great choice for the grill because it's good cooked anywhere from rare to medium. Recipes used to advise us to cook fish until it flaked, but now we know that flaky fish is overcooked. Although nothing beats the flavor of food prepared on an outdoor grill, this recipe is also successful when prepared indoors on a grill pan.

Makes 6 servings

6	(6-oz.) salmon fillets	2	tsp. dried crushed red pepper
½	cup vegetable oil	1½	tsp. ground ginger
¼	cup reduced-sodium soy sauce	1	tsp. sesame oil
¼	cup balsamic vinegar	½	tsp. salt
1	Tbsp. honey	¼	tsp. onion powder
2	tsp. finely chopped garlic		

1. Place salmon fillets in a large bowl or zip-top plastic freezer bag. Whisk together vegetable oil, soy sauce, balsamic vinegar, honey, garlic, crushed red pepper, ginger, sesame oil, salt, and onion powder. Reserve ¼ cup oil mixture. Pour remaining oil mixture over salmon. Cover or seal, and chill 30 minutes. Remove salmon, and discard marinade.

2. Preheat grill to 350° to 400° (medium-high) heat. Place fillets skin-side down on a well-oiled grill grate (close lid if using gas grill) until skin is crisp and well-browned on the bottom, about 4 minutes. With a wide spatula, carefully turn pieces; brush tops with marinade and continue to cook, basting often, until salmon is opaque but still moist in the center of the thickest part, 3 to 4 minutes longer.

From the kitchen of Amy Clarke
Fairfax, Virginia

DEVILED CRAB

This recipe has nearly disappeared in recent years, but it used to be a popular treat at seafood restaurants and fish camps. The filling is quite similar to a delectable crab cake, but the mixture is spooned into baking shells and popped into the oven until hot and golden. It is called "deviled" because that was once a common adjective for dishes seasoned with mustard and bold spices.

Makes 6 servings

⅓ cup butter	¼ cup whipping cream
¾ cup finely chopped celery	1 tsp. dry mustard
¾ cup finely chopped onion	½ tsp. freshly ground black pepper
¼ cup finely chopped bell pepper	¼ tsp. salt
1 lb. fresh lump crabmeat, drained and picked	1 Tbsp. Dijon mustard
1 cup saltine cracker crumbs, divided	½ tsp. hot sauce
½ cup chopped fresh parsley	1 Tbsp. butter, melted
	Paprika

1. Preheat oven to 350°.

2. Melt ⅓ cup butter in a large skillet over medium-high heat. Add celery, onion, and bell pepper; cook, stirring constantly, 8 minutes or until tender. Remove from heat. Gently stir in crabmeat, ¾ cup cracker crumbs, and parsley.

3. Stir together cream, dry mustard, pepper, salt, Dijon mustard, and hot sauce in a small bowl. Fold into crabmeat mixture. Spoon into 6 baking shells or individual baking dishes.

4. Toss together remaining ¼ cup cracker crumbs and melted butter in a small bowl; sprinkle over crab filling. Sprinkle tops with paprika. Bake at 350° for 15 to 20 minutes or until golden brown.

From the kitchen of Mrs. Herbert W. Rutherford
Baltimore, Maryland

FRIED OYSTERS

All along the Atlantic Seaboard and around the Gulf Coast, Southerners have a deep history and abiding loyalty to their local oysters. There are all sorts of ways to cook them—including not cooking them at all—but many people find the pleasure of sitting down to a basket of perfectly fried oysters to be nothing short of luxury.

Makes 6 servings

2 large eggs	1 qt. fresh oysters, drained and rinsed
1 sleeve saltine crumbs, finely crushed (about 1½ cups)	Canola oil

1. Whisk eggs until well-beaten in a shallow bowl. Pour cracker crumbs in a second shallow bowl.

2. Working with a few at a time, dip oysters in egg and dredge in cracker crumbs. Place on a pan in a single layer. Chill 2 hours.

3. Pour oil to depth of 1 inch in a Dutch oven; heat to 350°.

4. Working in batches, fry oysters 3 to 4 minutes or until golden brown. Do not add more oysters at one time than can float freely in the oil. Drain on paper towels. Serve immediately.

From the kitchen of Kathleen Wissinger
McGaheysville, Virginia

SLOW-COOKER PORK and PINTO CHALUPAS

A chalupa is a fried corn tortilla (sometimes shaped like a bowl or boat) that is filled with a savory mixture and finished with an assortment of tempting toppings. This recipe makes the dish easy to prepare. A package of taco salad shells works perfectly as premade chalupa bowls, and the delicious stew of pulled pork roast and pinto beans simmers in a slow cooker.

Makes 8 servings

1	(3½-lb.) bone-in pork loin roast	4	cups chicken broth
1	lb. dried pinto beans	1	(10-oz.) can diced tomatoes and green chiles with lime juice and cilantro
2	(4-oz.) cans chopped green chiles		
2	garlic cloves, chopped	8	taco salad shells
1	Tbsp. chili powder	1	small head iceberg lettuce, shredded
2	tsp. salt		Toppings: shredded Monterey Jack cheese,
1	tsp. dried oregano		pickled jalapeño slices, halved grape
1	tsp. ground cumin		tomatoes, sour cream, chopped avocado

1. Place pork in a 6-qt. slow cooker.
2. Rinse and sort beans according to package directions. Add beans to cooker.
3. Add green chiles, garlic, chili powder, salt, oregano, cumin, and broth. Cover and cook on HIGH 1 hour; reduce to LOW, and cook 9 hours.
4. Remove and discard bones and fat from roast. Pull meat into large pieces with two forks, and return to cooker. Stir in diced tomatoes.
5. Cook, uncovered, on HIGH 1 hour more or until liquid thickens slightly.
6. Heat taco salad shells according to package directions. Divide shredded lettuce evenly among shells. Spoon about 1 cup pork mixture into each shell using a slotted spoon.
7. Serve with desired toppings.

From the kitchen of Nora Henshaw
Okemah, Oklahoma

SPLENDOR IN THE BLUEGRASS

The Junior League of Louisville, Kentucky, 2000

As one might expect from a cookbook born in the land of bluegrass and brown liquor, this one offers 230 recipes submitted by JLL members, their family and friends, and local chefs and restaurants, each appropriate for gracious entertaining. The book also includes plenty of tips and hints, pictures from local photographers, and quotes from well-known Kentucky authors, such as this declarative bon mot from Corbin native Ronni Lundy: "There are those who will tell you that real cornbread has just a little sugar in it. They'll say it enhances the flavor or that it's an old tradition in the South. Do not listen to them. If God had meant for cornbread to have sugar in it, he'd have called it cake."

Bourbon—surely one of Kentucky's most appreciated and celebrated gifts to the world—features prominently in the beverage recipes. There's more to bourbon than juleps, but the city that hosts the Derby is bound to have thoughts on the subject. On the first Saturday in May, thousands of visitors flock to Louisville for "the most exciting two minutes in sports," capping the two-week-long Kentucky Derby Festival. When it comes to horse racing, astonishing hats, and the contents of heirloom silver julep cups, the stakes are high.

OLD KENTUCKY BOURBON MARINADE

Makes about 2 cups

¾	cup soy sauce	2	Tbsp. light brown sugar
½	cup bourbon	1	Tbsp. spicy brown mustard
¼	cup canola or corn oil	4	garlic cloves, minced
¼	cup Worcestershire sauce	1	tsp. ground white pepper
3	Tbsp. coarsely ground black pepper	½	tsp. ground ginger

Whisk together first 10 ingredients and ¼ cup water in a medium bowl. Use soon, or cover and chill for up to 3 days. Whisk just before using.

Splendor in the Bluegrass
Junior League of Louisville, Kentucky

SAUSAGE GRAVY

Sometimes gravy is the sauce. Sometimes it's the meal, served as a hearty breakfast or comforting supper. Most folks ladle sausage gravy generously over hot biscuits, although it can be served over grits or a skillet of home fries. One beloved Southern breakfast restaurant spoons it over their fried chicken biscuits.

Sausage gravy is called sawmill gravy in some communities, perhaps because it was often fed to ravenous sawyers working in lumber mills, or perhaps because the rough bits of cooked sausage resemble sawdust in the gravy.

Makes about 4 cups

1 lb. bulk pork sausage	Salt and freshly ground black pepper,
¼ cup all-purpose flour	to taste
2¼ cups whole milk, warmed	Chopped fresh parsley

1. Cook sausage in a large skillet over medium heat, stirring until it crumbles and is no longer pink. Remove sausage to a bowl using a slotted spoon, leaving drippings in skillet.
2. Whisk flour into hot drippings until smooth; cook, whisking constantly, 2 minutes.
3. Gradually whisk in milk and cook, whisking constantly, 5 to 7 minutes or until thickened and bubbly.
4. Stir in reserved sausage. Season with salt and plenty of pepper. Serve immediately.

From the kitchen of Art Shealey
St. Cloud, Florida

❧

PORK ROAST with CAROLINA GRAVY

If you don't own an instant-read thermometer, it's worth purchasing one. You'll soon learn to rely on it to ensure perfectly cooked meat in any recipe. This budget-friendly roast cooks to between 180° and 185° here. This is a higher temperature than recommended for most cuts of pork, but in this recipe it ensures incredibly tender slices.

Makes 8 servings

1 (5- to 6-lb.) bone-in pork shoulder roast (Boston butt)	3 medium onions, halved and sliced
2 tsp. salt	1 Tbsp. vegetable oil
2 tsp. freshly ground black pepper	2½ cups reduced-sodium chicken broth
4 medium leeks	½ cup dry white wine
3 thick bacon slices, chopped	10 fresh thyme sprigs
10 garlic cloves, halved	4 bay leaves
	1 Tbsp. butter

1. Preheat oven to 350°. Tie pork roast with kitchen string, securing at 2-inch intervals. Season with salt and pepper.

2. Remove and discard root ends and dark green tops of leeks. Thinly slice leeks; rinse well and drain. Cook bacon in an ovenproof Dutch oven or large, deep cast-iron skillet over medium-high heat 3 minutes.

3. Add leeks, garlic, and onions, and cook, stirring frequently, 15 to 17 minutes or until mixture is golden brown; transfer to a bowl.

4. Heat oil in Dutch oven. Add pork roast, fat side down, and cook 3 minutes on all sides or until browned. Remove pork.

5. Return leek mixture to Dutch oven. Top with pork. Add broth, wine, thyme, and bay leaves, stirring to loosen browned bits from bottom of pot. Bring to a boil. Remove from heat, and cover with tight-fitting lid or heavy-duty aluminum foil.

6. Bake at 350° for 3 to 3½ hours or until an instant-read thermometer inserted into thickest part of roast registers 180° to 185°. Remove pork from Dutch oven, cover with foil, and let stand 20 minutes before slicing.

7. Meanwhile, pour pan juices through a wire mesh strainer into a saucepan to equal 4 cups. Discard solids and any excess liquid. (Add equal parts broth and white wine to pan juices to equal 4 cups, if necessary). Let stand 5 minutes; skim fat from surface of pan juices.

8. Bring to a boil over medium-high heat; cook 20 to 25 minutes or until liquid reduces to 1 cup. Remove from heat. Stir in butter until melted. Serve with pork.

SHREDDED PORK WITH CAROLINA GRAVY:

Prepare recipe as directed through Step 6. Bake at 350° for 4 to 5 hours or until a meat thermometer inserted into thickest part of roast registers 195°. Remove from Dutch oven, cover with foil; let stand 20 minutes. Shred pork with two forks. Proceed with recipe as directed.

From the kitchen of Amy Tornquist
Durham, North Carolina

CUBAN BLACK BEANS and RICE

Makes 6 to 8 servings

Beans

1 lb. dried black beans
6 thick bacon slices, diced
1 large yellow onion, chopped
3 garlic cloves, minced
1 red bell pepper, chopped
8 cups chicken broth
2 bay leaves
1 tsp. salt
½ tsp. ground cumin

Mojo

2 garlic cloves, minced
1 Tbsp. chopped fresh cilantro
2 Tbsp. fresh lime juice
1 Tbsp. fresh orange juice
½ cup olive oil

Sofrito

7 garlic cloves
2 shallots, coarsely chopped
1 green bell pepper, coarsely chopped
1 cup chopped fresh cilantro
1 Tbsp. olive oil
1 Tbsp. smoked paprika
2 Tbsp. tomato sauce
2 Tbsp. chopped roasted red bell peppers
1 Tbsp. tomato paste

Plantain

Vegetable oil
1 unripe green plantain, peeled and cut into ½-inch cubes or thinly sliced
Hot cooked rice
Garnishes: fresh cilantro, lime wedges

1. To prepare beans, rinse and sort beans according to package directions. Place beans in a large Dutch oven. Cover with cold water to a depth of 2 inches above beans. Bring to a boil over high heat. Boil 1 minute, remove from heat, cover, and let stand 1 hour. Drain and set aside until needed.

2. Cook bacon in Dutch oven over medium heat, stirring often, 8 to 10 minutes or until crisp. Remove bacon to drain on paper towels. Leave drippings in Dutch oven.

3. Add onion, garlic, and bell pepper to hot drippings; cook, stirring often, 10 minutes or until tender.

4. Add broth, bay leaves, salt, cumin, and reserved beans. Bring to a boil over medium-high heat. Reduce heat to medium-low. Simmer, stirring occasionally, 2 hours or until beans are tender. Meanwhile, prepare mojo, sofrito, and plantain.

5. To prepare mojo, stir together garlic, cilantro, lime juice, and orange juice in a medium bowl. Heat ½ cup olive oil in a small saucepan over medium heat 2 to 3 minutes; whisk into juice mixture. Season with salt and pepper to taste.

6. To prepare sofrito, pulse garlic, shallots, bell pepper, and cilantro in a food processor until finely chopped. Heat oil in a medium saucepan over medium-high heat. Add garlic mixture; cook 5 to 7 minutes or until soft, stirring often. Add paprika, tomato sauce, roasted peppers, and tomato paste; cook, stirring, 3 minutes.

7. To prepare plantain, pour oil to depth of 1 inch in a 10-inch cast-iron skillet; heat to 340°. Fry plantain cubes or slices 2 to 3 minutes or until golden. Drain on paper towels.

8. Spoon desired amount of hot cooked rice onto individual serving plates. Top each with 1 cup black bean mixture and 1 Tbsp. sofrito. Drizzle each with 1 Tbsp. mojo. Sprinkle with reserved bacon and plantain cubes or slices.

From the kitchen of José Mendin
Miami Beach, Florida

JOHN'S NEW ORLEANS RED BEANS and RICE

Red beans and rice is a favorite comfort food. The dish originated in Louisiana and was a common dinner dish served on Mondays, the traditional wash day. The beans could simmer unattended while the cook was busy with the laundry and other chores. Plus, the long, slow simmer gives the nuanced flavors in this dish plenty of time to develop.

Makes 10 to 12 servings

1	lb. dried red kidney beans	3	bay leaves
¼	cup vegetable oil	3	garlic cloves, chopped
1	lb. mild smoked sausage, cut into ¼-inch-thick slices	2	Tbsp. salt-free Cajun seasoning
1	(½-lb.) smoked ham hock, cut in half	1	tsp. kosher salt
3	celery ribs, diced	1	tsp. dried thyme
1	medium-size yellow onion, diced	1	tsp. freshly ground black pepper
1	green bell pepper, diced	12	cups reduced-sodium chicken broth
			Serve with: hot cooked long-grain rice

1. Rinse and sort beans according to package directions. Place beans in a large Dutch oven. Cover with cold water to a depth of 2 inches above beans. Bring to a boil over high heat. Boil 1 minute, remove from heat, cover, and let stand 1 hour. Drain and set aside until needed.

2. Heat oil in the Dutch oven over medium-high heat. Add sausage and hock, and cook 8 to 10 minutes or until browned. Drain sausage and ham hock on paper towels, reserving 2 Tbsp. drippings.

3. Add celery, onion, bell pepper, bay leaves, garlic, Cajun seasoning, salt, thyme, and pepper to drippings. Cook over low heat, stirring occasionally, 15 minutes or until vegetables soften.

4. Add broth, beans, sausage, and ham hock to Dutch oven. Bring to a simmer. Cook, stirring occasionally, 2 hours or until beans are tender. Discard ham hock and bay leaves. Serve with hot cooked rice.

NOTE: Dried beans benefit from a rehydrating soak before cooking. This recipe calls for the quick-soak method in hot water, which renders the beans ready to cook in only 1 hour, as opposed to an overnight soak at room temperature.

From the kitchen of John Harris
New Orleans, Louisiana

PORK PICADILLO EMPANADAS

These dynamite filled turnovers are a popular Latin American street food. In this savory recipe, the pork filling gets subtle sweetness from raisins, crunch from toasted almonds, and a smoky kick from chipotle salsa.

Makes 16 empanadas

12 oz. ground pork
½ jalapeño pepper, seeded and minced
1 tsp. chili powder
1 tsp. ground cumin
¾ tsp. ground cinnamon
1 tsp. salt
¼ cup golden raisins
2 cups chipotle salsa, divided

2 Tbsp. fresh lime juice
3 Tbsp. chopped slivered almonds, toasted
½ cup sour cream
1 (16.3-oz.) can refrigerated buttermilk biscuits
1 large egg, beaten

1. Cook pork in a large skillet over medium-high heat 8 to 10 minutes or until meat crumbles and is no longer pink; drain.
2. Add jalapeño pepper, chili powder, cumin, cinnamon, and salt; cook, stirring occasionally, 2 minutes.
3. Stir in raisins, ½ cup salsa, and lime juice. Remove from heat, and stir in almonds and sour cream. Cool.
4. Separate dough into 8 biscuits. Separate each biscuit in half to make 16 rounds. Roll each round on a lightly floured surface to a 4-inch circle.
5. Spoon pork mixture evenly in center of each dough circle. Fold dough over filling, pressing edges with a fork to seal. Cover with plastic wrap, and chill up to 8 hours.
6. Preheat oven to 350°. Place empanadas on lightly greased baking sheets. Brush tops with egg.
7. Bake at 350° for 15 to 20 minutes or until golden. Cool 5 minutes on baking sheets. Serve with remaining 1½ cups chipotle salsa.

NOTe: For a more authentic touch, substitute frozen empanada wrappers for the biscuits. Follow instructions to prepare wrappers; proceed with recipe as directed.

From the kitchen of Gloria Bradley
Naperville, Illinois

BAKED HAM with BOURBON GLAZE

This is a center-of-the-table ham intended to feed a large group, often gracing tables at holidays and other special occasions. It's odd to think that this beloved Southern main dish started with a fully cooked product, but such is the case with most baked hams. It's the cook's way of making a good thing better.

Hams are a big deal. In addition to the main meal, a large baked ham generates plenty of great leftovers to enjoy for several days. A survey of old cookbooks and food magazines would suggest that cooks once had to grapple with too much leftover ham, always looking for tasty ways to use it up. That's likely what generated the quip that "eternity is two people and one ham." (Pictured on page 50)

Makes 12 to 14 servings

1	cup honey	2	Tbsp. Dijon mustard
½	cup light molasses or sorghum syrup	1	(6- to 8-lb.) smoked fully cooked,
½	cup bourbon		semiboneless ham
¼	cup orange juice		

1. Preheat oven to 325°. Microwave honey and molasses in a 1-qt. microwave-safe dish at HIGH 1 minute; whisk to blend. (Alternatively, heat honey and molasses in a small saucepan over medium heat.) Whisk in bourbon, orange juice, and mustard.
2. Remove skin and excess fat from ham, and place in a roasting pan.
3. Bake on lower oven rack at 325° for 1½ hours or until an instant-read thermometer inserted into thickest part of the ham registers 140°, basting occasionally with honey mixture. Transfer ham to a serving platter, reserving drippings.
4. Pour drippings into a small saucepan. Stir in remaining honey mixture. Bring to a boil over medium heat. Serve with sliced ham.

From the kitchen of Roevis McKay
New York, New York

SIDES, SALADS, and SAUCES

SPOONBREAD

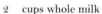

Spoonbread is an ethereal creamy-centered cornbread that rises like a soufflé. Although some people serve spoonbread with gravy, its true companions are butter, salt, and pepper.

Makes 6 servings

2   cups whole milk
1   cup plain cornmeal
1   tsp. kosher salt
¼   cup butter
4   large eggs, separated
Freshly ground black pepper

1. Preheat oven to 375°. Generously butter a 1½-qt. shallow baking dish.
2. Bring milk just to a boil in a large saucepan over medium-high heat. Gradually add the cornmeal, whisking constantly. Cook, stirring, 3 to 4 minutes or until mixture is smooth and thick, but not stiff.
3. Remove from heat, and quickly stir in salt and butter. Let stand 5 minutes, stirring occasionally. Whisk in egg yolks.
4. Beat egg whites (at room temperature) at medium speed with an electric mixer 5 minutes until soft peaks form. Fold whites into cornmeal mixture, one-third at a time. Pour into prepared baking dish.
5. Bake at 375° in center of oven for 45 to 50 minutes or until puffed, lightly browned, and set. Sprinkle with freshly ground black pepper.

From the kitchen of Winifred Green Cheney
Jackson, Mississippi

SIT and CHAT

Winifred Green Cheney was a noted cook in Jackson. She was also a close friend and near neighbor of Eudora Welty, often taking over a "tray lunch" when Miss Welty was facing a tight writing deadline. To express her gratitude and admiration, Miss Welty penned the introduction to Mrs. Cheney's cookbook.

GRANDE DAME

Charleston Receipts
(Copyright 1950; The Junior League of Charleston, Inc.)

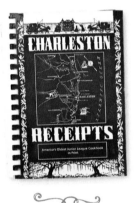

As the oldest Junior League cookbook still in print, this is the doyenne of spiral-bound community cookbooks. These recipes immortalize Charleston's culinary history and yet continue to inspire new generations of cooks. They reflect the closely woven culinary heritages of the Lowcountry aristocracy and the accomplished Gullah cooks who worked in their kitchens, often anonymously. The Gullah people, descendants of the enslaved Africans who worked on the colonial rice plantations of South Carolina and Georgia, used their impressive cooking skills and masterful understanding of local ingredients to create and influence much of Charleston's legendary cuisine. In addition to 750 recipes, *Charleston Receipts* includes sketches by local artists and Gullah verses. A section in the back includes "Gullah translations" for readers not familiar with the mellifluous dialect.

A small committee of about 21 league members came together to create the first edition of *Charleston Receipts* as a fund-raiser, starting with an investment of $150. They debated at length about how many copies to print before settling on 2,500, despite doubts about whether they could possibly sell that many. They did, plus at least 750,000 more. Other than some minor editing and reformatting, not a word has changed since the first copies were printed.

The word "receipt" might puzzle some readers who are not familiar with the Lowcountry tradition of using that term for recipes. Coincidentally, or perhaps not considering the many French and Italian immigrants to colonial Charleston, the French word for recipe is recette and the Italian is ricetta. The book addresses their word choice in the introduction, saying: "Throughout this book, as you will see, We never mention recipe—The reason being that we felt, (Though well aware how it is spelt!), That it is modern and not meant To use in place of old receipt To designate time-honored dishes According to ancestral wishes."

Charleston Receipts is a beloved cookbook in many kitchen collections. Who can guess how many visitors to Charleston carried home a copy as a souvenir? We hear of mothers buying a new copy as a wedding gift to each daughter or new daughter-in-law, carefully transcribing her handwritten notes into the margins.

Man w'en 'e hungry, 'e teck sum egg or cheese an' ting an' eat till e' full.
But 'ooman boun' fuh meck wuck an' trouble. 'E duh

~ TRANSLATION ~

"When a man is hungry, he takes some eggs or cheese and things and
eats until he is full, but a woman is bound to make work and trouble.
She cooks!"

MRS. RALPH IZARD'S AWENDAW

Makes 6 to 8 servings

1½ tsp. salt, divided
1½ cups uncooked quick grits (not instant)
1½ Tbsp. butter
3   large eggs, lightly beaten
1½ cups milk
¾   cup plain white cornmeal
2   Tbsp. butter

1. Preheat oven to 375°. Lightly grease 8 (1-cup) ramekins. Bring 1 tsp. salt and 6 cups water to a boil in a large saucepan over medium-high heat. Gradually whisk in grits, and return to a boil. Reduce heat to medium-low and cook, whisking often, 15 minutes or until thickened.

2. Remove grits from heat, and whisk in 1½ Tbsp. butter. Whisk about one-fourth of hot grits mixture into eggs; whisk egg mixture into remaining hot grits mixture. Gradually whisk in milk. Whisk in cornmeal and remaining ½ tsp. salt. Pour grits mixture into prepared ramekins.

3. Bake at 375° in center of oven for 30 to 35 minutes or until golden brown and set. Dot with 2 Tbsp. butter.

CHEESE AWENDAW:

Prepare recipe as directed, stirring in 2 cups (8 oz.) shredded smoked Gouda cheese and ½ tsp. ground red pepper after cornmeal.

GARLIC-&-HERB AWENDAW:

Prepare recipe as directed, stirring in 1 cup (4 oz.) freshly grated Parmesan cheese; ¼ cup each finely chopped fresh flat-leaf parsley, basil, and chives; 2 Tbsp. chopped fresh tarragon; 3 garlic cloves, pressed; and 1 tsp. freshly ground black pepper after cornmeal.

Charleston Receipts
Junior League of Charleston, South Carolina

SIT and CHAT

Awendaw is a very old Southern dish, but it wasn't always known beyond its community, also called Awendaw, which is the name given by the Sewee tribe of Native Americans to a small area near Charleston, South Carolina.

TOMATO DUMPLINGS

Fluffy dumplings are the feather beds of Southern comfort food. Here they float atop homemade chunky tomato sauce. This old-fashioned recipe is homey and filling, the type once served in meat-and-three diners or made by grandmothers for the Sunday table. Many family recipe boxes include a handwritten recipe for tomato dumplings.

Makes 4 to 6 servings

Sauce
¼ cup butter
½ cup finely diced onion
¼ cup finely diced green bell pepper
¼ cup finely diced celery
1 (28-oz.) can whole tomatoes, undrained and coarsely chopped
1 Tbsp. firmly packed brown sugar
½ tsp. dried basil
1 tsp. salt
¼ tsp. freshly ground black pepper
1 bay leaf

Dumplings
1 cup all-purpose flour
1½ tsp. baking powder
½ tsp. salt
1 Tbsp. butter, cut into small cubes and chilled
1 large egg, lightly beaten
⅓ cup milk
1 Tbsp. minced fresh parsley
1 Tbsp. chopped fresh basil

1. To prepare sauce, melt ¼ cup butter in a medium saucepan over medium-high heat. Add onion, bell pepper, and celery. Cook 5 minutes or until tender.

2. Stir in tomatoes, brown sugar, basil, salt, pepper, and bay leaf. Bring to a boil; reduce heat, and simmer 3 minutes.

3. To prepare dumplings, whisk together flour, baking powder, and salt in a medium bowl. Cut in chilled butter with a pastry blender until mixture is crumbly. Add egg, milk, parsley, and basil, stirring until dry ingredients are moistened.

4. Bring tomatoes to a low boil. Drop dough by tablespoonfuls onto surface of tomato mixture.

5. Cover and cook 20 minutes or until a wooden pick inserted into one of the dumplings comes out clean. Discard bay leaf. Serve immediately.

From the kitchen of Hilda Marshall
Culpepper, Virginia

HINT:

To prevent leaden, soggy dumplings, be sure the cooking liquid is gently boiling, and cover the pan until the cooking time is complete. Dumplings break apart when the cooking liquid is too cool.

WEST INDIES SALAD

This recipe is worth the splurge for top-quality jumbo lump crabmeat. The ice cubes sound like a peculiar ingredient, but their effect is an important part of the marinade, not to mention the charm and appeal of authentic West Indies Salad.

This salad is a quintessential regional dish in L.A. (Lower Alabama). It was invented by the late Bill Bayley, who owned a popular steak and seafood restaurant on the Gulf Coast. This well-guarded recipe was finally shared and published in 1964.

Makes 4 servings

1	medium-size sweet onion, very finely chopped
1	lb. jumbo lump crabmeat, picked
¾	tsp. salt
½	tsp. freshly ground black pepper
½	cup vegetable oil
⅓	cup cider vinegar
½	cup ice cubes

Serve with: assorted crackers
Garnish: chopped fresh parsley

The first cookbook of the Junior League of Mobile was originally published in 1964 and has been reprinted 13 times. This cookbook reflects the history of the city with updated recipes that have French, Spanish, and Southern influence.

1. Spread half of the onion in the bottom of a large bowl. Cover with crabmeat. Add the rest of the onion. Season with salt and pepper.
2. Pour oil and vinegar over the crabmeat mixture. Top with ice cubes.
3. Cover and chill at least 8 hours or up to 48 hours (the longer, the better).
4. Toss gently just before serving. Serve with crackers.

Recipe Jubilee!
The Junior League of Mobile

HOT Curried FRUIT

To Market,
To Market
Kentucky Junior
League of Owensboro

This curious side dish was quite popular at dinner parties and bridge club luncheons during the 1960s and '70s. It's a great accompaniment to baked ham and other roasted meats, although it is sweet enough to double as ice cream topping. For best flavor, make this a day ahead.

INGREDIENTS

1 can (29 oz) pear halves, drained

1 can (29 oz) peach halves, drained

1 can (29 oz) pineapple chunks, drained

2 cans (15 oz) apricot halves, drained

1 cup firmly packed brown sugar

1 x cup BUTTER softened

2 x tsp CURRY POWDER

1 tbsp. cornstarch

MAKES 8 SERVINGS

1 Preheat oven to 325°.

2 Place pears, peaches, pineapple and apricots in a 13- x 9- x 2- inch baking dish.

3 Whisk together brown sugar, cornstarch, and curry powder in a small bowl sprinkle over fruit. Dot with butter.

4 Bake at 325° for 30 minutes, basting occasionally with cooking liquid. Cool, cover, and chill overnight.

5 Preheat oven to 325°. Let mixture stand at room temperature for 15 minutes. Bake at 325° for 30 minutes or until bubbling, stirring occasionally. Serve warm.

CHICKEN and WILD RICE SALAD with TARRAGON VINAIGRETTE

Chicken and rice is a popular pairing all over the world, often appearing in casseroles and one-pot meals. Here, those ingredients form the heart of a crunchy chicken salad that is dressed with bright herbal vinaigrette.

Makes 4 to 6 servings

Vinaigrette
½ cup olive oil
¼ cup white wine vinegar
1 Tbsp. chopped fresh tarragon
1 tsp. kosher salt
½ tsp. freshly ground black pepper

Salad
½ cup uncooked wild rice
1 tsp. salt
2 cups chopped cooked chicken tenders
½ cup thinly sliced green onions
½ cup chopped celery
½ cup chopped toasted, blanched almonds
1 cup loosely packed watercress leaves

More than just a cook- book, The Junior League of Spartanburg, South Carolina, has produced a book that's illustrated with watercolors and also features beautiful local gardens. Originally pub- lished in 2001, this handy volume features over 200 recipes organized by season.

1. To prepare vinaigrette, gradually add olive oil to vinegar in a small bowl, whisking constantly until smooth. Whisk in tarragon, salt, and pepper.
2. To prepare salad, rinse rice in a fine wire-mesh strainer. Bring 1½ cups water and salt to a boil over medium-high heat in a small saucepan. Stir in rice, and return to a boil. Reduce heat to low, cover, and simmer, stirring occasionally, 40 to 50 minutes or until tender. Drain rice. Rinse under cold water; drain.
3. Stir together chicken, green onions, celery, almonds, and rice in a large bowl until combined. Drizzle desired amount of vinai- grette over salad; toss to coat. Cover and chill 1 hour. Toss with watercress and desired amount of remaining vinaigrette just before serving.

Meet Me at the Garden Gate
Junior League of Spartanburg, South Carolina

FAIRFIELD GROCERY'S CHICKEN SALAD

This is classic chicken salad, featuring lots of chicken and real mayonnaise with bits of finely chopped vegetables for crunch and color. It's been on the menu for ages at Fairfield Grocery & Market Cafe in Shreveport.

Makes 8 servings

3	lb. skinned and boned chicken breasts	1	cup finely chopped celery
6	cups chicken broth	½	cup finely chopped water chestnuts, drained
3	cups mayonnaise	½	cup finely chopped red bell pepper
1	tsp. ground red pepper	½	cup finely chopped yellow bell pepper
2	tsp. salt	½	cup finely chopped red onion
½	tsp. ground white pepper		

1. Place chicken breasts in a shallow layer in large skillet or pot. Add chicken broth. Cover and bring to a simmer over medium heat. Reduce heat to medium low, cover, and simmer 30 minutes or just until chicken is done. Drain. Discard broth or save for another use. Shred chicken with two forks.

2. Stir together mayonnaise, ground red pepper, salt, and white pepper in a large bowl until well-blended.

3. Add shredded chicken, celery, water chestnuts, bell peppers, and onion, stirring to coat. Cover and chill at least 4 hours.

SHRIMP SALAD:

Substitute 3 lb. chopped cooked shrimp for the cooked chicken breasts. Reduce mayonnaise to 2 cups and salt to 1 tsp. Proceed with recipe as directed.

From the kitchen of Gina Jester
Shreveport, Louisiana

HINT:

Boneless, skinless chicken breasts are very lean and can dry out quickly. Simmer them gently and only until done. Overcooked breast meat is tough and stringy.

BLUE and WHITE'S CHICKEN SALAD

The Collection by Mountain Brook Baptist Church was published in 1994 to celebrate the church's fiftieth anniversary. The compilation of recipes from church members and friends is an enduring reminder of the special occasion.

Clever and persistent cookbook committees could often woo coveted recipes from local cafes and restaurants. Birmingham's Blue & White Cafe closed years ago, but its chicken salad still receives rave reviews whenever it's served. The specified brands of mayonnaise and mustard are essential to the unique flavor. When great cooks share secrets about signature recipes, we should heed the advice.

Makes 4 to 6 servings

1¾ lb. cooked chicken breast tenders, chilled and chopped (about 4 cups)
3 to 4 celery ribs, diced (including some leaves)
1 cup toasted walnuts, coarsely chopped
1 cup Hellmann's mayonnaise
½ cup Honeycup Uniquely Sharp Mustard
1 tsp. freshly ground black pepper

Stir together all ingredients in a large bowl until blended. Serve immediately.

The Collection, an Anniversary Cookbook
of Mountain Brook Baptist Church
Mountain Brook, Alabama

TANGY TZATZIKI PASTA SALAD

Most summers don't go by without at least one batch of pasta salad. Well, move over, boring cold noodles. Here comes a salad that's full of flavor from ingredients inspired by the popular Greek yogurt and cucumber sauce known as tzatziki. This pasta salad goes great with grilled shrimp or chicken.

Makes 10 servings

2 cups low-fat plain Greek yogurt	1 red onion, sliced
¼ cup olive oil	1 cup pitted kalamata olives, sliced
2 Tbsp. chopped fresh dill	2 cucumbers, peeled, seeded, and diced
2 Tbsp. fresh lemon juice	½ cup sun-dried tomatoes in oil, drained and chopped
2 tsp. salt	1 (10-oz.) jar marinated artichoke hearts, drained and chopped
½ tsp. freshly ground black pepper	1½ cups crumbled feta cheese
3 garlic cloves, chopped	Grilled shrimp (optional)
16 oz. penne pasta	

1. Process yogurt, oil, dill, lemon juice, salt, pepper, and garlic in a food processor 30 seconds or until thoroughly blended. Transfer to a bowl; cover and chill 1 to 24 hours.
2. Cook pasta according to package directions. Drain and cool 10 minutes. Place in a large bowl.
3. Stir in onion, olives, cucumbers, tomatoes, and artichoke hearts.
4. Add yogurt mixture, and stir to coat. Gently stir in feta cheese. Cover and chill 1 hour.

From the kitchen of Dawn Moore
Warren, Pennsylvania

HOPPIN' JOHN SALAD

This is a light and delicate way to enjoy Hoppin' John, the perennial New Year's Day favorite eaten for good luck. Although black-eyed peas are most common, Hoppin' John can be made with any type of field pea, so take advantage of the local favorites that grow in your community, such as purple hull peas, lady peas, or crowder peas. There are dozens of types, each with a subtle difference in taste and texture.

Makes 6 cups

2   cups cooked black-eyed peas, drained
3   cups cooked long-grain rice
½   cup chopped red onion
¼   cup chopped celery
1   jalapeño pepper, seeded and minced
¼   cup loosely packed fresh chervil or parsley
¼   cup loosely packed fresh mint
1   garlic clove
1   tsp. salt
3   Tbsp. fresh lemon juice
¼   cup olive oil
¼   tsp. freshly ground black pepper

1. Combine peas, rice, onion, celery, and jalapeño in a large bowl.
2. Place chervil, mint, and garlic on a cutting board; sprinkle evenly with salt, and finely chop. Sprinkle over rice mixture, and stir gently.
3. Combine lemon juice, oil, and pepper in a small bowl. Pour over rice mixture, and stir to coat.

NOTE: Cooked rice keeps well, so consider making extra to have on hand. Store cooled rice in an airtight container in the refrigerator up to 7 days and in the freezer up to 6 months. Freeze the rice in 1- or 2-cup containers—or whatever amount you are most likely to use at once. To reheat the rice, add 2 Tbsp. liquid for each cup of rice. Cover and reheat in a small saucepan over medium-low heat for 4 to 5 minutes. Or, microwave, covered, at HIGH about 1½ minutes per cup.

From the kitchen of John Martin Taylor
Charleston, South Carolina

SHOUT HALLELUJAH POTATO SALAD

When cooks come across a reliable, creative, memorable potato salad that never fails to please the people around their tables, they have reason to rejoice. With this recipe, they might just shout "hallelujah!"

Makes 12 servings

5 lb. Yukon gold potatoes	¼ cup yellow mustard
1 Tbsp. salt	1 (4-oz.) jar diced pimiento, drained
4 large hard-cooked eggs, peeled	2 Tbsp. seasoned rice wine vinegar
1 cup plus 2 Tbsp. mayonnaise	2 Tbsp. fresh lemon juice
1 cup sweet salad cube pickles, drained	1 Tbsp. extra virgin olive oil
½ cup chopped red onion	1 to 2 jalapeño peppers, seeded and minced
½ cup chopped green bell pepper	1 to 2 tsp. celery salt
½ cup chopped celery	4 drops hot sauce
¼ cup chopped fresh flat-leaf parsley	½ tsp. smoked paprika

1. Cook potatoes and 1 Tbsp. salt in boiling water to cover 20 minutes or until tender; drain and cool 15 minutes. Peel potatoes, and place in a large bowl. Add eggs, and chop mixture into bite-size pieces.
2. Stir together mayonnaise, pickles, onion, bell pepper, celery, parsley, mustard, pimiento, vinegar, lemon juice, oil, jalapeño, celery salt, and hot sauce in a small bowl. Gently stir into potato mixture. Toss to coat. Season to taste with salt and pepper.
3. Sprinkle top with paprika. Serve immediately, or cover and chill up to 2 days.

From the kitchen of Blair Hobbs
Oxford, Mississippi

LAYERED CORNBREAD SALAD

Cornbread salad is a great choice for big family meals and casual entertaining. This one is similar to a classic chef's salad mixed with cornbread croutons. Because it is best when made a day ahead, cornbread salad travels very well—just right for tailgating and picnics. Some cooks prefer to make individual portions of salad in pint jars so that they can quickly pull them from the cooler and pass them around at their destination.

Makes 6 servings

1   (6-oz.) package buttermilk cornbread mix
1   (12-oz.) bottle Parmesan-peppercorn dressing
½   cup mayonnaise
¼   cup buttermilk
1   large bunch romaine lettuce, shredded (about 9 oz.)
2½ cups chopped smoked turkey (about 12 oz.)

2   large yellow bell peppers, chopped
2   large tomatoes, seeded and chopped
1   red onion, chopped
1   cup diced celery
2   cups (8 oz.) shredded Swiss cheese
10 bacon slices, cooked and crumbled
2   green onions, sliced

1. Prepare cornbread according to package directions; cool and crumble. Set aside.
2. Stir together dressing, mayonnaise, and buttermilk in a small bowl until blended.
3. Layer half each of crumbled cornbread, lettuce, turkey, peppers, tomatoes, red onion, celery, cheese, and bacon. Spoon half of dressing mixture evenly over top.
4. Repeat layers, ending with dressing mixture.
5. Cover and chill at least 8 hours or up to 24 hours. Sprinkle with green onions just before serving.

NOTE: If you prefer to use your own homemade cornbread, you'll need about 4 cups when crumbled.

LAYERED SOUTHWEST CORNBREAD SALAD:

Substitute 1 (6-oz.) package Mexican cornbread mix for 1 (6-oz.) package buttermilk corn-bread mix; 1 (16-oz.) bottle buttermilk-ranch dressing for Parmesan-peppercorn dressing; 1 (11-oz.) can sweet whole kernel corn, drained, and 1 (15-oz.) can black beans, drained and rinsed, for yellow bell peppers; and 1 (8-oz.) package finely shredded Cheddar and Monterey Jack cheeses with jalapeño peppers for shredded Swiss cheese. Prepare recipe as directed, omitting mayonnaise.

From the kitchen of Joanna L. Hay
Arcadia, Florida

SOUTHERN CONGEALIALITY

Gelatin salads bring back memories of supper at Grandma's.

Some of us believe that a celebration table, no matter how full, is lacking when there is no congealed salad. A cool little number with a come-hither jiggle can be appealing, so we don't understand those who poke fun at our beloved congealed creations, even when we call them salads and serve them as a side dish.

We are not alone; nine boxes of flavored gelatin are sold every second in the United States. That mind-boggling number confirms what many of us have suspected all along: A whole lot of folks embrace congealed creations with gusto, even if they are unwilling to admit it. Congealed salads suffer the slings and arrows from many naysayers, but even those folks can succumb to a little sentiment around the holidays. Perhaps it's the bemused recollection of a beloved grandmother, aunt, or other family member who prepared a quirky signature creation each year. It makes us smile, and perhaps shake our heads, to recall Nana's pride when she turned a jiggling jewel-toned creation out of the mold and trotted it into the dining room.

A review of family recipe cards and community cookbooks confirms that there was practically nothing that a cook could not congeal with a little determination and an overactive imagination. For better and for worse, cooks have congealed salads, soups, side dishes, and entrées with abandon. When gelatin recipes turn out well, it is easy to see why busy cooks like them. They are easy, nostalgic, pretty, refreshing, and open to endless customization through the addition of extra ingredients.

Because it can be difficult to unmold the congealed salad, there are several tips we have discovered over the years. First, lightly mist the inside of the mold with vegetable cooking spray before filling. Be sure the gelatin is firm before unmolding. It should spring back and jiggle when you gently press the top with your finger. And, before unmolding, carefully run a thin knife blade around the outer edge. You can also dip the bottom of the mold in warm water for about 15 seconds before unmolding. If salad sticks on the first try, dip in warm water again for about 5 seconds. Alternatively, wrap the outside of the mold in a warm, damp towel for 1 to 2 minutes.

To serve the salad on a platter, moisten the platter with a little water to help gelatin adhere to the surface and stay put. To serve it on crisp lettuce leaves, turn the leaves face down on top of the mold, top with the platter, and invert. If a small piece breaks while transferring it, put it back in place and use a drop of water to seal the edges. If you have a major mishap, cut the entire salad and serve it in a large bowl. We doubt you'll have leftovers, but if you do, spoon into parfait glasses with a mixture of cream cheese and whipped cream.

HOLIDAY CRANBERRY MOLD

Makes 8 servings

2   (6-oz.) packages raspberry-flavored gelatin
2   cups boiling water
1   (14-oz.) can whole-berry cranberry sauce
1   cup finely chopped celery
2   cups pineapple juice
1   Tbsp. fresh lemon juice
1   (20-oz.) can crushed pineapple, drained
1   (8-oz.) package cream cheese, softened
½   cup mayonnaise
½   cup finely chopped pecans
Garnishes: green leaf lettuce, chopped pecans

1. Dissolve gelatin in boiling water in large bowl, stirring until gelatin dissolves.

2. Stir in cranberry sauce, celery, pineapple juice, lemon juice, and crushed pineapple. Cover and chill 3 hours or until slightly set. The mixture should be the consistency of uncooked egg whites.

3. Beat cream cheese and mayonnaise until smooth in medium bowl with an electric mixer set to medium speed. Stir in chopped pecans.

4. Spoon cream cheese mixture evenly into 8 lightly greased 1-cup molds. Top with gelatin mixture. Cover and chill 8 hours.

5. Gently run a sharp knife around edges of mold to loosen. To serve the salad on crisp lettuce leaves, turn the leaves face down on top of the mold, top with the plate, and invert.

NOTE: If you don't have small molds, prepare the salad in ramekins or tea cups. To avoid unmolding the salads, prepare the mixture in wineglasses or compotes.

From the kitchen of Shirley Schmidt
Pass Christian, Mississippi

LIME GELATIN and COTTAGE CHEESE SALAD

Known as the best-selling community cookbook of all time, The Junior League of Baton Rouge has sold around 1.3 million copies of River Road Recipes since the first printing in 1959. With 650 recipes, this is a must-have for experiencing the heritage and tradition of Creole cooking.

This venerated recipe offers everything people adore (or cannot abide) about over-the-top congealed salads. Not everyone enjoys a congealed salad, not even when they harbor fond memories of a grandmother or other family member serving these molded creations on special occasions. That just means there's more for the rest of us.

Makes 16 servings

1 (6-oz.) package lime gelatin
1 (6-oz.) package lemon gelatin
1½ cups boiling water
1½ cups ice water
1 cup well-drained crushed pineapple
2 cups cottage cheese
1 cup mayonnaise
1 (14-oz.) can sweetened condensed milk
3 Tbsp. prepared horseradish
3 Tbsp. fresh lemon juice
¼ tsp. salt
1 cup finely chopped nuts

1. Dissolve gelatin in boiling water in a large bowl. Add ice water, and stir until ice melts and gelatin mixture cools. Stir in pineapple. Cover and chill 45 minutes or until slightly set. The mixture should be the consistency of uncooked egg whites.
2. Stir together cottage cheese, mayonnaise, sweetened condensed milk, horseradish, lemon juice, and salt in a medium bowl; stir into gelatin mixture. Fold in nuts.
3. Pour into a mold, if desired. Cover and chill overnight.

River Road Recipes: The Textbook of Louisiana Cuisine
Junior League of Baton Rouge

GRANDMA'S AMBROSIA

Ambrosia is a holiday tradition for many families, especially during the winter months when citrus is at its best. Grandmothers often served ambrosia in a sparkling glass bowl reserved for this special dish. As Dot put it, "When Grandmother took her cut-glass bowl from the cabinet, good things were sure to follow. That bowl always meant ambrosia. We had it for holidays, state occasions, and when the minister ate with us."

Makes 8 servings

8 oranges, peeled
¼ cup sugar

2 cups sweetened flaked coconut
1 cup coarsely chopped pecans

1. Section oranges over small bowl to catch juice. Reserve ¼ cup juice.
2. Cut orange sections in half. Place half of oranges in a serving bowl. Sprinkle with 2 Tbsp. sugar and top with 1 cup coconut. Repeat layers.
3. Sprinkle with pecans, and pour reserved juice over fruit.
4. Cover and chill.

From the kitchen of Dot Moore
Birmingham, Alabama

CREAMY SPICY CUCUMBERS

Part relish and part slaw, this easy side dish will perk up any plate or sandwich.

Makes about 6 cups

1   cup mayonnaise
¼   cup white vinegar
¼   cup evaporated milk
3   Tbsp. sugar
1   Tbsp. finely chopped parsley
2   tsp. hot sauce

½   tsp. salt
½   tsp. garlic powder
½   tsp. freshly ground black pepper
8   small cucumbers
1   bunch green onions, sliced

1. Stir together mayonnaise, vinegar, evaporated milk, sugar, parsley, hot sauce, salt, garlic powder, and pepper in a large bowl.
2. Peel, seed, and slice cucumbers. Add to bowl. Add green onions, and toss to coat.
3. Cover and chill 8 to 24 hours. Serve with a slotted spoon.

From the kitchen of Vickie Moses Perkins
Deridder, Louisiana

WATERMELON REFRESHER

This salad provides sweet, salty, and spicy relief on a hot summer day. It makes a huge amount, plenty for family reunions and weekend getaways. It is also versatile—try it in place of salsa on fish tacos, or dice the fruit a little smaller and serve with crisp corn chips.

Makes 12 to 16 servings

½	cup fresh lime juice	1	small seedless watermelon
2	Tbsp. turbinado sugar	1	small cantaloupe
2	Tbsp. fresh orange juice	2	English cucumbers
1	jalapeño or 2 serrano peppers, seeded and minced	1	jicama
2	tsp. sea salt or kosher salt	2	mangoes
½	tsp. dried crushed red pepper	½	cup coarsely chopped fresh cilantro
1	small red onion, diced	2	Tbsp. coarsely chopped fresh mint

1. Stir together lime juice, sugar, orange juice, jalapeño, salt, and crushed red pepper in a small bowl, stirring to dissolve sugar.
2. Place red onion in a large bowl. Dice watermelon and cantaloupe into 1-inch pieces; add to bowl. Peel and dice cucumbers, jicama, and mangoes; add to bowl.
3. Stir in lime juice mixture.
4. Cover and chill 20 minutes. Stir in cilantro, and mint and season with salt and pepper just before serving.

From the kitchen of Carolyn Kumpe
El Dorado, California

Taste of THE SOUTH

watermelon

Watermelon hits its prime in August, sweetening backyard barbecues, lazy-day picnics on the grass, and beach parties. It boasts an unbeatable combination for long, hot days: It's colorful, sweet, crunchy, refreshing, and portable. Choose a firm, symmetrical unblemished melon with a dull rind, without cracks or soft spots, that barely yields to pressure. Store uncut watermelon at room temperature for up to 1 week. If serving it chilled, refrigerate for 8 to 10 hours.

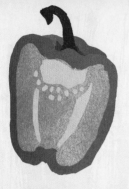

CONFETTI SWEET and SOUR SLAW

This appealing slaw is an updated version of the classic sweet-and-sour slaw made without mayonnaise, so it keeps well. It also travels well. You can transport the vegetables in a large zip-top bag and the dressing in a jar, and then assemble the slaw when you arrive at your destination.

Makes 8 to 12 servings

1   large red cabbage, shredded (9 cups)
1   lb. carrots, shredded (3 cups)
2   red or yellow bell peppers, cut into thin strips (3 cups)
1   small red onion, cut into thin strips (1 cup)
1   celery rib, thinly sliced
½   cup golden raisins
½   cup cider vinegar
¼   cup vegetable oil
¼   cup honey
1   Tbsp. fresh lemon juice
2   tsp. salt
½   tsp. freshly ground black pepper
Garnish: fresh cilantro leaves

1. Toss together cabbage, carrots, bell peppers, onion, celery, and raisins in a large bowl or heavy-duty zip-top plastic bag.
2. Combine vinegar, oil, honey, lemon juice, salt, and pepper in a jar; cover tightly, and shake vigorously. Pour over cabbage mixture, and toss to coat.
3. Chill.

From the kitchen of Bonnie Phillips
Weaverville, North Carolina

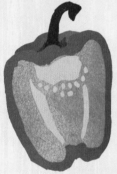

HINT:

If your favorite cabbage slaw recipe releases a lot of milky liquid as it sits, try this technique for removing excess moisture. Toss the shredded cabbage with 1 Tbsp. salt. Drain in a colander for 1 to 2 hours, then press or squeeze firmly. The cabbage will start to look soggy and wilted as it sits, but it turns out amazingly crisp, and stays that way after the slaw is made. When you use this method, the recipe might not need additional salt.

COLLARDS and KIMCHI

Many people who love collards appreciate a touch of hot pepper seasoning, so marrying this traditional Southern dish with a traditional spicy Korean dish is a smart move. Kimchi is a pleasantly pungent fermented Korean vegetable relish, similar to sauerkraut with a little kick. Look for jars or pouches of kimchi in the refrigerated produce section of well-stocked grocery stores. It's also popular at many local farmers' markets.

Makes 6 to 8 servings

1 Tbsp. butter	2½ cups reduced-sodium chicken broth
1½ tsp. lard or bacon drippings	2 tsp. soy sauce
1 cup chopped onion	1½ Tbsp. cider vinegar
1 cup large-diced country ham	1½ cups mild kimchi, drained and chopped
1½ lb. fresh collard greens, trimmed and coarsely chopped	

1. Melt butter with lard in a Dutch oven over medium-high heat until butter begins to foam. Add onion; cook 8 minutes or until onion just begins to brown.
2. Add ham, and cook 3 minutes.
3. Stir in collards, broth, and soy sauce. Cover and cook over medium heat, stirring occasionally, to desired degree of doneness, from 10 to 30 minutes. At 10 minutes, collards will be vibrant green and still have a little chewiness to them. At 30 minutes, collards will be drab green and fully tender.
4. Add vinegar; cook, stirring constantly, 1 minute.
5. Transfer mixture to a large bowl, and toss with kimchi. Serve immediately.

From the kitchen of Edward Lee
Louisville, Kentucky

SAUTÉED GREENS and WINTER SQUASH with OLIVE OIL-FRIED EGGS

To call this a side dish might be selling it short. Served with crusty bread, this is brunch or supper for two. Frying the eggs in very hot oil makes the whites firm and lacy along the edge while the yolks remain a little soft. The effect of the egg as it blends with the other ingredients in this sophisticated warm salad is fantastic.

Makes 2 servings

Salad
2   cups butternut squash cubes (1 small squash)
4   Tbsp. olive oil, divided
1   tsp. kosher salt, divided
1   medium onion, halved and thinly sliced
10 oz. mixed baby braising greens
¼   cup hazelnuts, toasted and coarsely chopped
2   Tbsp. dry sherry

Eggs
Olive oil
2   to 4 large eggs
¼   cup (1 oz.) crumbled goat cheese

1. To prepare salad, preheat oven to 450°. Toss squash with 2 Tbsp. olive oil; spread in a single layer on a baking sheet, and sprinkle with ½ tsp. salt. Bake 20 minutes or until squash is tender and golden brown, stirring occasionally.

2. Cook onion in remaining 2 Tbsp. hot oil in a large skillet over medium heat 10 minutes or until onion is tender.

3. Add greens, hazelnuts, sherry, and squash, tossing to coat. Sprinkle with remaining ½ tsp. salt. Cook, stirring often, 2 minutes or just until greens begin to wilt. Divide between 2 serving plates. Cover to keep warm.

4. To prepare eggs, pour olive oil to depth of ⅛ inch into a small nonstick skillet (about 1 cup oil for a 6-inch skillet). Heat oil over medium-high just until it begins to smoke. Reduce heat to medium. Break 1 egg into a ramekin or small bowl. Holding ramekin as close to surface as possible, carefully slip egg into oil. (Egg should sizzle, and oil might splatter.) Baste egg by rapidly spooning hot oil over it for about 30 seconds or until white is firm and crispy on edges. Remove egg from oil using a slotted spoon, carefully dabbing bottom of spoon with paper towels to absorb excess oil. Place egg atop cooked green mixture, and sprinkle with kosher salt to taste. Quickly cook the remaining eggs, one at a time.

5. Sprinkle goat cheese over greens mixture. Serve immediately.

NOTE: If you cannot find baby braising greens, substitute a quick-cooking leafy green such as spinach, chard, or baby kale. Discard stems, and tear leaves into large, bite-size pieces.

From the kitchen of Katie Button
Asheville, North Carolina

SPINACH PARMESAN

This lightly creamed spinach is a great side dish, and any leftovers can be used as a decadent omelet filling. Don't be alarmed by the huge pile of fresh spinach. It cooks down to the perfect amount. Avoid the temptation to use frozen spinach, which is far too mushy and wet for this recipe.

Makes 6 servings

Originally published in 1961, this cookbook has sold well over 100,000 copies in its lifetime. With over 700 recipes, the cookbook features dishes from famous West Coast Florida restaurants in addition to recipes with Greek, Spanish, Cuban, and Italian influence.

4   lb. fresh baby spinach
½   cup (2 oz.) freshly grated Parmesan cheese
½   cup whipping cream
⅓   cup butter
⅓   cup finely chopped onion
⅛   tsp. freshly ground black pepper
⅓   cup fine, dry breadcrumbs

1. Preheat oven to 450°. Lightly grease an 11- x 7-inch baking dish.
2. Bring ½ cup water to a simmer in a Dutch oven over medium heat. Add spinach in large handfuls, letting each addition wilt down a little before adding more. Cover and simmer 5 minutes or until tender. Drain well in a colander, pressing firmly to remove all excess liquid. Pour into large bowl.
3. Stir in Parmesan, cream, butter, onion, and pepper. Pour into prepared baking dish. Top with breadcrumbs.
4. Bake at 450° for 10 to 15 minutes or until thoroughly heated. Serve warm.

The Gasparilla Cookbook
Junior League of Tampa, Florida

SWEET POTATO CASSEROLE

This is the type of over-the-top sweet potato casserole that many of us expect to see on the Thanksgiving table. However, some people expect, if not demand, marshmallows on top. Other people prefer a crunchy topping that balances some of the casserole's unapologetic sweetness. This one delivers both, and if neither of those options will do, there are two more variations at the end. What an agreeable recipe.

Makes 6 to 8 servings

4½	lb. small sweet potatoes		¼	tsp. salt
1	cup granulated sugar		1½	cups cornflakes cereal, crushed
¼	cup milk		¼	cup chopped pecans
½	cup butter, at room temperature		1	Tbsp. brown sugar
2	large eggs		1	Tbsp. butter, melted
1	tsp. vanilla extract		1½	cups miniature marshmallows

1. Preheat oven to 400°. Grease an 11- x 7-inch baking dish.

2. Place sweet potatoes in single layer on baking sheet. Pierce potatoes with a fork. Bake at 400° for about 1 hour or until tender. Reduce oven temperature to 350°. Let potatoes cool to touch (about 20 minutes), peel, and place pulp in a large bowl. Beat at low speed with an electric mixer until smooth.

3. Add granulated sugar, milk, butter, eggs, vanilla, and salt. Beat at medium speed until smooth. Spoon into prepared baking dish.

4. Toss together cornflakes, pecans, brown sugar, and melted butter in a medium bowl. Sprinkle diagonally over casserole in rows that are 2 inches apart.

5. Bake at 350° for 30 minutes. Remove from oven, and let stand 10 minutes. Sprinkle marshmallows into rows not covered with cornflake mixture. Bake 10 minutes more. Let stand 10 minutes before serving.

GOLDEN MERINGUE-TOPPED SWEET POTATO CASSEROLE:

Omit cornflake topping and marshmallows. Bake sweet potato mixture at 350° for 30 minutes. Remove from oven; let stand 10 minutes. Beat 4 large egg whites at high speed with an electric mixer until foamy. Gradually add ¼ cup granulated sugar, 1 Tbsp. at a time, beating until stiff peaks form and sugar is dissolved. Spread meringue over sweet potato mixture; bake 10 more minutes or until golden.

PECAN-TOPPED SWEET POTATO CASSEROLE:

Omit cornflake topping and marshmallows. Pulse 3 Tbsp. all-purpose flour and ¼ cup firmly packed brown sugar in a food processor until combined. Add 1 Tbsp. cold butter, cut into small pieces, and process 45 seconds or until mixture is crumbly; stir in ⅓ cup finely chopped pecans. (Alternatively, stir together flour and brown sugar in a small bowl. Cut in 1 Tbsp. cold butter with a pastry blender until mixture is crumbly.) Sprinkle flour mixture over sweet potato mixture in baking dish. Bake at 350° for 40 to 45 minutes or until topping is golden brown.

From the kitchen of Jennifer Reich
Birmingham, Alabama

LEMON RICE

Makes 8 servings

1	garlic clove, very finely chopped	½	tsp. salt
2	cups chicken broth	1	cup basmati rice
2	Tbsp. butter	1	Tbsp. freshly grated lemon zest

1. Stir together garlic, broth, butter, and salt in a large saucepan. Bring to a boil over high heat. Stir in rice; reduce heat to low, cover, and cook 20 minutes or until broth mixture is absorbed and rice is tender. Do not lift lid until rice is likely to be done.
2. Fluff rice and stir in lemon zest using a fork.

LEMON-DILL RICE:

Prepare recipe as directed, stirring 1 Tbsp. finely chopped fresh dill into cooked rice along with the lemon zest.

From the kitchen of Lora Krug
Barrington Hills, Illinois

GOLDEN MACARONI and CHEESE

This is old-fashioned, simple, satisfying, straight-up baked macaroni and cheese. It comes from the oven golden and bubbly with a smattering of buttered crumbs on top. Some of us might recall our mothers or grandmothers shaking up flour and milk in a jar to remove any lumps. In the days before blenders, whisks, and other gadgets, it was a quick solution—and it still is.

Makes 8 servings

8   oz. elbow macaroni (about 2 cups)
2   cups milk
¼   cup all-purpose flour
1   tsp. salt
½   tsp. onion powder (optional)
½   tsp. freshly ground black pepper (optional)
¼   tsp. ground red pepper (optional)
¼   tsp. granulated garlic (optional)
¼   tsp. dry mustard (optional)
4½   cups (20 oz.) freshly shredded sharp Cheddar cheese, divided
1   cup soft, fresh breadcrumbs
¼   cup butter, melted

1. Preheat oven to 350°. Lightly grease a 13- x 9-inch baking dish.
2. Cook macaroni according to package directions until al dente. Drain well. Place in a large bowl. Set aside.
3. Place milk, flour, and salt in a qt. jar; cover tightly, and shake vigorously 1 minute. If using, add onion powder, pepper, ground red pepper, granulated garlic, and dry mustard; shake well. Pour over macaroni.
4. Stir in 3½ cups cheese. Pour into prepared baking dish. Sprinkle remaining 1 cup cheese over macaroni mixture.
5. Toss breadcrumbs and butter in a small bowl; sprinkle evenly over top.
6. Bake at 350° for 45 minutes or until golden brown. Let stand 5 minutes before serving.

NOTE: A 20-oz. loaf of pasteurized prepared cheese product, shredded or cut into small cubes, may be substituted for the Cheddar. For some of us, this is the secret ingredient that makes old-fashioned mac and cheese one of our favorite comfort foods.

From the kitchen of Louise Floyd
Potters Station, Alabama

RED RICE

Great cooks in the Lowcountry have been making red rice for nearly 300 years, a dish that draws on Native American, Italian, and African cultures. Red rice is a type of rice pilaf, a classic recipe with a long list of names and even more spellings, such as pillau, perloo, perlou, or perlow. The use of long-grain rice is essential to the texture of a proper pilaf because the grains can absorb every drop of the delicious cooking liquid and yet retain their shape without turning mushy.

Makes 8 servings

1   (28-oz.) can whole tomatoes, undrained
6   bacon slices, chopped
½   cup chopped onion
½   cup chopped celery
¼   cup chopped green bell pepper
2   cups long-grain rice, uncooked
2   tsp. salt
1   tsp. sugar
¼   tsp. freshly ground black pepper
1   tsp. hot sauce

1. Preheat oven to 350°. Lightly grease a 3-qt. baking dish.
2. Puree tomatoes with their juices in a blender. Set aside.
3. Cook bacon in a large skillet over medium-high heat, stirring often, 12 minutes or until crisp. Remove bacon with slotted spoon to drain on paper towels, leaving drippings in skillet.
4. Stir onion, celery, and bell pepper into drippings. Cook over medium-high heat 5 minutes or until tender. Stir in tomato puree, rice, salt, sugar, pepper, and hot sauce.
5. Cook 10 minutes over medium heat. Pour into prepared baking dish.
6. Bake, covered, at 350° for 25 to 30 minutes or until rice is tender and has absorbed the cooking liquid. Uncover, fluff rice with fork, and bake 10 more minutes.

Savannah Style
Junior League of Savannah, Georgia

Many of the over 450 recipes featured in this cookbook have been served in Savannah families since the colonial days. Other recipes are the most popular fare found at the city's landmark restaurants. The Junior League of Savannah shares with the reader a taste of the area's finest food mixed with Southern hospitality.

MAQUE CHOUX *with* ANDOUILLE SAUSAGE

This beautiful traditional dish of southern Louisiana benefits from both Cajun and Native American influences. There are several theories about its name, which is pronounced "mock shoe." Some culinary historians say it's derived from a French interpretation of a Native American word for corn. Maque choux is a tasty way to showcase fresh summer produce. This version gets a little oomph from spicy smoked andouille sausage.

Makes 8 servings

4 oz. andouille sausage, diced	1 cup peeled, seeded, and diced fresh tomato
½ cup sliced sweet onion	
½ cup chopped green bell pepper	¼ cup chopped green onion tops
2 garlic cloves, minced	1 cup sliced fresh okra (optional)
3 cups fresh corn kernels	1 tsp. Cajun seasoning

1. Cook sausage in a large skillet over medium-high heat 3 minutes or until browned.
2. Add onion, bell pepper, and garlic, and cook 5 minutes or until almost tender.
3. Add corn, tomato, onion tops, and okra, if desired. Cook, stirring often, 10 minutes or until tender. Add Cajun seasoning.
4. Season to taste with salt and pepper. Serve warm.

From the kitchen of Georgette M. Dugas
Crowley, Louisiana

DOWN-HOME SNAP BEANS with NEW POTATOES

This traditional recipe isn't as common as it once was, but it still deserves a place on our tables. Fresh beans and potatoes are finished in a sweet-and-sour bacon sauce that might remind you of German potato salad.

Makes 6 servings

1½ lb. small red potatoes, scrubbed and quartered

3 tsp. salt, divided

1 lb. fresh green beans, strings removed; beans broken into 1½-inch lengths

3 bacon slices, chopped

1 large onion, sliced

¼ cup cider vinegar

2 tsp. chopped fresh rosemary

½ tsp. sugar

1. Simmer potatoes, 1 tsp. salt, and water to cover in a large saucepan over medium-high heat for 10 minutes or until tender. Drain and set aside.

2. Simmer beans, 1 tsp. salt, and water to cover in saucepan over medium-high heat for 15 minutes or until tender. Drain and set aside.

3. Cook bacon in a large skillet until crisp. Remove bacon with slotted spoon, reserving drippings in skillet.

4. Cook onion in hot drippings 5 minutes or until tender. Stir in remaining 1 tsp. salt, vinegar, rosemary, and sugar. Add potatoes and green beans, and stir to coat. Cook, stirring occasionally, until heated through. Season to taste with salt and pepper. Sprinkle with bacon.

From the kitchen of Rubelene Singleton
Scotts Hill, Tennessee

HINT:

For best results, use old-timey green beans (such as half-runners and pole beans) that need to have their strings removed before they are broken into bite-size pieces. When you hear a reassuring snap, you know you have the right kind of bean. Many people contend that old-fashioned snap beans have superior flavor to contemporary stringless varieties. Keep in mind that although crisp-tender is best for tiny, fragile beans, sturdier beans need to be cooked until tender. That's appropriate cooking, not overcooking.

GERMAN POTATO SALAD *with* HOT BACON *and* BUTTERMILK DRESSING

There's always room in the family recipe collection for another great potato salad.

Makes 6 to 8 servings

8   new red potatoes (2 lb.)
8   slices bacon
1   small onion, chopped (1 cup)
2   Tbsp. all-purpose flour
2   Tbsp. sugar
1   tsp. salt
½   tsp. ground black pepper
¼   cup cider vinegar
½   cup buttermilk

1. Cook potatoes in a large saucepan of salted water 25 minutes or until tender.

2. Meanwhile, cook bacon in large heavy skillet over medium heat until crisp, about 15 minutes. Drain bacon on paper towels. Leave drippings in skillet.

3. Drain potatoes, peel if desired, and cut into thick slices. Place in serving bowl.

4. Add onion to skillet, and stir to coat in drippings; cook, stirring often, 5 minutes or until tender. Sprinkle flour, sugar, salt, and pepper over onions, and cook, stirring, 2 minutes. Stirring constantly, gradually add vinegar and ¼ cup water. Cook, stirring, 5 minutes or until mixture thickens and bubbles. Gradually stir in buttermilk. Cook, stirring, 3 minutes or until mixture thickens and bubbles. Pour warm dressing over warm potatoes, and stir gently to coat. Crumble bacon over potatoes. Serve warm or at room temperature.

Dining in the Smoky Mountain Mist: A Collection of Seasonal Delights
The Junior League of Knoxville, Tennessee

Published in 1995 by the Junior League of Knoxville, this 254-page cookbook features recipes from members as well as local celebrities and chefs. It's organized by seasons and contains quotes from writer and lecturer Wilma Dykeman.

BOK CHOY and CRUNCHY RAMEN SALAD

Not too long ago, many of us were unfamiliar with leafy green bok choy. Now we see it everywhere and appreciate that is just another form of inexpensive and easy-to-use cabbage, perfect for slaws and salads, such as this one. Uncooked ramen noodles team up with sunflower seeds and almonds to give this salad plenty of crunch.

Makes 6 to 8 servings

2   (3-oz.) packages ramen noodle soup mix
½   cup sunflower seeds
3   Tbsp. slivered almonds, chopped
½   cup sugar
¼   cup olive oil
¼   cup cider vinegar
2   Tbsp. soy sauce
1   bok choy, shredded
6   green onions, chopped

1. Preheat oven to 350°.
2. Discard flavor packets from soup mix. Crumble noodles onto a large baking sheet. Add sunflower seeds and almonds, and toss to combine. Spread in a single layer. Bake at 350° for 8 to 10 minutes or until golden brown. Cool.
3. Bring sugar, oil, vinegar, and soy sauce to a boil in a small saucepan over medium heat, stirring until sugar dissolves. Remove from heat, and cool completely.
4. Place bok choy and green onions in a large bowl. Drizzle with sugar mixture. Add ramen noodle mixture, and toss well. Serve immediately.

From the kitchen of Pat Hagedorn
Marco Island, Florida

OLD-FASHIONED CREAMED CORN

Makes 6 to 8 servings

12 ears freshly picked sweet corn
¼   cup butter
1   tsp. salt
¼   tsp. freshly ground black pepper
1   Tbsp. sugar (optional)
¼   cup milk
1   Tbsp. cornstarch

1. Shuck corn, and brush away the silks. Cut corn kernels off the cobs into a large bowl. Scrape the cobs with the back of the knife or a spoon to remove the milk; add to bowl.
2. Melt butter in a large, heavy skillet over medium heat. Stir in corn, salt, pepper, and, if desired, sugar. Cook, stirring slowly and constantly, 10 to 12 minutes or until corn is tender.
3. Stir together milk and cornstarch in a small bowl until smooth. Pour into corn; cook, stirring constantly, until mixture thickens. Serve immediately.

From the kitchen of Sharon Mould
Largo, Florida

DECADENT SCALLOPED POTATOES

This dish sounds fancy, but it's easy. The key to this recipe's great texture is warming up the potatoes in the cream before spooning them into the baking dish, which gives the potatoes a chance to release a little starch to hold everything in place.

Makes 6 to 8 servings

¼ cup butter
2 cups whipping cream
2 garlic cloves, chopped
1½ tsp. salt
½ tsp. freshly ground black pepper
1 tsp. dried Italian seasoning
¼ cup fresh flat-leaf parsley, chopped
2 lb. Yukon gold potatoes, peeled and thinly sliced
½ cup (2 oz.) freshly shredded Gruyère cheese

1. Preheat oven to 400°. Lightly grease a 13- x 9-inch baking dish.
2. Melt butter in a Dutch oven over medium-high heat. Stir in cream, garlic, salt, pepper, Italian seasoning, and parsley. Stir in potatoes.
3. Bring just to a boil, reduce heat to medium-low, and cook 15 minutes or until potatoes are tender. Stir gently to avoid breaking potato slices.
4. Spoon mixture into prepared dish, and spread evenly. Sprinkle with cheese.
5. Bake at 400° for 25 to 30 minutes or until bubbly and golden brown. Remove to a wire rack, and let stand 10 minutes before serving.

NOTE: Substitute freshly shredded Parmesan cheese for the Gruyère, if you like.

From the kitchen of Andrew Lewis
Birmingham, Alabama

SQUASH CASSEROLE

All cooks need at least one great summer squash casserole in their repertoire. It's awfully easy to grow too much squash, so even if we don't grow our own, we probably have friends or family members who will want to share theirs. If we had a nickel for every dish of squash casserole that has graced the tables at Southern covered-dish dinners, we'd have a whole lot of nickels, and, thankfully, a lot less squash. The best defense against too much summer squash is a good offense.

Makes 8 servings

1½ lb. small yellow squash
1   lb. small zucchini
1   small sweet onion, chopped
2½ tsp. salt, divided
1   cup grated carrots
1   (10¾-oz.) can cream of chicken soup
1   (8-oz.) container sour cream
1   (8-oz.) can water chestnuts, drained (optional)
1   (8-oz.) package herb-seasoned stuffing mix
½   cup butter, melted

1. Preheat oven to 350°. Lightly grease a 13- x 9-inch baking dish.
2. Cut squash and zucchini into ¼-inch-thick slices; place in large glass bowl. Add chopped onion, 2 tsp. salt, and 2 Tbsp. water. Cover tightly with plastic wrap, and microwave at HIGH for 5 minutes or until tender; drain well. (Alternatively, cook squash mixture in a steamer basket over simmering water.)
3. Stir together carrots, soup, sour cream, and remaining ½ tsp. salt in a large bowl. Stir in water chestnuts, if desired. Fold in squash mixture.
4. Stir together stuffing and melted butter. Spoon half of stuffing mixture in bottom of prepared baking dish. Spoon squash mixture over stuffing mixture. Top with remaining stuffing mixture.
5. Bake at 350° for 30 to 35 minutes or until bubbly and golden brown, shielding with aluminum foil during last 10 to 15 minutes to prevent excessive browning, if necessary. Let stand 10 minutes before serving.

From the kitchen of Marie T. Scott
Augusta, Georgia

HINT:

When using aluminum foil to shield a dish from excessive browning, just place the flat sheet over the top of the dish without tucking under the edges. Folding the foil tightly closed, such as when using foil as a lid, holds in moisture, which makes crumb toppings soggy.

GRILLED ROMAINE SALAD with BUTTERMILK-CHIVE DRESSING

This salad might sound unusual, but a touch of char and smoke is a wonderful way to make a crisp romaine salad memorable. The Buttermilk-Chive Dressing is similar to homemade Ranch dressing. It is so appealing and versatile that it might become your house dressing.

Makes 8 servings

4   romaine lettuce bunches
1   small red onion
2   Tbsp. olive oil

Buttermilk-Chive Dressing (recipe follows)
½   cup (2 oz.) freshly shaved Parmesan cheese

1. Coat cold grill cooking grate evenly with vegetable cooking spray, and place on grill over medium (300° to 350°) heat.
2. Discard tough outer leaves of romaine bunches. Cut bunches in half lengthwise, keeping leaves intact.
3. Peel onion, and cut in half vertically, keeping core (root end and top) intact. Cut each half into 4 wedges. Brush lettuce and onion evenly with olive oil.
4. Place onion wedges on cooking grate, and grill, covered with grill lid, 3 to 4 minutes on each side or to desired degree of doneness. Remove onion wedges.
5. Place romaine halves, cut sides down, on cooking grate. Grill, without grill lid, 2 to 3 minutes or just until wilted.
6. Divide grilled lettuce, cut sides up, evenly among serving plates. Top each with 1 onion wedge (separate into slices, if desired), and drizzle with Buttermilk-Chive Dressing.
7. Sprinkle evenly with Parmesan. Season to taste with kosher salt and freshly ground black pepper. Serve immediately.

BUTTERMILK-CHIVE DRESSING

Makes 1¼ cups

¾   cup buttermilk
½   cup mayonnaise
2   Tbsp. chopped fresh chives
1   Tbsp. minced green onion

1   garlic clove, minced
½   tsp. salt
¼   tsp. freshly ground black pepper

Combine all ingredients in a 1-pt. jar with a tight-fitting lid. Shake vigorously to combine. Chill until ready to use. Store refrigerated up to 3 days. Shake well just before serving.

From the kitchen of Laura Zapalowski
Birmingham, Alabama

OKRA FRIES with YOGURT SAUCE

Fresh okra is as prolific in parts of India as it is in the American South. This fantastic recipe is full of bold flavors and great textures, and it just might change the way you think about okra.

Thin okra strips are prepared like crisp French fries, generously seasoned, and tossed with fresh tomatoes, peanuts, and lots of fresh herbs. A quick yogurt sauce is the perfect way to tame the heat.

Makes 4 to 6 servings

Yogurt Sauce
1   cup plain Greek yogurt
1   tsp. cider vinegar
2   Tbsp. finely diced apple
2   Tbsp. finely diced red onion
1   Tbsp. chopped fresh chives
2   Tbsp. fresh lime juice

Okra
¼   cup fresh lime juice
2   Tbsp. Worcestershire sauce
1   Tbsp. dark molasses

Vegetable oil
2   lb. medium okra, cut lengthwise
     into thin strips
2   shallots, minced
½   cup roasted peanuts, coarsely chopped
1   Tbsp. garam masala
¼   tsp. ground red pepper
2   medium tomatoes, seeded and diced
¼   cup chopped fresh mint
¼   cup chopped fresh cilantro

1. To prepare sauce, whisk together yogurt and vinegar in a small bowl. Whisk in apple, onion, chives, and lime juice. Cover and chill until needed.
2. To prepare okra, stir together lime juice, Worcestershire, and molasses in a small bowl.
3. Pour oil to depth of 2 inches into a Dutch oven; heat to 375°. Working in batches, fry okra 7 to 10 minutes or until crispy and deep golden brown; drain on paper towels. Place in large bowl.
4. Add shallots, peanuts, garam masala, ground red pepper, tomatoes, mint, cilantro, and 3 Tbsp. of lime mixture. Toss to mix. Serve immediately with Yogurt Sauce and remaining lime juice mixture.

From the kitchen of Vishwesh Bhatt
Oxford, Mississippi

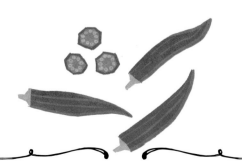

CRISP OKRA, ONION, and TOMATOES

Stewed okra and tomatoes is a classic Southern side dish, but this recipe reinvents the idea, making it brighter and fresher. Tender okra pods are quickly sautéed, then tossed with zesty red onion, juicy ripe tomatoes, and fresh lime. Come summer, when our gardens and farmers' markets are bursting with fresh okra and sun-ripened tomatoes, you'll want to keep this easy recipe close at hand.

Makes 8 servings

1	medium-size red onion, thinly sliced	2	lb. small fresh okra pods
1	pt. grape tomatoes, halved	¼	cup vegetable or olive oil
2	Tbsp. fresh lime or lemon juice	½	tsp. salt
2	tsp. Creole seasoning blend	¼	tsp. freshly ground black pepper

Stir together onion, tomatoes, lime juice, and seasoning blend in a large bowl. Cut okra pods in half lengthwise. Heat oil in a large skillet over medium-high heat. Working in batches, cook okra, red onion, and tomatoes 6 minutes or until browned, turning occasionally. Drain well on paper towels. Sprinkle hot vegetables with salt and pepper. Add more oil to skillet between batches, if needed. Serve at room temperature.

From the kitchen of Romey Johnson
Woodbridge, Virginia

RATATOUILLE

Ratatouille is a summertime miracle because it scoops up everything that surges into ripeness at the same time. Is your garden bursting at the seams? Did you get carried away and come home from the farmers' market with enough produce to feed an army? Want to cook a whole bunch of one delicious thing on the weekend and then use it creatively throughout the week? Ratatouille is the answer. Consider a double or triple batch.

The vegetable medley is one of the most versatile dishes you can make. It's a side dish, a salad to serve with fresh mozzarella cheese, a pasta sauce, a topping for bruschetta and pizza, an omelet filling, a lasagna layer, a relish for grilled meats, and so on. It is just as delicious served at room temperature as it is warm. Ratatouille freezes well, although it is a little softer and juicier when thawed.

Makes 4 to 6 servings

1 green bell pepper	1 large onion, coarsely chopped
1 red bell pepper	2 garlic cloves, minced
1 yellow bell pepper	3 medium-size ripe tomatoes, chopped
½ lb. zucchini	with their juices (about 1 lb.)
½ lb. yellow squash	1 tsp. salt
1 small eggplant (about 1 lb.)	¼ cup thinly sliced fresh basil
3 Tbsp. olive oil	Freshly ground black pepper to taste

1. Cut bell peppers into 1-inch pieces. Cut zucchini and squash into 1-inch slices. Set aside.

2. Cut eggplant into 1-inch cubes. Set aside separately.

3. Heat oil in a large skillet over medium heat. Add onion, and cook 5 to 7 minutes or until tender. Add garlic, and cook 1 minute.

4. Stir in tomatoes, eggplant, and salt. Cook 8 to 10 minutes or just until eggplant begins to soften. Stir in bell peppers, zucchini, and squash; cover and cook, stirring occasionally, 8 to 10 minutes or until vegetables are tender and liquid reduces and thickens slightly.

5. Stir in basil. Season to taste with additional salt and freshly ground black pepper. Serve warm or at room temperature.

NOTE: Most of the vegetables in ratatouille are available year-round, but not great sun-ripened local tomatoes, which are exclusively a summertime delight. The rest of the year, use high-quality canned tomatoes, which have more flavor than so-called fresh. Substitute 2 (14½-oz.) cans diced tomatoes for the fresh. The key to cooking with produce is to select it in the best form available at that time.

From the kitchen of Carolyn Flournoy
Shreveport, Louisiana

TOMATO PIE

Fresh tomato pie is a summertime staple on many Southern tables, but isn't well known outside the region. However, most people are won over by their very first bite. (Pictured on page 98)

Makes 6 servings

Sour Cream Pastry Crust
1¼ cups all-purpose flour
2   tsp. baking powder
½   tsp. salt
½   cup shortening
½   cup sour cream
Filling
4   medium heirloom tomatoes, cut into ½-inch-thick slices (about 1½ lb.)

1   tsp. salt
1   cup (4 oz.) shredded Parmesan cheese, divided
½   cup mayonnaise
3   green onions, chopped
2   Tbsp. chopped fresh basil
Garnishes: shaved Parmesan cheese, basil leaves

1. To prepare crust, whisk together flour, baking powder, and salt in a large bowl. Cut shortening into flour mixture with a pastry blender until mixture is crumbly. Add sour cream; stir with a fork until combined. Gently gather dough into a flat disk; wrap in plastic wrap, and chill 1 to 24 hours. Roll pastry into a 13-inch circle on a lightly floured surface. Fit into a 9-inch pie plate; fold edges under, and crimp. Cover and chill until needed.
2. To prepare filling, place tomatoes in a single layer on a wire rack lined with paper towels. Sprinkle with salt. Let stand 30 minutes. Pat dry with paper towels.
3. Preheat oven to 400°. Bake crust for 10 to 12 minutes or until lightly browned. Remove from oven.
4. Sprinkle ¼ cup cheese over bottom of warm crust. Arrange tomato slices over cheese.
5. Stir together mayonnaise, green onions, chopped basil, and remaining ¾ cup of cheese. Spread over tomatoes. Bake 20 to 25 minutes or until lightly browned. Let cool at least 5 minutes before serving hot, warm, or at room temperature.

From the kitchen of Libbo McCollum
Jasper, Alabama

HINT

Excellent sun-ripened tomatoes are the heart and soul of this dish.
However, ripe tomatoes are juicy. To keep the crust from turning soggy,
sprinkle the tomatoes with salt, and let them drain for a few minutes.
The tomatoes benefit from the seasoning, and the pie benefits from
less moisture. Although you can purchase a crust, this homemade
pastry is very easy and dependable. The sour cream makes the dough a
dream to handle and the pastry light and flaky.

BAKED BARBECUE BEANS

If there were such a thing as a list of the Top 5 Must-Haves for a Cook Out, baked beans would be on it. These are meaty, tangy, sweet, savory, and smoky. In short, they are just plain good. For best results, make them a day ahead so that the flavors have time to meld.

Makes 10 servings

1	tsp. vegetable oil	1	(15-oz.) can butter beans, drained and rinsed
1	small onion, chopped		
8	oz. ground beef or pork sausage (optional)	1	(15-oz.) can pork and beans, undrained
10	bacon slices, cooked and crumbled	2	Tbsp. molasses or sorghum syrup
⅔	cup firmly packed brown sugar	1	Tbsp. Dijon mustard
¾	cup barbecue sauce	1	tsp. salt
1	(15-oz.) can kidney beans, drained and rinsed	1	tsp. chili powder
		1	tsp. paprika
		½	tsp. freshly ground black pepper

1. Heat oil in a Dutch oven over medium-high heat. Add onion and, if desired, ground beef. Cook, stirring until meat crumbles and is no longer pink; drain.
2. Stir in bacon, brown sugar, barbecue sauce, beans, molasses, mustard, salt, chili powder, paprika, and pepper.
3. Spoon into a lightly greased 2½-qt. baking dish. Cover and chill 8 hours, if desired.
4. Preheat oven to 350°. Bake at 350° for 1 hour, stirring once.

***From the kitchen of** Patty Renwick*
Mount Airy, Maryland

OYSTER DRESSING

Many of us maintain a lifelong affection for the type of dressing we enjoyed while growing up. For most of the South, that is some sort of cornbread dressing. The additions and variations tend to follow regional and hometown preferences. This recipe comes from a chef who learned it from his mom while growing up in New Orleans, a place partial to oyster dressing.

Makes 12 servings

3	Tbsp. olive oil	2	tsp. ground black pepper
2	medium onions, finely chopped	1	tsp. salt
4	celery ribs, finely chopped	1	tsp. dried crushed red pepper
2	red bell peppers, finely chopped	1	tsp. hot sauce
2	green bell peppers, finely chopped	2	(8-oz.) containers fresh oysters, drained and coarsely chopped
4	garlic cloves, minced	2	large eggs, beaten
¼	cup butter	1	cup (4 oz.) finely grated Parmigiano-Reggiano cheese
⅔	cup dry white wine		
½	cup chicken broth	8	cups crumbled cornbread
3	bay leaves		
2	Tbsp. fresh thyme leaves		

1. Preheat oven to 375°. Lightly grease a shallow 3-qt. or 13- x 9-inch baking dish.
2. Heat oil in a large skillet over medium heat. Add onion, celery, bell peppers, and garlic; cook 15 to 20 minutes or until tender and lightly browned.
3. Stir in butter, wine, broth, bay leaves, thyme, pepper, salt, crushed red pepper, hot sauce, and oysters. Cook 3 to 4 minutes or until edges of oysters begin to curl. Remove from heat; let stand 10 minutes. Discard bay leaves. Pour into a large bowl.
4. Stir in eggs and cheese. Fold in cornbread. Spoon mixture into baking dish.
5. Bake at 375° for 40 to 45 minutes or until lightly browned.

From the kitchen of John Currence
Oxford, Mississippi

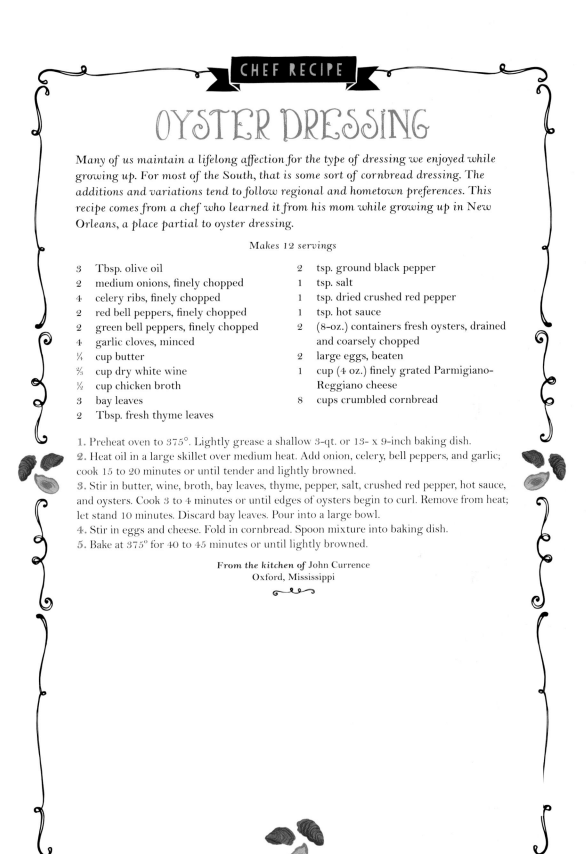

SOUPS, STEWS, and GUMBO

OLD-FASHIONED CHICKEN and DUMPLINGS

Makes about 2½ qt.

SIT and CHAT

We are grateful for the chicken, but this dish is really all about the dumplings. Perfect dumplings are simultaneously substantial and ethereal, both filling and light as a feather. We might never guess that cooks started adding inexpensive dumplings to the pot in an effort to stretch one chicken into enough to feed a large family. Chilled fat and the even distribution of ingredients are keys to dumpling success.

Chicken and Chicken Broth
1   (3¾-lb.) whole chicken
3   carrots, cut into quarters
3   celery ribs, cut into quarters
2   yellow onions, cut into quarters
3   garlic cloves
6   fresh thyme sprigs
1   tsp. salt

Dumplings
3   cups self-rising flour
½   tsp. poultry seasoning
½   tsp. salt
⅓   cup vegetable shortening, chilled
2   tsp. bacon drippings, chilled
1   cup milk
Garnish: celery leaves

1. To prepare broth, bring chicken, carrots, celery, onions, garlic, thyme, salt, and water to cover to a boil in a Dutch oven over medium heat. Reduce heat to medium-low, and simmer 45 minutes or until chicken is done. Remove chicken, reserving liquid and vegetables in Dutch oven. Cool chicken 30 minutes; skin, bone, and shred chicken. Return skin and bones to Dutch oven. Loosely cover chicken meat, and refrigerate until needed.

2. Continue to simmer broth over medium heat 1 hour or until broth reduces to about 6 cups. Pour broth through a wire-mesh strainer into a large saucepan; discard solids.

3. To prepare dumplings, combine flour, poultry seasoning, salt, and broth in a medium bowl. Cut in shortening and bacon drippings with a pastry blender until mixture is crumbly. Add milk, stirring only until dry ingredients are moistened.

4. Turn dough out onto a lightly floured surface. Roll to ⅛-inch thickness, and sprinkle lightly with flour; cut into 4- x ½-inch strips.

5. Bring broth mixture to a boil. Drop dumplings, 1 piece at a time, into boiling broth, stirring gently after each addition. Reduce heat, and simmer, stirring often, 20 minutes. Serve hot.

From the kitchen of Mrs. Alex B. Snyder
Monroe, North Carolina

POT LIKKER SOUP

Pot likker is the delicious broth produced when greens simmer in well-seasoned cooking liquid, and is many people's favorite part of a pot of greens. Great cornbread is a required accompaniment because it will sop up every last drop. Collards are traditional, but feel free to substitute other sturdy leafy greens, such as kale, mustard, or turnip.

Makes 10 cups

HINT:

Many of us appreciate the convenience of canned field peas and beans. However, some of us prefer to cook fresh, frozen, or dried legumes from scratch. You'll need 1¾ cups of fresh or frozen peas to replace each 15-oz. can. One pound of dry beans makes 5 to 6 cups of cooked beans, equivalent to about 3 cans.

2   lb. fresh collard greens
¾   lb. smoked ham hocks
3   Tbsp. olive oil
1½ lb. cooked ham, chopped
2   Tbsp. hot sauce
3   medium onions, chopped
1   garlic clove, minced
10 cups chicken broth
½   cup vermouth
6   red potatoes, diced
2   (15-oz.) cans field peas with snaps, drained and rinsed
2   (15-oz.) cans crowder peas, drained and rinsed
1   Tbsp. white vinegar
2   tsp. salt

1. Remove and discard stems and discolored spots from collards; rinse with cold water. Drain; tear leaves into 1-inch pieces.
2. Place collards, ham hocks, and water to cover in a large Dutch oven. Bring to a boil; remove from heat; drain. Repeat procedure. Drain and set aside.
3. Heat oil in Dutch oven over medium-high heat. Toss together ham and hot sauce. Cook 6 to 8 minutes or until browned. Add onion and garlic; cook 5 minutes or until tender.
4. Stir in broth, vermouth, potatoes, field peas, crowder peas, collards, and ham hocks. Bring to a boil, reduce heat, and simmer, stirring occasionally, 45 minutes.
5. Remove meat from hocks; discard skin and bones, and return meat to soup.
6. Stir in vinegar and salt. Serve hot.

From the kitchen of Brooks Hart
Woodbury, Connecticut

OYSTER STEW

Many families around the South just cannot imagine the holiday season without enjoying a tasty batch of homemade oyster stew. At one time in history, the briny taste of fresh oysters was a rare and exotic treat for families who lived far from the ocean. These folks were able to get oysters only during the coldest winter months when they could be safely shipped on ice, often just in time for Christmas.

Makes about 4 cups

¼   cup butter
½   tsp. Worcestershire sauce
Dash of celery salt
½   cup diced celery

2   cups whole milk
1   pt. shucked oysters with their liquor, undrained
2   Tbsp. sherry

1. Melt butter in medium saucepan over medium-low heat. Stir in Worcestershire sauce, celery salt, celery, and milk. Cook, stirring, 4 minutes or until milk begins to steam and form bubbles around the edge.
2. Gently stir in oysters with their liquor. Heat slowly, stirring, for 1 to 2 minutes or until edges of oysters begin to curl.
3. Stir in the sherry. Season to taste with salt and pepper. Serve immediately.

From the kitchen of Miss Mavis Womack
Ackerman, Mississippi

GAME DAY CHILI

Some Southerners can stretch watching a ballgame into a full day of celebration. That day features all sorts of good things to eat, often including a big pot of chili. This is reliable game day chili—not too fancy and not too plain. Offer hot sauce to people who want to fire up their bowl. Almost all chili tastes best when made a day ahead and reheated.

Makes about 14 cups

2   lb. ground chuck
1   medium onion, chopped
3   to 4 garlic cloves, minced
2   Tbsp. chili powder
2   tsp. ground cumin
1   to 2 tsp. ground red pepper
1   tsp. paprika
1   (6-oz.) can tomato paste

2   cups beef broth
12 oz. bottle dark beer
3   (8-oz.) cans tomato sauce
2   (15-oz.) cans pinto beans, drained and rinsed
1   (4.5-oz.) can chopped green chiles, undrained
1   Tbsp. Worcestershire sauce

1. Cook ground chuck, onion, and garlic in a Dutch oven over medium heat, stirring occasionally, 10 minutes or until meat crumbles and is no longer pink.
2. Add chili powder, cumin, ground red pepper, and paprika. Cook 1 minute.
3. Add tomato paste, and cook 1 minute.
4. Add broth, beer, tomato sauce, beans, chiles, and Worcestershire sauce.
5. Bring to a boil. Cover, reduce heat to low, and simmer 2 hours. Serve hot.

***From the kitchen of** Courtney Bush*
Austin, Texas

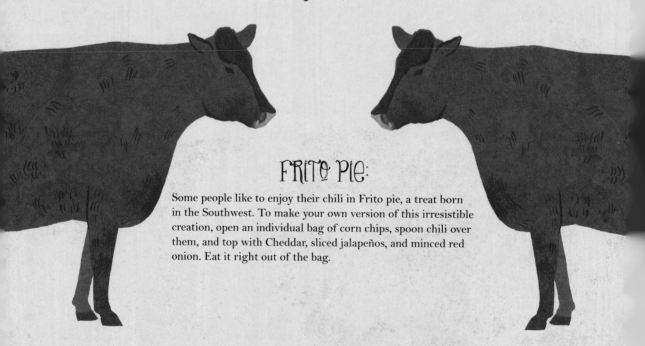

FRITO PIE:

Some people like to enjoy their chili in Frito pie, a treat born in the Southwest. To make your own version of this irresistible creation, open an individual bag of corn chips, spoon chili over them, and top with Cheddar, sliced jalapeños, and minced red onion. Eat it right out of the bag.

QUICK SHRIMP CHOWDER

How quick it is! By combining fresh shrimp with a few ingredients you likely keep on hand, you can have a pot of freshly made chowder on the table in minutes. Serve this with oyster crackers, if you have them. People just love those little things.

Makes 10 cups

- 2 Tbsp. butter
- 1 medium onion, chopped
- 2 (10¾-oz.) cans cream of potato soup, undiluted
- 3½ cups milk
- ¼ tsp. ground red pepper
- 1½ lb. peeled, medium-size raw, fresh shrimp
- 1 cup (4 oz.) shredded Monterey Jack cheese

Garnishes: fresh parsley, freshly ground black pepper
Serve with: oyster crackers

1. Melt butter in a Dutch oven over medium heat. Add onion, and cook 5 minutes or until tender.
2. Stir in soup, milk, and pepper. Bring to a boil, stirring.
3. Reduce heat, add shrimp, and simmer, stirring often, 3 to 5 minutes or only until shrimp turn pink. Remove from heat.
4. Add cheese, and stir until melted.
5. Serve immediately with oyster crackers.

NOTE: 1½ lb. frozen shrimp, thawed; 1½ lb. peeled crawfish tails; or 3 cups chopped cooked chicken may be substituted for the fresh shrimp.

From the kitchen of Cynthia J. Strickland
Bethel, North Carolina

CHICKEN, MUSHROOM, and WILD RICE SOUP

More than 100 years ago, the Cathedral Church of the Advent in Birmingham sought a way to encourage people to attend weekday sermons during the 30 days of Lent. Their tactic? Great food. These days, hundreds of locals gather to enjoy a congenial meal after services. This soup is a popular menu item. Volunteers at the church prepare the chicken broth from scratch, making this hearty soup doubly delicious.

Makes about 12 cups

2   (6-oz.) packages long-grain and wild rice mix
10 cups chicken broth, divided
7   Tbsp. butter, divided
1   cup sliced fresh mushrooms
1   cup chopped onion
1   cup chopped celery
½   cup all-purpose flour
½   cup half-and-half
2   Tbsp. dry white wine
2   cups shredded cooked chicken breast
Garnishes: fresh parsley leaves, freshly cracked pepper

1. Bring rice, 4 cups chicken broth, and 1 seasoning packet from rice mix to a boil in a saucepan over medium-high heat. Cover, reduce heat to low, and simmer 20 minutes or until liquid is absorbed and rice is tender. (Reserve remaining seasoning packet for another use.)

2. Meanwhile, melt 3 Tbsp. butter in a large skillet over medium heat. Add mushrooms, onion, and celery, and cook, stirring often, 10 to 12 minutes or until tender.

3. Melt remaining 4 Tbsp. butter in a Dutch oven over medium heat. Whisk in flour, and cook, whisking constantly, 2 minutes or until thick and bubbly. Gradually whisk in remaining 6 cups broth, and cook, stirring often, 8 to 10 minutes or until slightly thickened.

4. Whisk in half-and-half and wine. Stir in mushroom mixture, chicken, and rice.

5. Cook, stirring occasionally, 5 to 10 minutes or until thoroughly heated. (Do not boil.)

From the kitchen of the volunteers at the Cathedral Church of the Advent
Birmingham, Alabama

LOADED BAKED POTATO SOUP

This is a wonderful mashup of creamy potato soup and broccoli Cheddar soup.
(Pictured on page 148)

Makes about 12 cups

4 Tbsp. butter	½ cup heavy cream
1 small yellow onion, chopped	½ cup sour cream
3 Tbsp. all-purpose flour	1 cup (4 oz.) shredded Cheddar cheese
6 cups chicken broth	3 cups frozen broccoli florets, thawed
½ tsp. kosher salt	Toppings: chopped cooked bacon, sliced
½ tsp. freshly ground black pepper	green onions, shredded Cheddar cheese
2 medium-size russet potatoes, peeled and diced	

1. Melt butter in a Dutch oven over medium heat; add onion, and cook, stirring often, 3 to 5 minutes or until tender.
2. Sprinkle onion mixture with flour, and cook, stirring constantly, 1 minute. Gradually whisk in chicken broth, salt, and pepper.
3. Add potatoes, and bring to a boil, stirring often. Reduce heat to medium-low; simmer, stirring occasionally, 15 minutes or until potatoes are tender.
4. Whisk together heavy cream and sour cream in a bowl. Gradually stir about 1 cup hot potato mixture into cream mixture; add cream mixture to remaining hot potato mixture, stirring constantly.
5. Stir in cheese and broccoli. Cook 5 minutes or until thoroughly heated. Serve with desired toppings.

From the kitchen of Julie Deily
Orlando, Florida

VIRGINIA HOSPITALITY

The Junior League of Hampton Roads, Virginia, 1975

First published in 1975, *Virginia Hospitality* includes more than 600 recipes and features 26 sketches of famous Virginia homes by local artists. It is also full of hints for successful entertaining from accomplished hostesses.

A drawing of a pineapple graces the bright red cover of *Virginia Hospitality*. Many of us regard a whole pineapple to be the symbol of colonial hospitality. Although some historians cast doubt on the authenticity of the tale, the story is told that the practice started with the sea captains who returned to the colonial ports bearing cargo from the Caribbean, including pineapples, spices, and rum. One captain allegedly speared a pineapple on the fence post near his door to signal his safe return and as an invitation for his friends and neighbors to come over to sample his haul and hear his tales from the high seas. Colonial innkeepers soon added pineapples to their signs and bedposts as

a sign of welcome. Hostesses of sufficient means copied the practice and placed fresh pineapples over their door frames and in centerpieces as a sign of welcome, or at least a sign of affluence and opulence.

Hampton Roads is a city located in southeastern Virginia, part of the area known as the Tidewater. Hampton Roads is also the name of a body of water that includes one of the world's largest natural harbors. Beyond the harbor is a roadstead or "roads," which is the term for an area of open water that is less enclosed than a harbor where ships can ride at anchor. At the point where the waters of the Elizabeth, Nansemond, James, and several other smaller rivers empty in the Chesapeake Bay on their way to the Atlantic Ocean, Hampton Roads soon became a center of colonial commerce. The area boasts 400 years of American history, drawing visitors from around the world to hundreds of historical sites and attractions. It's little wonder that the area is known for its hospitality and great food.

Deep Creek Plantation

This Eastern Shore Plantation was begun in the mid 1700s but was developed and beautified over a period of a hundered years. The house suffered many years of neglect and abuse until about 1950 when the owners did extensive repair work to preserve the home for ultimate restoration. Under the present ownership of Brigadier General and Mrs. Chester B. deGavre, the house and gardens have taken on a new life with reconstruction of many dependencies and the addition of a rose garden, which is a delight to all. The house is handsomely furnished with family heirlooms, English and American antiques, and reproductions of museum pieces made by General deGavre from measured drawings.   –*Virginia Hospitality*

CREAM of PEANUT SOUP

This is a very old Virginia recipe with deep ties to the groundnut stews of Senegal. The oldest versions of this recipe call for finely chopped peanuts, but this updated soup relies on peanut butter. Many people enjoy their first taste of peanut stew when touring Colonial Williamsburg or other historical sites in the Tidewater area. This soup is quite rich, which is why it is often served in small cups for sipping.

Makes about 5 cups

¼ cup butter
1 small onion, finely chopped
2 celery ribs, finely chopped
2 Tbsp. all-purpose flour
¼ tsp. ground red pepper
2 cups chicken broth
1 cup whole milk

1 cup half-and-half
1 cup creamy peanut butter (not all-natural)
½ tsp. salt
¼ tsp. freshly ground black pepper
Garnishes: chopped peanuts, paprika

1. Melt butter in a large saucepan over medium heat. Add onion and celery, and cook 5 minutes or until tender.
2. Whisk in flour and ground red pepper until smooth; cook, stirring constantly, 2 minutes.
3. Add broth, and bring to a boil. Gradually stir in milk and half-and-half. Pour mixture through a wire-mesh strainer into a bowl. Discard solids.
4. Place peanut butter in Dutch oven. Gradually add milk mixture, salt, and pepper, whisking until smooth.
5. Bring to a simmer over medium heat. Simmer, stirring constantly, 5 minutes or until thoroughly heated. (Do not boil.)
6. Garnish, if desired.

Virginia Hospitality
Junior League of Hampton Roads, Virginia

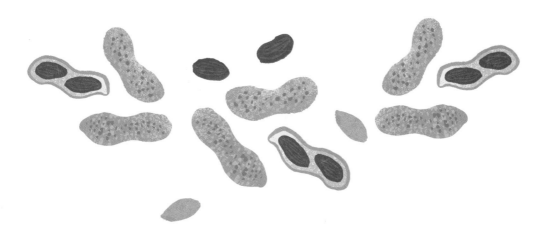

CHILLED AVOCADO SOUP

This is a perfect soup for summer. To turn this into a light meal, top each serving with grilled or poached shrimp or crabmeat.

Makes about 8 cups

3	avocados, quartered
¼	cup coarsely chopped onion
¼	cup coarsely chopped green onions
½	cup coarsely chopped fresh cilantro
¼	cup coarsely chopped fresh parsley
3	Tbsp. fresh lime juice
1	tsp. chili powder
2	tsp. salt
½	tsp. freshly ground black pepper
½	tsp. ground cumin
½	tsp. hot sauce
4	cups chicken broth
2	cups sour cream

Garnishes: grilled shrimp, cilantro, avocado slices, dried crushed red pepper

1. Process avocado, onion, green onions, cilantro, parsley, lime juice, chili powder, salt, pepper, cumin, and hot sauce in a blender or food processor until mixture is smooth, stopping to scrape down sides. Pour into a large bowl.

2. Stir in chicken broth and sour cream. Cover and chill 3 hours.

From the kitchen of Sheryl Davidson
Atlanta, Georgia

HERBED LEMON and EGG SOUP

The Greek name for this classic soup is avgolemono. The flavor of this soup relies heavily on the chicken broth, so it's worth making rich broth from scratch.

Makes about 10 cups

8	cups chicken broth
1	cup uncooked rice
½	cup chopped green onions
½	cup chopped fresh parsley
1	Tbsp. chopped fresh dill
1	Tbsp. chopped fresh mint
6	large eggs
⅓	cup fresh lemon juice
½	tsp. salt
¼	tsp. freshly ground black pepper

Garnish: fresh dill sprigs

1. Bring broth to a boil in a large saucepan over medium-high heat. Add rice; reduce heat, cover, and simmer 20 minutes or until rice is tender.
2. Stir in green onions, parsley, dill, and mint.
3. Whisk eggs until frothy in a medium bowl. Gradually add lemon juice, whisking constantly.
4. Whisk about 1 cup of the hot broth into the egg mixture.
5. Whisk the egg mixture into the saucepan. Stir slowly 1 to 2 minutes, or just until the soup becomes opaque and thickens as the eggs cook.
6. Season with salt and pepper. Serve immediately.

From the kitchen of Margie Spanos
Birmingham, Alabama

HINT:

When making broth, it is essential to use chicken pieces with bones and skin, which contribute far more flavor and body than meat alone. When you need only broth, use inexpensive boney chicken pieces—such as wings, thighs, and necks—that can stay in the broth until they fall apart. Be sure to remove the chicken meat as soon as it is done, well before it turns tough and stringy. Return the skin and bones to the pot and continue to simmer the broth until it has rich, delicious chicken flavor.

Yellow Tomato and PEACH Gazpacho

This inventive version of chilled gazpacho combines three summertime Southern treasures: sun-ripened tomatoes, glorious fresh peaches, and sweet Vidalia onions. This gorgeous soup is the color of a summer sunset.

3 medium size yellow tomatoes, seeded and chopped (about 2 lb)

1 yellow bell pepper, seeded and chopped

1 medium size cucumber, peeled, seeded & chopped

1 garlic clove, chopped

3 fresh peaches, peeled and chopped

1 small Vidalia onion, chopped

1/4 cup fresh lime juice

1/2 tsp hot sauce

1/2 tsp salt

2 tbsp rice wine vinegar

1 tbsp Worcestershire sauce

1/2 tsp freshly ground black pepper

Garnish: fresh peach slices

1 Process tomatoes, bell pepper, cucumber, garlic, peaches and onion in a blender or food processor until smooth, stopping to scrape down sides. Pour into a large bowl.

2 Stir in lime juice, vinegar, Worcestershire, hot sauce, salt, and pepper.

3 Cover and chill at least 4 hours.

4 hours

MAKES ABOUT 8 CUPS

From the Kitchen of John Fleer
Asheville, North Carolina

BUTTERNUT SQUASH TORTILLA SOUP

This recipe adds winter squash to this classic soup, a vegetable that works beautifully with Southwestern and Tex-Mex flavors. Some cooks like to add a handful of crushed tortilla chips or a chopped corn tortilla to the soup to thicken it a bit before serving.

Makes about 10 cups

2	Tbsp. olive oil
1	large red onion, chopped
1	jalapeño pepper, seeded and chopped
4	garlic cloves, finely chopped
1	Tbsp. ground cumin
1	tsp. salt
1	Tbsp. tomato paste
1	(2-lb.) butternut squash, peeled and cut into ½-inch cubes
1	(14½-oz.) can petite diced tomatoes, drained
6	cups chicken broth
2	cups fresh cilantro leaves

Toppings: tortilla chips or strips, shredded cooked chicken, crumbled queso fresco (fresh Mexican cheese), diced avocado, lime wedges

1. Heat oil in Dutch oven over medium heat. Add onion and jalapeño pepper; cook 5 minutes or until tender.
2. Add garlic, cumin, salt, and tomato paste; cook 2 minutes, stirring.
3. Add butternut squash and diced tomatoes. Cook, stirring often, 10 minutes.
4. Add chicken broth, and bring to a boil. Reduce heat to low; simmer, stirring occasionally, 20 minutes or until squash is tender.
5. Stir in cilantro just before serving. Serve hot with desired toppings.

From the kitchen of Russell Van Kraayenburg
Houston, Texas

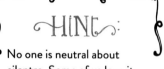

HINT:

No one is neutral about cilantro. Some of us love it. Others don't care for what they perceive as its soapy taste, and that's putting it mildly. If you fall into the latter category, replace the cilantro in the soup with fresh parsley leaves or finely chopped baby spinach so that the soup still benefits from the flavor and color of something green and leafy. Offer the cilantro as one of the toppings, if you wish.

SWEET POTATO CURRY
with SHRIMP

Makes about 14 cups

2 Tbsp. vegetable oil
2 cups diced sweet onion
1 cup diced celery
1 cup diced carrots
2 garlic cloves, finely chopped
1 Tbsp. curry powder
1 lb. Yukon gold potatoes, peeled and diced
1 lb. sweet potatoes, peeled and diced
2 cups chicken broth

1 (13.5-oz.) can unsweetened coconut milk
2 tsp. salt
1 tsp. freshly ground black pepper
3 cups fresh corn kernels (about 6 ears)
1 lb. peeled, large raw shrimp
Toppings: toasted coconut, thinly sliced green onions, coarsely chopped roasted peanuts

1. Heat oil in a Dutch oven over medium-high heat. Add onion, celery, and carrots; cook 8 minutes or until tender. Add garlic and curry powder, and cook, stirring, 1 minute.
2. Add potatoes, sweet potatoes, broth, coconut milk, salt, and pepper. Bring to a boil, stirring often. Reduce heat, and simmer, stirring occasionally, 20 to 25 minutes or until potatoes are tender.
3. Stir in corn and shrimp; cook 4 to 5 minutes or just until shrimp turn pink. Serve immediately with desired toppings.

VEGETARIAN SWEET POTATO CURRY:

Substitute 2 cups shelled frozen edamame (green soybeans), thawed, for the shrimp. Substitute vegetable broth for chicken broth.

From the kitchen of Patricia Gleason
Lynchburg, Virginia

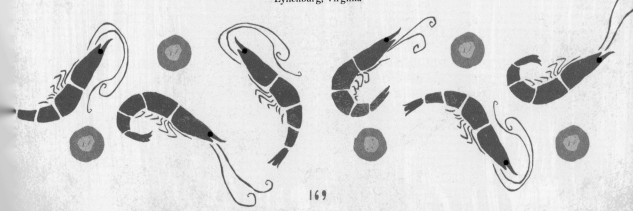

STATES' RIGHTS

Battling over the stew's origin.

Some things are quick. Brunswick stew is not one of them, but the results are worth every minute. You wind up with enough to feed a crowd, or enough to freeze for several great meals to come.

Raconteur and humorist Roy Blount Jr. quips that Brunswick stew is what happens when small mammals carrying ears of corn fall into barbecue pits. It's true that Brunswick stew was once made with a variety of wild game, particularly squirrels and rabbits, but it's now usually made with chicken and pork. For this version, the chicken and pork are smoked for hours—either at home or at a local barbecue joint—before they go into the pot. The vegetables matter just as much. Each cook has a secret combination of vegetables and seasonings, but nearly all agree that corn, butter beans or lima beans, and tomatoes are required.

The good people of both the town of Brunswick, Georgia, and Brunswick County, Virginia, equally and passionately claim to be the point of origin for the eponymous stew.

Some decades ago, Brunswick, Georgia, mounted a 25-gallon iron pot atop a town monument. The inscription declares the pot to be the very one in which the very first Brunswick stew did bubble on July 2, 1898. Georgian Brunswick stew tends to be made in relatively small batches, often in local cafes where it is served as a barbecue side dish.

In 1988, the Virginia General Assembly issued a decree naming Brunswick County the home of Brunswick stew, claiming they can trace their stew back to 1828. These days, stew making in Virginia is often a male-dominated ritual. Men known as stewmasters tend huge cauldrons, stirring the contents with boat oars, cooking up hundreds of quarts to be sold at fund-raisers for community causes. These stews are very thick, often not declared done until an oar can stand upright in the center. Virginian Brunswick stew is served as a main dish with bread on the side.

Bickering over who made it first and who makes it best is one of those (mostly) good-natured battles that will never be settled. Both communities continue to declare their provenance, and certainly their take on the way to make it, to be unassailable. This version incorporates a little of both iconic styles, and comes from a neutral state.

BRUNSWICK STEW

Makes about 6 qt.

Hickory wood chips
2 (2½ lb.) whole chickens
1 (3-lb.) Boston butt pork roast
3 (14½-oz.) cans diced tomatoes
6 cups frozen whole kernel yellow corn, thawed
6 cups frozen butter beans, thawed
2 medium onions, chopped
4 cups chicken broth
3 cups ketchup
½ cup white vinegar
½ cup Worcestershire sauce
¼ cup firmly packed brown sugar
1 Tbsp. salt
1 Tbsp. freshly ground black pepper
2 Tbsp. hot sauce

1. Soak wood chips in water for at least 30 minutes. Prepare charcoal fire in smoker; let burn 20 minutes. Drain wood chips, and place on coals. Place water pan in smoker; add water to depth of fill line. Remove and discard giblets from chicken. Tuck wings under; tie with string, if desired. Place chicken and pork on lower food rack; cover with smoker lid. Cook chicken 2¼ hours; cook pork 6 hours or until a meat thermometer inserted into thickest portion registers 155°. Let cool. Remove chicken from bone. Chop chicken and pork.

2. Stir together chicken, pork, tomatoes, corn, butter beans, onions, broth, ketchup, vinegar, Worcestershire, brown sugar, salt, pepper, and hot sauce in a 6-qt. Dutch oven. Cover and simmer over low heat, stirring occasionally, 2½ to 3 hours or until thickened. Stir more often as stew gets thicker.

From the kitchen of Tim Smith
Birmingham, Alabama

GARBANZO BEAN and SPINACH STEW

This recipe combines pantry staples with a few fresh ingredients to create a light yet filling homemade stew in minutes. Keeping a few seasoning blends on hand, such as the Greek seasoning used in this recipe, is a quick and easy way to add great flavor to recipes.

Makes 4 servings

1 Tbsp. olive oil	1 (28-oz.) can diced tomatoes
1 large onion, diced	2 (15-oz.) cans garbanzo beans, drained and rinsed
2 garlic cloves, minced	
2 Tbsp. tomato paste	2 cups vegetable broth
1½ tsp. chopped fresh rosemary	8 oz. fresh baby spinach
2 tsp. dried oregano	2 Tbsp. chopped fresh parsley
1 Tbsp. Greek seasoning	1 Tbsp. fresh lemon juice
2 tsp. salt	Serve with: hot cooked couscous or rice
½ tsp. freshly ground black pepper	Crumbled feta cheese (optional)

1. Heat oil in large saucepan over medium-high heat. Add onion; cook 5 minutes or until tender. Add garlic, and cook 1 minute.

2. Stir in tomato paste, rosemary, oregano, Greek seasoning, salt, and pepper; cook 1 minute.

3. Stir in tomatoes, beans, and broth. Bring to a boil; reduce heat to low, and simmer, stirring occasionally, 15 minutes.

4. Stir in spinach and parsley; cook 5 minutes or until spinach wilts. Stir in lemon juice.

5. Serve immediately over couscous. Top each serving with crumbled feta, if desired.

From the kitchen of Karen Greenlee
Lawrenceville, Georgia

KENTUCKY BURGOO

Makes about 8 qt.

1   (3- to 4-lb.) whole chicken, cut up
1   (2-lb.) beef chuck roast, cut into chunks
2   lb. boneless pork loin, cut into chunks
2   Tbsp. salt, divided
1   dressed rabbit (optional)
1   lb. tomatoes, chopped
5   potatoes, peeled and diced
5   celery ribs, sliced
4   carrots, chopped
2   onions, chopped
2   green bell peppers, chopped
1   small cabbage, shredded
2   cups frozen whole kernel corn
1   cup frozen baby lima beans
1   cup frozen English peas
3   garlic cloves, minced
2   qt. beef broth
4   cups ketchup
2   cups dry red wine
1   cup Worcestershire sauce
½   cup white vinegar
1   Tbsp. freshly ground black pepper
1   Tbsp. dried thyme

1. Place chicken, beef, pork, 1 Tbsp. salt, and rabbit, if using, in a large heavy stockpot. Add water to cover. Bring to a boil. Cover, reduce heat, and simmer 2 to 3 hours or until meats are tender. Strain. Return liquid to pot. Skin, bone, and shred meats, and return to pot. Cool, cover, and refrigerate overnight.

2. Remove fat layer from surface. Return stew to a simmer.

3. Stir in tomatoes, potatoes, celery, carrots, onions, bell peppers, cabbage, corn, lima beans, peas, garlic, broth, ketchup, wine, Worcestershire, vinegar, pepper, thyme, and remaining 1 Tbsp. salt.

4. Simmer, covered, 1 hour. Uncover and simmer 2 hours longer or until thick, stirring frequently. Serve hot.

From the kitchen of Mrs. Sue Sue Hartstern
Louisville, Kentucky

SIT *and* CHAT

"*If it walked or it flew, it goes in burgoo.*" *At one time, this meaty stew was made with an assortment of game and livestock cooked in giant cauldrons called burgoo kettles. We're told that in 1895 Chef Gustav Jaubert and his 10 assistants prepared 6,000 gallons of burgoo for a single event. That feat is, of course, extreme, but even now cooks who make burgoo don't bother with making only a little. Burgoo is a community event, meant to be shared.*

GUMBO Z'HERBES

Chef Leah Chase is famous for her Gumbo Z'Herbes. Every year on Maundy Thursday, she prepares 100 gallons of her gumbo at the famed Dooky Chase restaurant. Chef Chase advises to never use an even number of greens in this gumbo because it is considered unlucky. She uses nine greens in her recipe, and reminds us, "You will acquire a new friend for every kind of green in the pot—and we hope one of them's rich."

She also tells us, "People always ask if I serve soul food. I remind them that all food is soul food, it just depends on where your soul resides. I do good, simple cooking from my Creole background. But if you tell me what your soul likes, I'll cook it for you."

Makes about 4 qt.

5 cups chopped mustard greens	½ lb. smoked ham, diced
5 cups chopped collard greens	½ lb. uncooked beef brisket, diced
5 cups chopped turnip greens	½ lb. dry Spanish chorizo or andouille
3 cups chopped beet tops	sausage, diced
2 cups chopped cabbage	3 Tbsp. vegetable oil
2 cups chopped romaine lettuce	¼ cup all-purpose flour
2 cups chopped watercress	2 tsp. salt
1½ cups coarsely chopped spinach	½ tsp. fresh thyme leaves
1 cup chopped carrot tops	½ tsp. ground red pepper
2 garlic cloves, chopped	½ tsp. filé powder
1 medium onion, chopped	Serve with: hot cooked rice
½ lb. smoked sausage, diced	Garnish: fresh thyme

1. Combine mustard greens, collard greens, turnips greens, beet tops, cabbage, romaine, watercress, spinach, carrot tops, garlic, onion and water to cover in a 15-qt. stockpot; cover. Bring to a boil over high heat; boil 20 minutes. Uncover; boil, stirring occasionally, 30 minutes. Drain, reserving cooking liquid. Coarsely chop greens. Keep cooking liquid warm in large saucepan over very low heat.

2. Combine smoked sausage, smoked ham, and brisket in pot with 2 cups reserved cooking liquid. Bring to a boil. Boil, stirring once, 15 minutes.

3. Meanwhile, cook chorizo in hot oil in a medium skillet over medium-low heat, stirring occasionally, 10 minutes or until browned. Remove with a slotted spoon; drain on paper towels, reserving 3 Tbsp. drippings in skillet.

4. Make a roux by whisking flour into reserved drippings. Cook over medium heat, stirring constantly with a wooden spatula or wooden spoon, until roux is medium brown (about 15 minutes). Add roux to stockpot, and stir well.

5. Add chopped greens mixture and 5 cups reserved cooking liquid. Reduce heat to medium-low; simmer, stirring occasionally, 20 minutes.

6. Stir in salt, thyme, ground red pepper, and chorizo. Cook, stirring occasionally, 40 minutes.

7. Add filé powder and stir vigorously just before serving. Serve over rice.

From the kitchen of Leah Chase
New Orleans, Louisiana

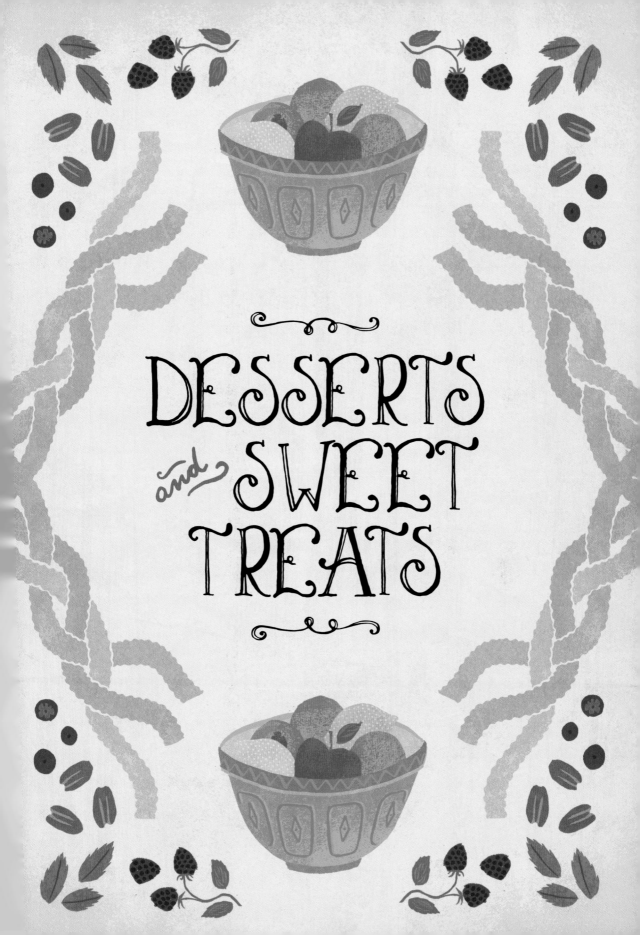

DESSERTS *and* SWEET TREATS

BANANA PUDDING

Southerners take banana pudding very seriously. Although tawdry shortcut versions abound, the formula for the real thing includes homemade custard, store-bought vanilla wafers, and meringue topping with toasted peaks. Perfect custard isn't difficult, but practice makes perfect. Custards are the soul of many great desserts. They are also essential comfort food. In some communities, making proper egg custard was part of the registered nurse licensing exam until the 1970s. Custards do make us feel better.

Makes 6 servings

1 cup granulated sugar, divided	1 Tbsp. butter
⅓ cup all-purpose flour	2 tsp. vanilla extract
Dash of salt	48 vanilla wafers
2 cups whole milk	4 large bananas (2½ lb. unpeeled; about
4 large eggs, separated	6 cups when thinly sliced)

1. Preheat oven to 325°. Whisk together ¾ cup sugar, flour, and salt in a large heavy saucepan. Gradually whisk in milk. Whisk in egg yolks. Cook over medium heat, stirring constantly with a heatproof spatula, 8 to 10 minutes or until pudding thickens and just begins to bubble around the edges. Remove from heat, and stir in butter and vanilla.
2. Arrange one-third of the vanilla wafers in the bottom of 6 (6-oz.) custard cups. Cover with one-third of the banana slices. Pour one-third of the warm pudding over the bananas. Repeat the layers twice more.
3. Beat egg whites (at room temperature) in a large bowl at medium speed with an electric mixer until foamy. Increase mixer speed to high, and add remaining ¼ cup sugar, 1 Tbsp. at a time, beating until mixture is glossy and stiff peaks form, 2 to 4 minutes. Spread meringue over warm pudding, spreading and sealing to edge of dish.
4. Bake at 325° for 15 to 20 minutes or until meringue is golden. Cool on a wire rack 30 minutes. Serve slightly warm, or cool completely and refrigerate until chilled.

From the kitchen of Mrs. Julia Moats
Birmingham, Alabama

HINT:

For best flavor, use firm, ripe bananas with a few
brown speckles. Older bananas quickly darken in the pudding.
Bananas keep better when left attached to the crown until
needed. If you want them to last, be sure to keep them away
from fresh apples, which make them ripen much more quickly.
On the other hand, if you need to ripen up green bananas, place
them in a brown paper bag with an apple overnight.

BREAD PUDDING *with* VANILLA SAUCE

Bread pudding is humble and rustic, yet somehow seems fancy. It's hard to imagine that this beloved dessert started as a way to salvage stale bread. Just about every culture that makes bread has its own version of bread pudding. French bread and other similar white breads work well because they are tender enough to soak up the custard but not so soft that they dissolve.

Makes 6 to 8 servings

Pudding
- 4 cups cubed crustless French bread
- 3 large eggs, lightly beaten
- 1½ cups granulated sugar
- 2 Tbsp. packed light brown sugar
- ½ tsp. ground nutmeg
- ¼ cup butter, melted
- 2¾ cups whipping cream
- ¾ cup raisins

Sauce
- ½ cup granulated sugar
- 3 Tbsp. light brown sugar
- 1 Tbsp. all-purpose flour
- Dash of ground nutmeg
- 1 large egg
- 2 Tbsp. butter
- 1¼ cups whipping cream
- 1 Tbsp. vanilla extract

1. To prepare bread pudding, preheat oven to 375°. Lightly grease a 2-qt. soufflé dish or baking dish.

2. Arrange bread in a single layer on a baking sheet. Bake at 375° for 8 minutes or until lightly toasted and slightly firm, but not crunchy. Cool.

3. Whisk together eggs, granulated sugar, brown sugar, and nutmeg in a large bowl until smooth. Whisk in melted butter and whipping cream. Gently stir in bread and raisins.

4. Pour into prepared dish. Let stand 20 minutes, occasionally pressing on bread to soak up custard.

5. Bake at 375° for 50 to 55 minutes, shielding with aluminum foil after 30 minutes to prevent excessive browning. Meanwhile, prepare sauce.

6. To prepare sauce, whisk together granulated sugar, brown sugar, flour, nutmeg, egg, butter, and cream. Cook over medium heat, whisking constantly, 10 to 12 minutes or until thickened. Remove from heat; stir in vanilla.

7. Let pudding stand 10 minutes before serving warm with warm Vanilla Sauce.

From the kitchen of Margaret Ajac
Raleigh, North Carolina

PUMPKIN CRISP *with* NUTMEG WHIPPED CREAM

This is one of those incredibly easy dump cake recipes that is ready for the oven in less than 10 minutes. The result is a heavenly dessert that is part warm cake and part pudding with buttery pecans scattered throughout, just waiting for a big dollop of freshly whipped cream.

Makes 12 servings

Crisp
1   (15-oz.) can pumpkin
1   cup evaporated milk
1   cup granulated sugar
1   tsp. vanilla extract
½   tsp. ground cinnamon
1   (18.25-oz.) package butter-flavored yellow cake mix

1   cup chopped pecans
1   cup butter, melted

Whipped cream
1   cup whipping cream, chilled
2   Tbsp. powdered sugar
Dash of ground nutmeg

1. To prepare crisp, preheat oven to 350°. Lightly grease a 13- x 9-inch baking dish.
2. Stir together pumpkin, milk, granulated sugar, vanilla, and cinnamon in a large bowl until smooth. Pour into prepared baking dish.
3. Sprinkle cake mix evenly over pumpkin mixture. Sprinkle pecans evenly over cake mix. Drizzle butter evenly over pecans.
4. Bake at 350° for 1 hour or until golden brown. Remove from oven, and let stand 10 minutes before serving.
5. To prepare whipped cream, beat cream in medium bowl at low speed with an electric mixer until foamy. Increase speed to medium-high, and gradually add powdered sugar and nutmeg, beating until soft peaks form.
6. Serve cake warm or at room temperature topped with whipped cream.

From the kitchen of Ann Goellner
Beaufort, North Carolina

TRES LECHES FLAN

Flan is a type of egg custard, so for the creamiest, silkiest texture, bake it in a water bath that is sometimes called a bain-marie. The water insulates the custard from the harsh and perhaps uneven heat of the oven. Custard continues to cook and firm up as it cools, so it is important to remove it from the oven when it is just shy of set. After a short rest, it will be perfect.

Makes 6 servings

½   cup sugar
1   (8-oz.) package cream cheese, softened
2   large eggs, at room temperature
2   large egg yolks, at room temperature

1   (14-oz.) can sweetened condensed milk
1   (12-oz.) can evaporated milk
1½ cups milk
1   tsp. vanilla extract

1. Preheat oven to 325°. Have ready 6 (6-oz.) custard cups.

2. Cook sugar in a small saucepan over medium heat. Cook, without stirring, 5 to 7 minutes or until sugar melts and turns the color of amber. Quickly pour into cake pan. Using oven mitts, tilt cake pan to evenly coat bottom of pan with caramel.

3. Beat cream cheese in large bowl at medium speed with an electric mixer 1 minute. Add eggs and egg yolks; beat at low speed until well blended.

4. Beat in sweetened condensed milk, evaporated milk, milk, and vanilla at low speed. Mixture should not be foamy and might be slightly lumpy. Pour over caramel in cake pan.

5. Place cake pan in roasting pan. Pour enough very hot tap water (170° to 175°) into roasting pan to come halfway up outside of cake pan.

6. Bake at 325° for 40 to 45 minutes or until edges are set. A 2-inch circle in center of custard should jiggle slightly when pan is gently shaken. Cool on a wire rack. Cover and chill at least 8 hours. The flan will continue to set as it cools.

7. Run a knife around edges to loosen. Invert onto a serving platter; let stand for 10 minutes, and then lift off cake pan.

From the kitchen of Kate, Grace, Rachel, and Hope Rovner
Plano, Texas

HUGUENOT TORTE

Makes 8 servings

2   large eggs
1½   cups sugar
¼   cup all-purpose flour
3   tsp. baking powder
¼   tsp. salt
1   tsp. vanilla extract
1   cup chopped crisp apple
1   cup chopped pecans
Serve with: whipped cream

1. Preheat oven to 325°. Grease a 2-qt. baking dish.

2. Beat eggs in a large bowl at high speed with an electric mixer for 5 minutes or until doubled in volume and lemon-colored. Reduce mixer speed to medium, and gradually add sugar, beating 5 minutes or until tripled in volume and pale yellow.

3. Whisk in flour, baking powder, and salt, whisking only until blended. Quickly stir in vanilla. Fold in apple and pecans. Pour into prepared dish.

4. Bake at 325° for 45 minutes or until top is crusty. (Torte will puff up and bubble and then fall.) Run a knife around edge of dish while still warm. Cool at least 10 minutes before serving warm or at room temperature with whipped cream.

Old St. *Andrew's* Parish Church
Charleston, South Carolina

Sit and Chat

Some people say that Huguenot torte is Charleston's most famous dessert. It's found on menus and on kitchen tables. It's also sometimes available at church. That's because congregations of several Charleston area churches operate tearooms each spring to raise funds for parish activities and local charities. Traditional recipes such as Huguenot torte are popular menu items. In some parts of the South, this dish is called Ozark Pudding.

FRUIT COBBLER with UNIVERSAL BLACK IRON SKILLET PIECRUST

The piecrust fits perfectly in a 10-inch cast-iron skillet. Like many of us, Jack Butler is devoted to his skillet and admires its superiority over flimsy nonstick pans, saying, "We don't talk nonstick in polite company; a well-cured iron skillet is as slippery as anything needs to get." Jack goes on to share how much he loves to cook because he finds it relaxing. As he puts it, "Now my favorite way to unwind after work is to spend an hour in the kitchen, an icy martini in hand, things bubbling or sizzling while I wash and peel and chop or roll out a rich crust, leaving floury fingerprints on my cold and beaded glass."

Makes 8 to 10 servings

Piecrust

3   cups all-purpose flour
½   tsp. salt
¾   cup butter
¾   cup ice water

Filling

1   Tbsp. butter
½   cup all-purpose flour
1   cup sugar, divided
4   to 5 cups fresh or frozen blueberries, raspberries, or blackberries

1. To prepare crust, whisk together flour and salt in a large bowl. Cut in butter with a pastry blender until mixture is crumbly with a few pieces of butter the size of small peas. Sprinkle ice water, 1 Tbsp. at a time, evenly over flour mixture, stirring with a fork only until dry ingredients are moistened. Pour onto a lightly floured work surface, gather into a ball, flatten into a disk, wrap well, and chill for at least 30 minutes.

2. Preheat oven to 375°. Roll pastry to ¼-inch thickness. Fit into a well-seasoned 10-inch cast-iron skillet. Trim away excess pastry; reserve trimmings. Prick bottom and sides of pastry all over with the tines of a fork. Bake at 375° for 8 minutes or until golden. Set aside.

3. To prepare filling, cut butter into flour with a pastry blender until crumbly. Stir in ½ cup sugar.

4. Spoon one-third of the blueberries into the cooled crust. Sprinkle with one-third of the sugar and the flour mixture. Repeat layers twice.

5. Arrange the crust trimmings over the top. Sprinkle with remaining sugar.

6. Bake at 375° for 50 minutes or until the crust is lightly browned and the filling is bubbly. Let stand at least 15 minutes before serving warm.

NOTE: You can make this cobbler with a 14.1-oz. package of refrigerated piecrusts. To ensure the cobbler crust is wide and thick enough to line the skillet, use both crusts in the package. Unfold one piecrust, and press out fold lines. Unfold second crust and stack on top of the first, turning so that the fold lines do not overlap. Press edges to seal. Roll stacked crusts to a 14-inch circle, and then proceed with the recipe. There will be no trimmings, so use a third crust for the top, if you wish.

From the kitchen of Jack Butler
Alligator, Mississippi

BANANA COBBLER with STREUSEL TOPPING

This creative cobbler is reminiscent of a delicious combination of warm banana bread, banana pudding, and great oatmeal cookies. For best results, use slightly overripe bananas that have yellow peels splotched with brown flecks. You won't get the same depth of flavor or moistness without them.

Makes 8 servings

Streusel Topping
¾ cup firmly packed light brown sugar
½ cup self-rising flour
½ cup butter, softened
1 cup uncooked regular oats
½ cup chopped pecans

Cobbler
1 cup self-rising flour

1 cup sugar
1 cup milk
½ cup butter, melted
4 medium-size ripe bananas, sliced (2 lb. unpeeled; about 4 cups when thinly sliced)

Serve with: vanilla or caramel ice cream

1. To prepare streusel, stir together brown sugar, flour, and butter in a large bowl until crumbly. Stir in oats and pecans. Chill until needed.
2. To prepare cobbler, preheat oven to 375°. Lightly grease an 11- x 7-inch baking dish.
3. Whisk together flour, sugar, and milk; mix only until blended. Whisk in melted butter. Pour batter into prepared dish. Top with banana slices. Sprinkle with Streusel Topping.
4. Bake at 375° for 40 to 45 minutes or until golden brown and bubbly. Let stand 10 minutes before serving warm, topped with ice cream.

From the kitchen of Ann Wilson
Lexington, North Carolina

EASY PEACH COBBLER

There are too many different types of cobbler to count across the South. Some are soft and cakey, some are juicy and topped with crisp pastry, and the rest are somewhere in between. As its name implies, this one is incredibly easy. Dori Sanders lives and works on her family orchard in upstate South Carolina, often greeting and regaling guests who stop by to buy fresh peaches by the basket and bushel. Dori also wrote two acclaimed novels. Needless to say, Dori can tell lyrical stories about peaches, farm life, and Southern cooking. She makes a fine cobbler, too.

Makes 8 to 10 servings

½ cup unsalted butter
1 cup all-purpose flour
2 cups sugar, divided
1 Tbsp. baking powder
Pinch of salt
1 cup milk
4 cups fresh peach slices
1 Tbsp. lemon juice
Ground cinnamon or nutmeg (optional)

1. Preheat oven to 375°. Place butter in a 13- x 9-inch baking dish, and place dish in oven only long enough for butter to melt.
2. Whisk together flour, 1 cup sugar, baking powder, and salt. Add milk, and stir only until dry ingredients are moistened. Pour batter over butter; do not stir.
3. Bring remaining 1 cup sugar, peach slices, and lemon juice to a boil in a large saucepan over high heat, stirring constantly. Pour over batter; do not stir. Sprinkle with cinnamon, if desired.
4. Bake at 375° for 40 to 45 minutes or until golden brown. Serve cobbler warm or cool.

From the kitchen of Dori Sanders
Filbert, South Carolina

HINT:

To peel only one or two pieces of soft, ripe fruit—such as peaches and tomatoes—use a serrated peeler. To easily peel large amounts, score an X on the bottom of each peach with a serrated knife. Bring a large saucepan of water to a boil. Have ready a medium bowl of ice water. Working with one peach at a time, place the peach in a ladle or large spoon and submerge it in boiling water for 15 to 45 seconds or until the skin begins to loosen around the X. The riper the peach, the less time it requires in the water. Transfer immediately into ice water. When peaches cool, slip off the peel, starting at the X.

1-2-3 BLACKBERRY SHERBET

This three-step, three-ingredient sherbet is so amazing that it can leave people speechless. The recipe calls for blackberries, but the sherbet is also delicious made with raspberries, strawberries, or peaches. Although it might sound unusual to use buttermilk in sherbet, that tangy flavor is essential to the unique flavor of this recipe. Be sure to use real buttermilk, not milk curdled with lemon juice.

Makes 1 qt.

4 cups fresh or frozen blackberries, thawed	2 cups sugar
	2 cups buttermilk

1. Stir together blackberries and sugar in a bowl; let stand 30 minutes, stirring occasionally. Process blackberry mixture in a blender or food processor until smooth, stopping to scrape down sides.

2. Pour mixture through a fine wire-mesh strainer into a 9-inch square pan; discard solids. Stir in buttermilk.

3. Cover and freeze 8 hours. Break frozen mixture into chunks, and place in a bowl. Beat with an electric mixer at medium speed until smooth. Return to pan; cover and freeze 3 hours or until firm.

NOTE: To freeze in 1½-qt. electric ice-cream maker: Pour blackberry mixture into a large glass or metal bowl, cover, and refrigerate until very cold, at least 4 hours. Pour into ice-cream maker, and freeze according to manufacturer's instructions. Transfer to an airtight container, and freeze until firm enough to scoop.

1-2-3 STRAWBERRY SHERBET:

Substitute fresh or frozen strawberries for the blackberries.

1-2-3 PEACH SHERBET:

Substitute fresh or frozen peaches for the blackberries.

1-2-3 RASPBERRY SHERBET:

Substitute fresh or frozen raspberries for the blackberries.

From the kitchen of Arlene P. Rogers
Louisville, Kentucky

We All Scream for Ice Cream

Here are a few tips on making sure your ice cream turns out great:

1. Most countertop electric ice-cream makers work best when the freezer bowl has been frozen for at least 24 hours. If you have space to store your bowl in your freezer, it will always be ready to go.

2. For the best ice-cream texture, be sure that the cooked custard mixture is thoroughly chilled (40 degrees or less) before pouring it into the freezer.

3. Ice cream expands when it freezes, so don't fill the freezer bowl more than three-quarters full. When the bowl is too full, the ice cream isn't as smooth and creamy, not to mention that spillovers make a sticky mess.

4. If your recipe calls for mix-ins, such as chocolate chips, nuts, or chunks of fruit, add them at the very end of freezing, after the ice cream has become firm. Continue churning only until the pieces are evenly distributed.

WALTER'S ULTIMATE VANILLA ICE CREAM

Homemade ice cream isn't just a sweet treat, it's an event. Waiting for the creamy mixture to freeze adds to the anticipation of the good things to come. One bite of this delicious homemade custard ice cream will remind you why vanilla remains the most popular ice cream flavor around.

Makes about 1½ qt.

6   large egg yolks
¾   cup sugar
⅛   tsp. salt
1   Tbsp. vanilla extract
2   cups whole milk, warmed
4   cups whipping cream

1. Whisk together yolks, sugar, salt, and vanilla until thick and pale. Gradually whisk in warm milk. Pour into a heavy saucepan. Cook over very low heat, stirring constantly, 5 minutes or until mixture thickly coats a spoon. Remove from heat. Pour through a wire-mesh strainer into a bowl.
2. Fill a large bowl with ice. Place bowl containing milk mixture in ice. Let stand, stirring occasionally, 20 minutes. Remove bowl from ice bath.
3. Stir in cream. Cover and chill 1 hour.
4. Pour into a 1½-qt. electric ice-cream maker, and freeze according to manufacturer's instructions. Transfer to an airtight container, and freeze until firm enough to scoop.

From the kitchen of Walter Royal
Raleigh, North Carolina

FRESH PEACH SORBET

This sorbet delivers the very essence of fresh Southern peaches. Only fully ripe peaches that fill the air with their perfume will do. In fact, this is a great way to use dead-ripe peaches that are too soft for most other recipes. The alcohol in the vodka or liqueur improves the texture of the sorbet by keeping it from getting too icy and coarse.

Makes 1 qt.

2 lb. ripe peaches, peeled and chopped
1 cup warm water
½ cup sugar

1 Tbsp. vodka, peach schnapps, or orange liqueur

1. Process peaches in a blender or food processor until smooth. Pour though a fine-mesh strainer into a large bowl.
2. Stir together warm water, sugar, and vodka in a medium bowl until sugar dissolves. Stir into peach puree. Cover and chill until very cold, at least 4 hours.
3. Pour into 1½-qt. electric ice-cream maker, and process according to manufacturer's instructions. Transfer to an airtight container, and freeze until firm enough to scoop.

From the kitchen of Rebecca Crump
Nashville, Tennessee

PRALINES

These classic pralines are the key ingredient in the cheese-cake on the opposite page, but they are so delicious that you might find yourself making a batch (or two, or 10) even when you don't plan to make the cheesecake.

Makes 1 dozen

¼ cup butter, divided
¾ cup firmly packed light brown sugar
¾ cup granulated sugar
¾ cup half-and-half
1¼ cups coarsely chopped pecans
½ tsp. vanilla extract

1. Use 1 Tbsp. butter to coat inside of a large heavy saucepan. Have ready a sheet of wax paper or parchment paper for the pralines.
2. Stir together brown sugar, granulated sugar, half-and-half, and remaining 3 Tbsp. butter in buttered saucepan. Cook over low heat, stirring constantly, until sugar dissolves. Stir in pecans.
3. Bring to a boil over medium heat. Cook, stirring constantly, until mixture reaches 235° to 245° (soft ball stage) on a candy thermometer (about 6 to 8 minutes). Remove from heat.
4. Stir in vanilla; let stand 3 minutes.
5. Beat vigorously with a wooden spoon 3 minutes or until mixture begins to thicken. Working quickly, drop pralines by tablespoonfuls onto wax paper.
6. Let stand until firm. Pralines keep in an airtight container for a few days, but they taste best on the first day.

From the kitchen of Georgia Kinney
Greensboro, North Carolina

SIT *and* CHAT

Culinary historians believe that pralines were introduced to New Orleans by the French in the early 19th century. French pralines were made with almonds, but locals soon started using Southern pecans. Pralines proved to be a perfect no-bake confection for hot and humid Louisiana. Those conditions might wreak havoc on other sweets, but when making pralines, we want the sugar to crystal-lize and turn grainy.

HINT

To clean the sticky saucepan, fill it with water, and simmer on the stove until the residue softens and loosens. It's easier to cook off a mess than to scrub it off.

PRALINE CHEESECAKE

Cheesecake is one of the most popular desserts around, but this one is made all the better by the generous addition of homemade pralines. No one will complain if you make extra pralines for nibbling.

Makes 12 servings

2 cups finely crushed shortbread cookies	1½ tsp. vanilla extract
3 Tbsp. butter, melted	4 large eggs
4 Pralines, coarsely crumbled (recipe on opposite page)	2 large egg yolks
	⅓ cup whipping cream
5 (8-oz.) packages cream cheese, softened	1 tsp. finely grated lemon zest
1¾ cups plus ⅓ cup sugar, divided	16 oz. sour cream
2 Tbsp. all-purpose flour	Garnish: crumbled Pralines

1. Preheat oven to 350°. Toss together cookie crumbs and melted butter in a medium bowl. Press into bottom and up sides of a greased 10-inch springform pan. Bake at 350° for 8 minutes. Cool on a wire rack. Sprinkle coarsely crumbled Pralines over crust. Place pan on a foil-lined baking sheet.

2. Beat cream cheese at medium speed with a heavy-duty stand mixer until smooth. Gradually add 1¾ cups sugar, beating until smooth. Beat in flour and vanilla.

3. Add eggs and egg yolks, 1 at a time, beating only until yellow disappears after each addition. Stir in whipping cream and lemon zest. Pour into crust.

4. Bake at 350° in lower third of oven 10 minutes. Reduce oven temperature to 325°, and bake 1 hour and 20 minutes or until filling is almost set. A 2-inch circle in center of custard will jiggle slightly when pan is gently shaken. Cool on a wire rack 1 hour.

5. Stir together sour cream and remaining ⅓ cup sugar in small bowl. Spread over cheesecake. Bake at 325° for 10 minutes. Gently run a knife around edge of cheesecake to loosen. Cool on wire rack. Cover and chill 8 hours. Remove sides of pan.

From the kitchen of Georgia Kinney
Greensboro, North Carolina

CINDERELLA CHEESECAKE

This showstopping cheesecake features a creamy peanut butter filling baked in a chocolate brownie crust.

Makes 10 to 12 servings

Brownie crust

3	(1-oz.) unsweetened chocolate baking squares
¼	cup unsalted butter
½	cup sifted all-purpose flour
⅛	tsp. salt
⅛	tsp. baking powder
2	large eggs
1	cup firmly packed light brown sugar
1½	tsp. vanilla extract
½	(1-oz.) bittersweet chocolate baking square, finely chopped

Cheesecake filling

12	oz. cream cheese, softened
1	cup firmly packed light brown sugar
3	large eggs
½	cup sour cream
1⅓	cups creamy peanut butter

Topping

¾	cup sour cream
2	tsp. granulated sugar
	Chocolate curls

1. To prepare crust, preheat oven to 350°. Grease and flour a 9-inch springform pan.

2. Microwave 3 baking squares and butter in a small microwave-safe bowl at MEDIUM (50% power) 1½ minutes or until melted, stirring at 30-second intervals.

3. Stir together flour, salt, and baking powder in a large bowl.

4. Beat eggs and brown sugar in a large bowl at medium-high speed with an electric mixer 3 to 4 minutes or until batter forms thin ribbons when beaters are lifted.

5. Add vanilla, bittersweet chocolate, and melted chocolate mixture. Beat only until blended.

6. Stir in flour mixture just until combined. Spread 1 cup crust mixture on bottom of prepared pan.

7. Bake at 350° on center oven rack 13 to 15 minutes or until set. Cool on a wire rack 10 minutes; freeze 15 minutes. Remove from freezer; spread remaining batter up sides of pan to ¼ inch from top, sealing batter to bottom crust.

8. To prepare filling, beat cream cheese and brown sugar at medium speed with a heavy-duty electric stand mixer until blended. Add eggs, 1 at a time, beating only until yellow yolk disappears after each addition. Beat in sour cream only until blended. Beat in peanut butter until blended.

9. Pour filling into prepared crust. (Mixture will not completely fill crust.)

10. Bake at 350° for 35 minutes or until center is almost set. A 2-inch circle in center of filling should jiggle slightly when pan is shaken gently. Meanwhile, prepare topping. Stir together sour cream and sugar in a small bowl until smooth.

11. Remove cheesecake from oven. Spread topping over center of cheesecake, leaving a 2-inch border around edge. Bake for 1 minute more.

12. Remove from oven; gently run a knife around edge of cheesecake to loosen. Cool completely on a wire rack.

13. Cover and chill 8 to 12 hours. Remove sides of pan. Top with chocolate curls.

Savor the Moment: Entertaining Without Reservations
Junior League of Boca Raton, Florida

BOURBON BALLS

This classic candy is particularly popular during the winter holidays. A tin of bourbon balls makes a thoughtful gift.

Makes about 3 dozen

1   cup powdered sugar
2   Tbsp. unsweetened cocoa
¼   cup bourbon
2   Tbsp. light corn syrup
2   cups finely crushed vanilla wafers
     (about 12 oz.)
1   cup finely chopped toasted pecans
Powdered sugar

1. Sift together 1 cup powdered sugar and cocoa into a small bowl. Stir together bourbon and corn syrup in a large bowl. Gradually stir powdered sugar mixture into bourbon mixture, stirring until blended.
2. Add vanilla wafers and pecans; stir 1 minute or until well mixed. Try to form a small ball with some of the dough to be sure it holds its shape. If not, continue to stir and test in 20-second intervals.
3. Form mixture into 1-inch balls. Coat balls in powdered sugar, and place on a baking sheet lined with wax paper or parchment paper.
4. Chill 1 hour or until slightly firm. Store refrigerated in an airtight container.

From the kitchen of Mrs. E. A. Tunnells
Charleston, South Carolina

BUCKEYES

A real buckeye is an inedible tree nut that people used to carry in their pockets for good luck. They are small and round with a dark-brown hull and a little buff-colored spot on top. This peanut butter and chocolate candy is made to look like a buckeye, but can be eaten. That sounds much luckier.

Makes about 4 dozen

2   cups creamy peanut butter (not all-natural)
½   cup butter, softened
1   tsp. vanilla extract

4   cups powdered sugar
2   cups semisweet chocolate morsels
2   Tbsp. vegetable shortening

1. Beat peanut butter, butter, and vanilla in a large bowl at medium speed with an electric mixer until smooth.

2. Add powdered sugar; beat on low speed until mixture is well mixed. The mixture will be crumbly and look a little dry.

3. Form mixture into 1-inch balls. Press a wooden pick into the top of each ball (to be used later as the handle for dipping), and chill in freezer until firm, about 30 minutes.

4. Microwave chocolate and shortening in a small glass bowl at HIGH 1½ minutes or until melted, stirring twice.

5. Working with 1 at a time, hold ball by the pick and coat the lower three-fourths of ball in melted chocolate, leaving the brown tops exposed. (If the picks start to slip out, place a fork underneath the ball for stability while you dip.) Let excess chocolate drip back into the bowl. Place on wax paper or parchment paper to set. Remove pick. Cover loosely with plastic wrap, and chill. Store refrigerated in an airtight container.

From the kitchen of Peggy Heath
Tyler, Texas

HINT:

The peanut butter balls must be chilled and the chocolate
must be warm for the coating to adhere properly. Work in batches,
removing only about 1 dozen balls from the freezer at a time. Gently
reheat the chocolate when it starts to cool and solidify. Some
cooks prefer melting the chocolate and shortening in the top of
a double boiler over gently simmering water so that it stays
warm at a constant temperature.

MILDRED'S TOFFEE

Toffee is a sophisticated treat and a very welcome gift. It was once rather challenging to make perfect toffee because of the uncertainty about how long to cook the sugar. Testing the candy required cups of cold water and bits of lava-hot sugar syrup. No more. With help from a trusty candy thermometer, there's no mystery, only great results.

If you can make one kind of toffee, you can pretty much make them all. Be sure to try all the variations listed below.

Makes about 1½ lb.

1½ cups toasted slivered almonds, divided
1 cup sugar
1 cup butter
1 Tbsp. light corn syrup
1 cup semisweet chocolate morsels

1. Mist a baking sheet with vegetable cooking spray. Spread 1 cup almonds into a 9-inch round on baking sheet.
2. Bring sugar, butter, corn syrup, and ¼ cup water to a boil in a heavy saucepan over medium heat, stirring constantly. Cook until sugar mixture reaches 290° to 310° (hard crack stage) on a candy thermometer (about 15 minutes). The color will change to deep golden brown and the mixture will thicken slightly. Carefully pour hot sugar mixture over nuts.
3. Sprinkle chocolate morsels evenly on top, and let stand 30 seconds or until melted. Spread melted chocolate over surface.
4. Sprinkle remaining ½ cup almonds evenly over top.
5. Chill 1 hour or until firm. Break into bite-size pieces. Store in an airtight container.

PECAN TOFFEE:

Substitute 1½ cups toasted pecan pieces for the almonds. Proceed as directed.

BOURBON-PECAN TOFFEE:

Substitute 1½ cups toasted pecan pieces for the almonds. Substitute ¼ cup bourbon for ¼ cup water. Proceed as directed.

HAWAIIAN TOFFEE:

Substitute 1½ cups chopped toasted macadamia nuts for the almonds. Proceed as directed.

From the kitchen of Mildred Hayward
Kenosha, Wisconsin

SALTINE CRACKER CANDY

Many of us will remember making this candy as children. It sounds peculiar, but it is really good, especially if you like the combination of salty and sweet.

Makes 8 to 10 servings

24 saltine crackers
1 cup butter
1 cup firmly packed light brown sugar

12 oz. milk chocolate morsels
½ cup chopped pecans or walnuts

1. Preheat oven to 325°. Line bottom of a 13- x 9-inch baking pan with aluminum foil. Arrange crackers in a single layer in pan.
2. Microwave butter and brown sugar in a microwave-safe glass bowl at HIGH for 3 to 4 minutes or until sugar dissolves, stirring occasionally. Pour butter mixture over crackers.
3. Bake at 325° for 15 minutes or until bubbly. Remove from oven, sprinkle chocolate morsels evenly on top, and let stand 30 seconds or until melted. Spread melted chocolate over surface. Sprinkle evenly with pecans.
4. Cover and chill at least 2 hours. Cut into 1-inch squares or break into pieces. Store refrigerated in an airtight container.

From the kitchen of Pam Lutgen
Largo, Florida

DATE BALLS

Naturally sweet and sticky dates make these old-fashioned treats moist and tender. Part candy, part cookie, they might remind you of the popular rice cereal treats. The dried Medjool dates often found in the produce section of the grocery store are particularly tasty and successful in this recipe.

Makes about 4 dozen

½ cup butter, softened
1 cup sugar
1 (10-oz.) package pitted dates, chopped
1 large egg, lightly beaten
1 cup chopped pecans

1 tsp. vanilla extract
4 cups crisp rice cereal
Sweetened flaked coconut or powdered sugar

1. Stir together butter, sugar, dates, and egg in a medium saucepan; cook over low heat 6 to 8 minutes, stirring constantly, until sugar dissolves. Add pecans; cook, stirring constantly, 10 minutes.
2. Remove from heat, and stir in vanilla. Stir in cereal. Cool slightly.
3. Form mixture into 1½-inch balls. Coat balls in coconut, and place on a baking sheet lined with wax paper or parchment paper. Let stand until firm. Store in an airtight container.

From the kitchen of Kay Wallace
Eclectic, Alabama

OATMEAL CAKE with BROILED TOPPING

This is an old-fashioned spice sheet cake that is spiffed up by its amazing coconut and pecan topping. Don't be tempted by the aroma of the warm cake; let it cool completely after broiling so the topping has time to cool and stick to the tender cake. This cake is just right for when you need a nice dessert or snack that people can nibble on for a few days.

Makes 12 to 15 servings

Cake
1   cup uncooked regular rolled oats
½   cup butter, cut into pieces
1¼   cups boiling water
1⅓   cups all-purpose flour
1   tsp. baking soda
1   tsp. ground cinnamon
½   tsp. ground nutmeg
2   large eggs

1   cup firmly packed brown sugar
¾   cup granulated sugar

Broiled Topping
1   cup firmly packed brown sugar
1   cup chopped pecans or walnuts
1   cup sweetened flaked coconut
½   cup butter, softened
⅓   cup milk

1. To prepare cake, preheat oven to 350°. Grease and flour a 13- x 9-inch baking pan.

2. Place oats and butter in a large bowl. Pour 1¼ cups boiling water over oat mixture; cover and let stand 20 minutes.

3. Whisk together flour, baking soda, cinnamon, and nutmeg in a large bowl.

4. Add eggs, 1 at a time, to oat mixture, beating at medium speed with an electric mixer only until yellow yolk disappears after each addition.

5. Gradually add brown sugar and granulated sugar, beating only until blended. Gradually add flour mixture, beating only until blended. Pour batter into prepared pan.

6. Bake at 350° for 25 to 30 minutes or until a wooden pick inserted in center comes out clean. Meanwhile, make the Broiled Topping.

7. To prepare topping, beat together brown sugar, pecans, coconut, butter, and milk at medium speed with a mixer until well blended. Spoon onto warm cake. Gently spread topping over cake using back of a spoon.

8. Preheat broiler with oven rack in highest position. Broil cake for 3 to 5 minutes or until topping is bubbly and lightly browned. Cool completely.

From the kitchen of Rosemary Cole
Gulf Shores, Alabama

COCA-COLA CAKE

Don't make the frosting ahead; you need to pour it over the cake shortly after baking.

Makes 12 to 15 servings

Cake
1	cup Coca-Cola
½	cup buttermilk
1	cup butter, softened
1¾	cups granulated sugar
2	large eggs
2	tsp. vanilla extract
2	cups all-purpose flour
¼	cup unsweetened cocoa
1	tsp. baking soda
1½	cups miniature marshmallows

Frosting
½	cup butter
⅓	cup Coca-Cola
3	Tbsp. unsweetened cocoa
1	lb. powdered sugar
1	Tbsp. vanilla extract
¾	cup chopped pecans (optional)

1. Preheat oven to 350°. Grease and flour a 13- x 9-inch baking pan.

2. Stir together Coca-Cola and buttermilk in a small bowl; set aside.

3. Beat butter in large bowl at low speed with an electric mixer until creamy. Gradually add sugar; beat until blended. Add eggs, 1 at a time, beating only until yellow yolk disappears into the batter after each addition. Quickly beat in vanilla.

4. Whisk together flour, cocoa, and baking soda in medium bowl. Add to butter mixture in thirds, alternating with half of cola mixture, beginning and ending with flour mixture. Beat at low speed only until blended after each addition. Fold in marshmallows.

5. Pour batter into prepared pan. Bake at 350° for 30 to 35 minutes or until a wooden pick inserted in center comes out clean. (Avoid piercing a marshmallow, which might still be sticky even when cake is done.) Cool 10 minutes. Meanwhile, make the frosting.

6. To prepare frosting, bring butter, cola, and cocoa to a boil in a large saucepan over medium heat, stirring until butter melts. Remove from heat; whisk in powdered sugar and vanilla. Pour immediately over warm cake, spreading evenly. Sprinkle with pecans, if using. Cool completely.

From the kitchen of Mrs. Paul E. Grisham
Decatur, Alabama

SIT and CHAT

Many of the world's most famous soft drinks were invented in the South. That's not surprising. Worldwide, sweet drinks are most popular in hot, humid climes. Although we'll never know the name of the very first baker to pour soda into cake batter, the idea caught on quick. The acidic soda makes this chocolate cake very tender and moist. For best results, seek out Coke made with real cane sugar. Diet soda doesn't work well at all.

PRIZE CAKE

One of the South's Most Famous Desserts

When Emma Rylander Lane of Clayton, Alabama, self-published her cookbook in 1898, appropriately called *Some Good Things to Eat*, she probably never dreamed that her Prize Cake would become one of the most famous and beloved Southern cakes. Despite it becoming her namesake, it's unlikely that Miss Lane invented Lane Cake, but she appears to be the first to publish the recipe, and that secured her lifelong association with this beloved confection.

Southern Living first published a recipe for Lane Cake in 1966 in their second issue, but perhaps the most famous mention of a Lane cake is in Harper Lee's novel, *To Kill a Mockingbird*. Scout describes eating one "so full of shinny it made me tight." "Shinny," in this case, refers to bourbon. It's true. Bourbon is an essential ingredient in a real Lane Cake, which means that the cake improves in flavor as it ages and mellows. Covered and uncut, this cake can be made up to one week ahead.

This recipe for Lane Cake comes from Edna Lewis and Scott Peacock, two of the most respected experts on the art of Southern cooking. Mr. Peacock shares that Lane Cake was his favorite birthday cake when he was growing up in Alabama. Ms. Lewis, the grand-daughter of a former slave, was instrumental in bringing Southern cuisine to the world stage. Her cooking and writing revived the art of refined Southern cooking while offering a glimpse of African-American farm life in rural Virginia in the early 20th century. Her venerable cookbooks, especially *The Taste of Country Cooking*, are required reading for anyone seeking to learn more about Southern cookery. As Ms. Lewis said, "One of the greatest pleasures of my life has been that I have never stopped learning about good cooking and good food."

In her later years, Ms. Lewis teamed up with Mr. Peacock to write *The Gift of Southern Cooking*, a cookbook that aimed to keep Southern foodways honest. True Southern food, they both believed, is the enjoyment of the land. Their recipes showcase fresh, homegrown ingredients with only the barest of embellishments to enhance the food's natural flavors. In the words of Ms. Lewis: "When I grew up, everyone had a garden, and we ate bountiful foods—vegetables, fruits, grains, beans, and more fish than meat. People didn't know any better than to be good cooks, and good food bonded us together."

LANE CAKE

This recipe comes from Edna Lewis and Scott Peacock, two of the most respected experts on the art of Southern cooking. Ms. Lewis was instrumental in bringing traditional Southern dishes to the world stage. (Pictured on page 176)

Makes 12 servings

Cake
3½ cups all-purpose flour
1 Tbsp. baking powder
¼ tsp. salt
1 cup unsalted butter, softened
2 cups sugar
1 cup whole milk
8 large egg whites

Filling
12 large egg yolks
1½ cups sugar
¾ cup unsalted butter, melted
1½ cups finely chopped pecans
1½ cups finely chopped raisins
1½ cups sweetened flaked coconut
½ cup bourbon
1½ tsp. vanilla extract

1. To prepare cake, preheat oven to 325°. Grease and flour 3 (9-inch) round cake pans. Line bottoms with parchment paper rounds; grease and flour paper.

2. Whisk together flour, baking powder, and salt in a medium bowl.

3. Beat butter in a large bowl at medium speed with an electric mixer until creamy. Gradually add sugar. Beat at high speed 5 to 7 minutes or until mixture is light and fluffy.

4. Add flour mixture to butter mixture in thirds, alternately with half of milk, beginning and ending with flour mixture. Beat at low speed only until blended after each addition.

5. Beat egg whites in a large bowl at high speed until stiff peaks form. Stir one-third of egg whites into batter. Gently fold in remaining whites with a rubber spatula. Spoon batter into prepared cake pans. Smooth tops with spatula.

6. Bake at 325° for 20 to 25 minutes or until a wooden pick inserted in center comes out clean. Cool in pans on wire racks 10 minutes. Remove from pans, and cool completely on wire racks.

7. To prepare filling, whisk together egg yolks and sugar in large heavy saucepan until well blended. Whisk in melted butter, and cook over medium heat, stirring constantly, 3 minutes or until mixture thickly coats back of a spoon. Do not let mixture simmer or boil.

8. Stir in pecans, raisins, coconut; cook 1 minute. Stir in bourbon; cook 1 minute. Remove from heat, and stir in vanilla. Let stand 5 minutes.

9. Spread scant 1 cup filling between layers; use remainder on top and sides of cake. Cool completely.

From the kitchen of Edna Lewis and Scott Peacock
Freetown, Virginia, and Hartford, Alabama

BEST CARROT CAKE

A carrot cake with cream cheese frosting is one of the most-requested birthday cakes. This one is a real showstopper, with both pineapple and coconut added to the batter. The buttermilk glaze keeps the cake layers wonderfully moist. Carrot cake is easy and forgiving, making it a great layer cake for beginning bakers.

Makes 12 servings

Cake

2	cups all-purpose flour
2	tsp. baking soda
½	tsp. salt
2	tsp. ground cinnamon
3	large eggs
2	cups sugar
¾	cup vegetable oil
¾	cup buttermilk
2	tsp. vanilla extract
2	cups grated carrot
⅔	cup drained crushed pineapple
1⅓	cups sweetened flaked coconut
1	cup chopped pecans or walnuts

Buttermilk Glaze

1	cup sugar
1½	tsp. baking soda
½	cup buttermilk
½	cup butter
1	Tbsp. light corn syrup
1	tsp. vanilla extract

Cream Cheese Frosting

¾	cup butter, softened
1	(3-oz.) package cream cheese, softened
3	cups sifted powdered sugar
1½	tsp. vanilla extract

Garnish: chopped pecans

1. Preheat oven to 350°. Grease and flour 3 (9-inch) round cake pans. Line bottoms with parchment paper. Lightly grease and flour paper.

2. Whisk together flour, 2 tsp. soda, salt, and cinnamon in a medium bowl.

3. Beat eggs, 2 cups sugar, oil, ¾ cup buttermilk, and 2 tsp. vanilla in a large bowl at medium speed with an electric mixer until smooth.

4. Add flour mixture, beating at low speed until blended.

5. Fold in carrot, pineapple, coconut, and pecans. Pour batter into prepared pans. Gently tap pans on counter to remove air bubbles.

6. Bake at 350° for 25 to 30 minutes or until a wooden pick inserted in center comes out clean. Meanwhile, make the buttermilk glaze.

7. To prepare glaze, bring 1 cup sugar, 1½ tsp. soda, ½ cup buttermilk, ½ cup butter, and corn syrup to a boil in a large Dutch oven over medium-high heat. Boil, stirring often, 4 minutes. Remove from heat, and stir in 1 tsp. vanilla. Brush warm glaze evenly over cake layers.

8. Cool in pans on wire racks 15 minutes. Remove from pans, and cool completely on wire racks.

9. To prepare frosting, beat ¾ cup butter and cream cheese in a large bowl at medium speed with an electric mixer until creamy. Add powdered sugar and 1½ tsp. vanilla; beat until smooth. Spread frosting between layers and on top and sides of cake. Sprinkle with chopped pecans.

From the kitchen of Phyllis Vanhoy
Salisbury, North Carolina

CREAM CHEESE POUND CAKE

This is an old-fashioned pound cake. It contains no leavening, so the cake is dense with a moist crumb. For many of us, this cake is a lesson in perfect pound cake.

The recipe was submitted by Eddy McGee, who said in his letter, "I'm different than most letter carriers. I bake for the folks on my route." A great mailman is everyone's neighbor.

Makes 12 servings

1½ cups butter, at room temperature
1   (8-oz.) package cream cheese, at room temperature
3   cups sugar
6   large eggs
1   Tbsp. vanilla extract
3   cups all-purpose flour
⅛   tsp. salt
Garnish: fresh berries

1. Preheat oven to 300°. Grease and flour a 10-inch Bundt pan.
2. Beat butter and cream cheese in a large bowl with an electric mixer at medium speed until creamy. Gradually add sugar, beating 5 to 7 minutes or until mixture is light and fluffy. Add eggs, 1 at a time, beating only until yellow yolk disappears after each addition. Quickly beat in vanilla.
3. Whisk together flour and salt in a medium bowl. Add to butter mixture in thirds, beating at low speed only until blended after each addition. Pour batter into pan. Gently tap pan on counter to remove air bubbles.
4. Fill a 2-cup ovenproof measuring cup or small baking pan with water, and place it in the oven on the rack below the tube pan.
5. Bake at 300° for 1 hour and 40 minutes or until a wooden pick inserted in center comes out clean. Cool in pan on a wire rack for 10 to 15 minutes. Remove from pan, and cool completely on wire rack.

From the kitchen of Eddy McGee
Elkin, North Carolina

HINT:

Pick the Right Pan

Pound cake recipes that call for a tube pan won't always fit in a Bundt pan. Tube pans, which are sometimes called angel food pans, have straight, high sides with a removable bottom. One-piece Bundt pans are shallower and more fluted. Although both may measure 10 inches in diameter, each holds a different amount of batter. Most 10-inch Bundt pans hold 10 or 12 cups of batter. Most 10-inch tube pans hold 14 or 16 cups. When unsure of size, use a measuring cup to fill the cake pan with water to determine its capacity.

COLD-OVEN BROWN SUGAR POUND CAKE

Before baking any cake, or preparing any dish, for that matter, be sure to read the recipe. There might be some surprises. For example, this atypical pound cake starts in a cold oven rather than the usual preheated oven.

Be sure to use cake flour when that type of flour is called for in a recipe. It's different from all-purpose flour and behaves differently in the recipe.

Makes 12 servings

1	cup butter, softened	3	cups cake flour
½	cup shortening	1	tsp. baking powder
2	cups firmly packed light brown sugar	1	cup canned evaporated milk
1	cup granulated sugar	2	tsp. vanilla extract
6	large eggs	2	cups chopped toasted pecans

1. Do not preheat oven. Grease and flour a 10-inch tube pan.

2. Beat butter and shortening in a large bowl at medium speed with an electric mixer until creamy. Gradually add brown sugar and granulated sugar, beating at high speed for 5 to 7 minutes or until mixture is light and fluffy. Add eggs, 1 at a time, beating only until the yellow yolk disappears after each addition.

3. Sift together flour and baking powder into a medium bowl. Add to butter mixture in thirds, alternately with half of the milk, beginning and ending with flour mixture. Beat batter at low speed only until blended after each addition. Stir in vanilla and pecans. Pour batter into prepared pan.

4. Place pan in cold oven. Set oven temperature to 300°.

5. Bake at 300° for 1 hour and 30 minutes to 1 hour and 45 minutes or until a long wooden pick inserted in center comes out clean. Cool in pan on a wire rack 10 minutes. Remove from pan, and cool completely on wire rack.

From the kitchen of Ruth Rippetoe
Greensboro, North Carolina

HINT

How Soft Is Softened Butter?

To achieve that just-right stage, leave the butter in a cool, shaded spot on the kitchen counter for two hours. Test the softness by pressing the butter with your finger. If the indention shows and yet the butter holds its shape, it's perfect. If you forget to set out the butter and resort to the microwave, use the lowest power level in 20-second intervals. Overly soft or melted butter will not work properly in recipes, even if you let it solidify again.

TWO-STEP SOUR CREAM POUND CAKE with LEMON GLAZE

There is no reason to think this recipe would work at all, much less turn out perfectly. The method contradicts every bit of advice on how to make pound cake. Although this method is unconventional, it's not random—the ingredients must be placed in the bowl in the listed order, and the mixing requires a heavy-duty stand mixer.

Makes 12 servings

Cake
3   cups sugar
3   cups all-purpose flour
¼   tsp. salt
¼   tsp. baking soda
1   cup butter, softened
1   (8-oz.) container sour cream
6   large eggs

2   Tbsp. fresh lemon juice
½   tsp. vanilla extract

Lemon Glaze
1   cup powdered sugar
1   tsp. finely grated fresh lemon zest
2   Tbsp. fresh lemon juice
½   tsp. vanilla extract

1. To prepare cake, preheat oven to 325°. Grease and flour a 10-inch tube pan.
2. Place cake ingredients in the order listed in 4-qt. mixing bowl of a heavy-duty stand mixer.
3. Beat at low speed 1 minute, stopping to scrape down sides. Beat at medium speed 2 minutes. Spoon batter into prepared pan.
4. Bake at 325° for 1 hour and 30 minutes or until a long wooden pick inserted in center comes out clean. Cool cake in pan on a wire rack 10 minutes. Remove from pan, and cool completely on wire rack. Meanwhile, make the Lemon Glaze.
5. To prepare glaze, stir together powdered sugar, lemon zest, lemon juice, and vanilla in a small bowl until smooth. Drizzle glaze evenly over cake. Cool completely.

From the kitchen of Bettie Jo Sightler
West Columbia, South Carolina

CARMELITAS

These ooey, gooey bar cookies are so popular and beloved that you could say that they have a cult following. The chewy caramel and chocolate filling rests on an oatmeal-brown sugar crust. This is what all oatmeal cookies hope to be when they grow up.

INGREDIENTS

2 cups all-purpose Flour

1 tsp baking soda

2 cups uncooked quick-cooking oats

1 1/2 cups firmly packed light brown Sugar

OATS

1 x cup BUTTER melted

1/4 tsp salt

1 Package Semi (12 oz) -Sweet Chocolate morsels

1/2 cup chopped pecans or walnuts. (optional)

1/3 cup HALF & HALF

1 (14 oz.) package soft, chewy caramel candies

MAKES 2 DOZEN

1 Preheat oven to 350°. Lightly grease a 13-x 9 inch baking pan.

2 Whisk together flour, oats, brown sugar, baking soda, & salt in a large bowl.

3 Add butter, stirring until mixture is crumbly. Reserve half of mixture (about 2 3/4 cups) Press remaining half of mixture into bottom of prepared tin pan. Sprinkle evenly with chocolate morsels and nuts, if using.

4 Microwave caramels and half-and-half in a microwave-safe bowl at MEDIUM (50% power) 3 minutes. Stir and microwave at MEDIUM 1 to 3 more minutes or until mixture can be stirred smooth. Let stand 1 minute. Pour evenly over chocolate morsels. Sprinkle evenly with reserved crumb mixture.

5 Bake at 350° for 30 minutes or until light golden brown. Cool in pan on a wire rack. Cut into bars. Store in an airtight container at room temperature up to 3 days or freeze up to 1 month.

MRS. REAGAN'S VIENNA CHOCOLATE BARS

Makes 3 dozen

1 cup butter, softened
1½ cups granulated sugar, divided
2 large egg yolks
2½ cups all-purpose flour
1 (10-oz.) jar seedless raspberry preserves
1 cup semisweet chocolate morsels
4 large egg whites, at room temperature
¼ tsp. salt
2 cups finely chopped pecans, lightly toasted

1. Preheat oven to 350°. Line a 15- x 10-inch jelly-roll pan with aluminum foil; lightly grease foil.
2. Beat butter and ½ cup sugar at medium speed with a heavy-duty electric stand mixer until well blended. Add egg yolks, and beat until combined.
3. Gradually add flour, beating at low speed 1 to 2 minutes or just until combined. Press mixture onto bottom of prepared pan.
4. Bake at 350° for 15 to 20 minutes or until golden brown. Remove from oven. Spread preserves over crust. Sprinkle with chocolate morsels.
5. Beat egg whites and salt in bowl of a stand mixer at high speed, using whisk attachment, until foamy. Add remaining 1 cup sugar, 1 Tbsp. at a time, beating until stiff peaks form and mixture is glossy. Fold in pecans. Gently spread meringue mixture over chocolate mixture.
6. Bake at 350° for 30 to 35 minutes or until meringue is browned and crispy. Cool completely on a wire rack (1 hour). Cut into bars.

Giant Houseparty
Philadelphia-Neshoba County Chamber of Commerce

The occasional celebrity recipe can add a certain cachet to community cookbooks. After visiting the Neshoba County Fair (billed as Mississippi's Giant Houseparty) during Ronald Reagan's 1980 bid for the Presidency, Nancy Reagan shared this recipe for buttery layers of short-bread and fruit topped with crisp meringue.

ULTIMATE CHOCOLATE CHIP COOKIES

When people describe and discuss what constitutes the ultimate perfect classic chocolate chip cookie, any disagreements often center on whether the cookies should be soft or crisp. These cookies can turn out either way, depending on the baking time.

Other disagreements are often over whether a chocolate chip cookie should contain anything other than chocolate morsels. There are three variations offered below that will let you taste and compare your way through the debates.

Be sure to use dark brown sugar in the recipe; its extra moisture makes a big difference.

Makes about 5 dozen

¾ cup butter, softened
¾ cup granulated sugar
¾ cup firmly packed dark brown sugar
2 large eggs
1½ tsp. vanilla extract

2¼ cups plus 2 Tbsp. all-purpose flour
1 tsp. baking soda
¾ tsp. salt
1 (12-oz.) package semisweet chocolate morsels

1. Preheat oven to 350°. Lightly grease 2 baking sheets. (If you have only one baking sheet and plan to bake the cookies in batches, let the pan cool completely between batches.)
2. Beat butter, granulated sugar, and brown sugar in a large bowl at medium speed with an electric mixer until creamy. Add eggs and vanilla, beating until blended.
3. Whisk together flour, baking soda, and salt in a medium bowl. Add to butter mixture in thirds, beating well after each addition. Stir in chocolate morsels.
4. Drop dough by tablespoonfuls onto prepared baking sheets.
5. Bake at 350° for 8 to 14 minutes or until desired degree of doneness, 8 minutes for soft and gooey cookies, or up to 14 minutes for crisp results. Remove to wire racks to cool.

PEANUT BUTTER-CHOCOLATE CHIP COOKIES:

Decrease salt to ½ tsp. Add 1 cup creamy peanut butter with butter and sugars. Increase flour to 2½ cups plus 2 Tbsp. Proceed as directed. (Dough will look a little moist.)

OATMEAL-RAISIN CHOCOLATE CHIP COOKIES:

Reduce flour to 2 cups. Add 1 cup uncooked quick-cooking oats to dry ingredients and 1 cup raisins with morsels. Proceed as directed.

COCONUT-MACADAMIA CHUNK COOKIES:

Substitute 1 (12-oz.) package semisweet chocolate chunks for morsels. Add 1 cup white chocolate morsels, ½ cup sweetened flaked coconut, and ½ cup macadamia nuts with chocolate chunks. Proceed as directed.

From the kitchen of Susan Hefilfinger
Mandeville, Louisiana

SWEDISH ALMOND COOKIES

These delicate, shortbread-like cookies melt in your mouth. This recipe is an example of an heirloom family recipe that was likely brought over from the old country, made with love, celebrated with nostalgia, and passed down through the generations with pride.

Makes 3 dozen

½ cup shortening	2 cups all-purpose flour
½ cup butter, at room temperature	1½ cups ground almonds
1 cup sifted powdered sugar	1 Tbsp. vanilla extract
½ tsp. salt	Powdered sugar

1. Preheat oven to 325°.
2. Beat shortening and butter in a large bowl at medium speed with an electric mixer until creamy. Add powdered sugar and salt, and beat until mixture is light and fluffy.
3. Stir in flour. Stir in almonds, vanilla, and 1 Tbsp. water.
4. Form dough into 1-inch balls. Place on ungreased baking sheets.
5. Bake at 325° for 12 to 15 minutes or until light golden brown.
6. Cool slightly. Roll warm cookies in powdered sugar until evenly coated. Cool completely on wire racks.

From the kitchen of Mrs. J.W. Montgomery
Kinston, North Carolina

HINT:

Many stores now sell packages of ground almonds,
but you can use slivered almonds to make your own in
a food processor. Pulse the processor so that the nuts
bounce up and down over the blade, and be sure
to stop before the nuts grind into paste.

BENNE SEED WAFERS

These tiny, very crisp cookies are slightly nutty and delicately sweet. It might be impossible to eat only one.

Makes 10 dozen

½ cup white sesame seeds
½ cup butter, softened
1 cup sugar
1 large egg, lightly beaten
½ tsp. vanilla extract

1¾ cups all-purpose flour
2 tsp. baking powder
½ tsp. baking soda
½ tsp. salt

1. Preheat oven to 325°. Lightly grease a baking sheet.

2. Cook sesame seeds in a heavy skillet over low heat, stirring often, 5 minutes or until very lightly toasted. Pour in a single layer on a plate to cool. Seeds will continue to darken as they cool.

3. Beat butter in a large bowl at medium speed with an electric mixer until creamy. Gradually add sugar, beating well. Stir in sesame seeds, egg, and vanilla.

4. Whisk together flour, baking powder, baking soda, and salt in a medium bowl. Stir into butter mixture. Cover dough, and chill until firm, at least 1 hour.

5. Working in batches, form dough into ½-inch balls. (Pressing dough into a 1-tsp. measuring spoon creates about a ½-inch ball.) Place balls on prepared baking sheet. Flatten to ⅟₁₆-inch thickness with floured fingers or a flat-bottomed glass.

6. Bake at 325° for 8 to 10 minutes or until lightly browned. Transfer to wire racks to cool. The cookies will continue to firm up as they cool. Store in an airtight container.

From the kitchen of Clementa Florio
Wadmalaw Island, South Carolina

Taste of THE SOUTH
benne seeds

A round Charleston, South Carolina, many people use the word "benne" to describe what most of us call sesame seeds. It's true that benne seed is a type of sesame seed, but they aren't equivalent in terms of flavor. True benne nearly disappeared when growers turned to commercially viable sesame seed that could be pressed for oil. Thanks to restoration efforts, very limited amounts of domestic benne are being produced these days, but it is hard to find. The best substitute for authentic benne is very fresh white sesame seeds.

FRIED APPLE PIES

Makes 6 servings

1½ cups dried apples
1   Tbsp. butter
½   cup sugar
¾   tsp. ground cinnamon
½   tsp. ground nutmeg
2   cups all-purpose flour
½   tsp. salt
½   cup shortening
¼   to ½ cup whole milk
Vegetable oil
Sifted powdered sugar (optional)

1. Bring apples and water to cover to a boil in a medium sauce-pan. Reduce heat, and simmer, uncovered, 30 minutes or until apples are soft. Remove from heat, and let stand, uncovered, for 1 hour. Drain off any standing liquid. Mash apples coarsely with a fork or pastry blender. Again, drain off any standing liquid. The filling should be very thick. Stir in butter, sugar, cinnamon, and nutmeg. Cover and chill.
2. Whisk together flour and salt in a large bowl. Work in short-ening with pastry blender or fingertips until mixture is crumbly. Sprinkle milk, 1 Tbsp. at a time, evenly over surface; stir with a fork until dry ingredients are moistened.
3. Divide pastry into 6 equal portions. Roll each portion to ⅛-inch thickness on a lightly floured surface, and cut each into a 6-inch round. (A saucer makes a nice guide.)
4. Spoon one-sixth of apple filling on half of each round. Moisten edge of pastry, fold dough over apple filling, and press edges to seal. Crimp edges with a fork.
5. Pour oil to depth of ½ inch into a large heavy skillet. Heat over medium-high heat. Working in batches, fry pies 3 minutes on each side or until golden brown, turning once. Drain well on paper towels. Sprinkle warm pies with powdered sugar, if desired. Serve warm or at room temperature.

From the kitchen of Mrs. Denver W. Anderson
Eva, Tennessee

SIT *and* CHAT

The roster of famous Southern pies is long and honorable, but perhaps no type inspires more nos-talgia than a fried apple pie. Despite the implica-tions of their name, most homemade fried pies are not deep-fried, but cooked in a skillet until they are golden brown. Fried pies have long been popular in the Mountain South, where hearthside baking in a trusty iron skillet was perfected in the days before ovens were common.

MINI PECAN PIES

Makes 1 dozen

3 cups chopped pecans	2 Tbsp. melted butter
¾ cup sugar	1 tsp. vanilla extract
¾ cup dark corn syrup	⅛ tsp. salt
3 large eggs, lightly beaten	12 frozen tart shells

1. Preheat oven to 350°. Bake pecans at 350° in a single layer in a shallow pan 8 to 10 minutes or until toasted and fragrant. Pour onto plate to cool.

2. Stir together sugar and corn syrup in a medium bowl. Stir in pecans, eggs, melted butter, vanilla, and salt.

3. Arrange pastry shells on a large rimmed baking sheet. Spoon about ¼ cup pecan mixture into each shell.

4. Bake at 350° for 25 to 30 minutes or until set. Remove to wire racks to cool completely (about 30 minutes). Store in an airtight container for up to 3 days.

CRUNCHY PECAN PIE BITES:

Substitute 6 dozen frozen mini phyllo shells for the tart shells. Prepare recipe as directed through Step 2. Place pastry shells on a large baking sheet. Spoon about 1½ tsp. pecan mixture into each pastry shell. Bake at 350° for 20 minutes or until set.

From the kitchen of Rose M. Clinton
Alexandria, Louisiana

BEST-OF-THE-BEST

HEAVENLY RECIPES

The Church Ladies' Divine Desserts
(Copyright 2001)

Just think of it, a whole cookbook full of dessert recipes attributed to "church ladies," the affectionate nickname given to excellent community cooks who generously prepare and share great recipes with their church family. Experienced attendees of well-stocked church potlucks and dinners on the ground now seek out the specialties of these talented cooks.

The book's cover promises a collection of heavenly recipes and sweet recollections, so we know we're in for a serious sugar fix. In the introduction, we learn that "Desserts that take some doing, such as banana pudding topped with golden meringue, cheesecake covered with blueberry compote, and pound cake with a crumb as fine as face powder, will satisfy any sweet tooth....It was likely a church lady who first announced 'Save your fork!'."

COCONUT CUSTARD PIE

Custard pies, also known as cream pies, are a quintessential Southern confection. For many of us, coconut pie is the best of the bunch. Busy cooks will sing the praises of this easy recipe. Coconut lovers will swoon over the divine results.

Makes 8 servings

Crust
1½ cups graham cracker crumbs
⅓ cup butter, melted
¼ cup sugar
Filling
3 large eggs, well beaten

2 cups whipping cream
¾ cup sweetened flaked coconut
½ cup sugar
1 tsp. vanilla extract
Garnishes: whipped cream, toasted coconut

1. Preheat oven to 350°. To prepare crust, stir together graham cracker crumbs, melted butter, and ¼ cup sugar; press on bottom and up sides of a lightly greased 9-inch pie plate. Bake at 350° for 12 minutes. Cool completely on a wire rack. Increase oven temperature to 425°.
2. To prepare filling, whisk together eggs, whipping cream, coconut, ½ cup sugar, and vanilla; pour into crust. Bake at 425° for 15 minutes.
3. Reduce oven temperature to 325°. Shield edges of crust with foil to prevent excessive browning. Bake at 325° for 20 minutes or until set. Cool completely on a wire rack.

From the kitchen of Brenda Rhodes Miller
The Church Ladies' Divine Desserts

GERMAN CHOCOLATE PIE

German chocolate desserts did not originate in Germany. Instead, their name comes from a popular style of sweetened baking chocolate created in 1852 by a man named Samuel German, who worked for Baker's Chocolate Company. As with the frosting on a classic German chocolate cake, this rich, fudgy pie contains coconut and pecans.

The Junior League of Charleston, West Virginia, invites you to experience this collection of recipes from the Appalachian region of the United States. The theme of the cookbook is the pioneer woman and features many favorites from local cooks and restaurants, as well as famous West Virginians.

Makes 8 servings

1	(4-oz.) package sweet baking chocolate
¼	cup butter or margarine
1	(12-oz.) can evaporated milk
1½	cups sugar
3	Tbsp. cornstarch
⅛	tsp. salt
2	large eggs
1	tsp. vanilla extract
1	(9½-inch) unbaked deep-dish pie shell
⅔	cup flaked coconut
⅓	cup chopped pecans
1	cup sweetened whipped cream
3	Tbsp. chocolate shavings

1. Preheat oven to 375°.
2. Cook baking chocolate and butter in a medium saucepan over low heat, stirring until chocolate melts and mixture is smooth. Remove from heat, and gradually stir in evaporated milk; set aside.
3. Whisk together sugar, cornstarch, and salt in a large bowl.
4. Whisk in eggs and vanilla, mixing well.
5. Gradually whisk in chocolate mixture, using a wire whisk.
6. Pour mixture into pie shell. Sprinkle with coconut and chopped pecans.
7. Bake at 375° for 45 minutes. (Pie might appear soft, but will become firm as it cools.) Cool at least 4 hours. Top pie with whipped cream and chocolate shavings.

Mountain Measures
Junior League of Charleston, West Virginia

SWEET POTATO PIE *with* ROSEMARY-CORNMEAL CRUST

In parts of the South, sweet potato pie runs circles around pumpkin pie. A touch of fragrant rosemary and a bit of crunchy cornmeal in the crust makes this pie extra special.

Makes 8 servings

Crust
¾ cup all-purpose flour
½ cup plain white cornmeal
¼ cup powdered sugar
2 tsp. chopped fresh rosemary
¼ tsp. salt
½ cup cold butter, cut into pieces
¼ cup very cold water

Filling
1½ lb. small, slender sweet potatoes

3 large eggs
¾ cup granulated sugar
1 cup evaporated milk
3 Tbsp. butter, melted
2 tsp. finely grated fresh orange zest
1 Tbsp. fresh orange juice
½ tsp. ground cinnamon
¼ tsp. ground nutmeg
1½ tsp. vanilla extract

1. To prepare crust, whisk together flour, cornmeal, powdered sugar, rosemary, and salt in a medium bowl until well blended. Cut butter into flour mixture with a pastry blender until mixture is crumbly, with a few pieces of butter the size of small peas.

2. Sprinkle cold water, 1 Tbsp. at a time, over flour mixture, stirring with a fork until dry ingredients are moistened. Pour onto a work surface. Gather and form into ball, then flatten into a disk. Wrap well in plastic wrap, and chill 30 minutes.

3. Unwrap dough, and roll between 2 new sheets of lightly floured plastic wrap into a 12-inch round. Fit into a 9-inch pie plate. Fold edges under, and crimp. Chill 30 minutes.

4. Preheat oven to 400°. Bake crust at 400° for 20 minutes, shielding edges with aluminum foil to prevent excessive browning. Cool completely on a wire rack (about 1 hour).

5. To prepare filling, place sweet potatoes on a baking sheet, and bake at 400° for 45 minutes or until soft. Let stand 10 minutes. Cut potatoes in half lengthwise; scoop out pulp into a bowl. Mash pulp until smooth. Discard skins.

6. Whisk together eggs and granulated sugar in a large bowl until well blended. Stir in milk, melted butter, orange zest, orange juice, cinnamon, nutmeg, and vanilla. Stir in sweet potato pulp. Pour mixture into crust.

7. Bake at 400° for 20 minutes. Reduce oven temperature to 325°, and bake 20 to 25 minutes more or until center is set. Cool completely on a wire rack (about 1 hour).

NOTE: If you don't want to prepare a homemade crust, you can add cornmeal and fresh rosemary to a refrigerated crust. Substitute ½ (14.1-oz.) package refrigerated piecrusts for cornmeal crust ingredients. Unroll on a lightly floured surface. Sprinkle with 1 Tbsp. plain white cornmeal and 2 tsp. chopped fresh rosemary. Lightly roll cornmeal and rosemary into crust. Fit into a 9-inch pie plate according to package directions. Fold edges under; crimp. Proceed as directed, beginning with Step 5.

From the kitchen of Crystal Detamore-Rodman
Charlottesville, Virginia

CLASSIC CHESS PIE

If in the beginning there was pie, it was probably chess pie. Although there are as many versions of Southern chess pie as there are stars in the sky, this recipe features ingredients common in most old-timey chess pies: vinegar and cornmeal, plus other common farmstead ingredients. Cooks who had no access to fresh citrus fruit used ordinary vinegar to add acidity to the filling.

Makes 8 servings

1   (9-inch) unbaked piecrust shell, chilled
2   cups sugar
2   Tbsp. cornmeal
1   Tbsp. all-purpose flour
¼   tsp. salt
½   cup butter, melted
¼   cup milk
1   Tbsp. white vinegar
½   tsp. vanilla extract
4   large eggs, lightly beaten

1. Preheat oven to 425°. Line pie shell with aluminum foil or parchment paper, making sure it extends over the edge of the crust. Fill with pie weights or dry, uncooked rice or beans. Bake at 425° for 4 to 5 minutes or until pie shell no longer looks wet. Carefully remove foil and weights, and bake 2 to 3 more minutes or until crust looks dry and golden. Cool on wire rack.
2. Reduce oven temperature to 350°. Whisk together sugar, cornmeal, flour, and salt in a large bowl. Whisk in melted butter, milk, vinegar, and vanilla. Whisk in eggs. Pour mixture into piecrust.
3. Bake at 350° for 50 to 55 minutes or until set, shielding edges with aluminum foil after 10 minutes to prevent excessive browning. Cool completely on a wire rack.

COCONUT CHESS PIE:

Prepare filling as directed; stir in 1 cup toasted sweetened flaked coconut before pouring into piecrust. Bake as directed above.

From the kitchen of Mildred Wheeler
Richmond, Virginia

HINT:

Blind Baking

The crust for this pie is baked and cooled before it is filled. This technique, known as blind baking, is common when pie filling is thin and wet. Otherwise, the crust would remain soft and turn soggy before the filling sets. The unbaked pie shell is lined with aluminum foil or parchment paper and then filled with ceramic or metal pie weights or with uncooked rice or dried beans. The foil keeps the weights from sticking to the uncooked pastry, and the weights keep the pastry from buckling while it bakes. The rice or beans cannot be eaten after they have been used as weights, but many cooks save them to reuse in future piecrusts.

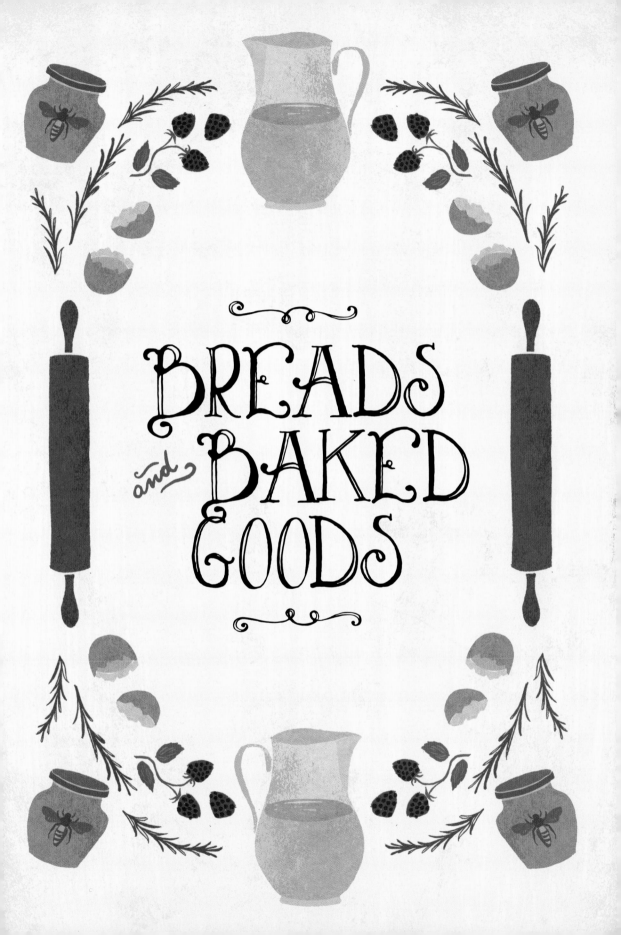

BREADS and BAKED GOODS

SKILLET CORNBREAD

No food in the world loves a cast-iron skillet more than cornbread. Some people believe the meal should be on the table and the eaters around it when cornbread comes from the oven. It tastes good as it cools, but nothing compares to those first piping hot bites when the crust is crisp and the center is tender.

Makes 1 (10-inch) cake

3   Tbsp. bacon drippings
1¾ cups cornmeal
1   tsp. baking powder
1   tsp. baking soda

¾   tsp. salt
2   cups buttermilk
1   large egg

1. Preheat oven to 450°. Place bacon drippings in a 10-inch cast-iron skillet, and heat in oven 8 to 10 minutes or until drippings begin to shimmer.
2. Meanwhile, stir together cornmeal, baking powder, baking soda, and salt in a large bowl, and make a well in the center. Stir together buttermilk and egg in a medium bowl. Pour buttermilk mixture into cornmeal mixture, and stir only until dry ingredients are moistened.
3. Remove hot skillet from the oven, pour hot drippings into cornmeal mixture, and quickly stir with a fork to incorporate. Pour batter into hot skillet, and immediately place in oven.
4. Bake at 450° for 18 to 20 minutes or until golden brown and cornbread pulls away from sides of skillet. Immediately remove from skillet, and serve piping hot.

From the kitchen of Mrs. Robert Lee Tyson
Broken Bow, Oklahoma

HINT:

For the best flavor, use very fresh cornmeal, preferably stone-ground. Most stone-ground cornmeal is whole grain, which means it should be stored in the freezer and used quickly. Some cooks and families have strong feelings about white versus yellow cornmeal. The truth is that the color makes no difference in the recipe, although it's fine to stick with what you know and prefer.

HOT-WATER CORNBREAD

These crisp little skillet cakes are a tad fancier than some versions of hot-water cornbread that are made with little more than cornmeal, boiling water, and a spoonful of grease. Some people call these pones or hoe cakes, especially when they literally were cooked on the blade of a garden hoe held over embers.

David advises making large pones for adults and small ones for children. "You always need to have one of these in hand when you sit down to a bowl of greens or butter beans." That is, if they make it to the table. Eager eaters have been known to stand around the skillet, ready to pounce on the piping hot cakes.

Makes 1 dozen

2	cups cornmeal	¼	cup half-and-half
¼	tsp. baking powder	1	Tbsp. vegetable oil
1¼	tsp. salt	1	to 2 cups boiling water
1	tsp. sugar		Vegetable oil

1. Whisk together cornmeal, baking powder, salt, and sugar in a large bowl. Stir in half-and-half and 1 Tbsp. oil.

2. Gradually add boiling water, stirring until batter is the consistency of soft mashed potatoes. The amount of boiling water needed varies, depending on the type of cornmeal used. Coarse stone-ground cornmeal requires more liquid.

3. Pour oil to depth of ½ inch into a large heavy skillet. Heat over medium-high heat. Working in batches, spoon batter in ¼-cupfuls into the hot oil. Fry 3 minutes on each side or until golden, turning once. Drain on paper towels. Serve hot.

SOUTHWESTERN HOT-WATER CORNBREAD:

After adding boiling water, stir in 1 seeded and minced jalapeño pepper; 1 cup (4 oz.) shredded Mexican cheese blend; 1 cup frozen whole kernel corn, thawed; and ¼ cup minced fresh cilantro.

BAKED HOT-WATER CORNBREAD:

Omit skillet procedure. Preheat oven to 475°. Pour ⅓ cup vegetable oil into a 15- x 10-inch jelly-roll pan, spreading to edges. Drop batter as directed into pan. Bake at 475° for 12 to 15 minutes. Turn and bake 5 more minutes or until golden brown.

From the kitchen of David Newell
Trussville, Alabama

HUSH PUPPIES

These hot cornbread fritters are irresistible. A fish fry (and many a barbecue plate) is incomplete without them.

Makes about 2 dozen

1	cup cornmeal	1	large egg, lightly beaten
½	cup all-purpose flour	1¼	cups buttermilk
1	tsp. salt	¾	cup finely chopped onion
1	tsp. baking soda		Vegetable oil, for deep-frying
1	Tbsp. sugar		

1. Whisk together cornmeal, flour, salt, baking soda, and sugar in a large bowl. Make a well in center of mixture.
2. Whisk together egg and buttermilk in a small bowl. Add to dry ingredients, and stir only until moistened, about 10 times around the bowl. Fold in onions. Let stand 10 minutes.
3. Meanwhile, pour oil to depth of 3 inches into a Dutch oven or large heavy pot that is at least 5 inches deep; heat to 375°.
4. Preheat oven to 225°. Working in batches, drop batter by rounded tablespoonfuls into hot oil. Make sure hush puppies can float freely. Fry 2 to 3 minutes on each side or until golden brown. Let oil return to 375° between batches. Drain on paper towels. Keep fried hush puppies warm in 225° oven up to 15 minutes.

From the kitchen of Miss Lucille Smith
Cleveland, South Carolina

❧

CORN LIGHT BREAD

Unlike crusty cornbread made in a skillet, this cornbread bakes in a loaf pan and can be sliced like sandwich bread. Its texture is similar to pound cake and makes fantastic toast.

Makes one 9-inch loaf

	Vegetable shortening	1	tsp. baking soda
1	Tbsp. plus 2 cups white cornmeal, divided	1	tsp. salt
1	cup all-purpose flour	2	cups buttermilk
½	cup sugar	3	Tbsp. bacon drippings or butter, melted

1. Preheat oven to 375°. Grease a 9- x 5-inch loaf pan with shortening. Sprinkle with 1 Tbsp. cornmeal.
2. Whisk together remaining 2 cups cornmeal, flour, sugar, baking soda, and salt in a large bowl.
3. Add buttermilk, stirring just until blended. Stir in bacon drippings.
4. Spoon batter into prepared pan. Let stand 10 minutes.
5. Bake at 375° for 40 minutes or until browned on top; a wooden pick inserted in center should come out clean. Cool in pan on a wire rack 10 minutes.

From the kitchen of Mrs. Eloise Haynes
Cleveland, Mississippi

❧

EGG BREAD

To many people, the term "egg bread" refers to yeast bread that is similar to challah or brioche. To other folks, especially those from the Cumberland Plateau, those words often conjure memories of thick, fluffier-than-usual corn-bread. This recipe can be traced back to once-popular and long-gone restaurants and department store cafeterias in downtown Nashville, where thick slices of hot egg bread were split and filled with creamed chicken.

Makes 6 to 8 servings

1 cup milk
2¼ cups yellow cornmeal, divided
3 large eggs
1 tsp. salt
2 cups buttermilk
1 tsp. baking soda
2 Tbsp. shortening

1. Preheat oven to 400°.
2. Stir together milk and 1 cup water in a large saucepan. Bring to a boil over high heat. Remove from heat, and gradually whisk in 2 cups cornmeal. Let stand until needed.
3. Beat eggs in a large bowl at high speed with an electric mixer until foamy. Add salt, and beat 5 minutes or until mixture is light and fluffy.
4. Stir together buttermilk and baking soda in a small bowl. Pour into egg mixture, and mix well. Add cornmeal mixture, and stir until smooth.
5. Place shortening in a 10-inch cast-iron skillet. Place skillet in oven 5 minutes. Pour melted shortening into cornmeal mixture, and mix well. Stir in remaining ¼ cup cornmeal. Pour mixture into hot skillet.
6. Bake at 400° for 25 to 30 minutes or until firm. Remove from skillet immediately, and serve hot.

The Nashville Cookbook
Nashville Area Home Economics Association

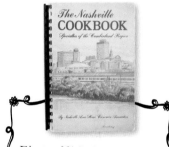

First published in 1976, this collection of the best recipes of the Cumberland region is also a celebration of history and hospitality. The illustrations through-out the book showcase the major influences as the city transformed from rural to contemporary.

SWEET POTATO BISCUITS

In 1976, Mildred Cotton Council opened Mama Dip's restaurant, named for the childhood nickname given to her by her siblings because her height and long arms allowed her to dip a ladle all the way into the bottom of the rain barrel. The restaurant is a Chapel Hill institution, serving up Southern-style family meals. Mama Dip's two cookbooks have been praised by some of the most famous chefs and food writers in the world.

Makes about 3 dozen

4   cups self-rising flour
⅛   tsp. baking soda
3   Tbsp. sugar
2   cups cooked, mashed sweet potatoes
½   cup butter, melted
1   to 1¼ cups whole milk
All-purpose flour

1. Preheat oven to 400°. Lightly grease 2 baking sheets.
2. Whisk together flour, baking soda, and sugar in a large bowl. Make a well in the center.
3. Stir together sweet potatoes, butter, and 1 cup milk in a large bowl until well blended. Pour into flour mixture, and stir with a fork just until dough comes together and pulls in the dry ingredients. The dough should be soft and sticky, but not wet; add remaining ¼ cup milk to moisten dough, if needed.
4. Sprinkle a work surface with all-purpose flour. Turn dough out, and knead gently 8 to 10 times. Pat or roll dough to ¾-inch thickness. Stamp out biscuits with a 2-inch round cutter; do not twist cutter. Dip cutter in all-purpose flour if dough sticks. Reshape scraps once. Place biscuits on prepared baking sheets.
5. Bake at 400° for 15 minutes or until firm and golden brown.

From the kitchen of Mildred (Mama Dip) Council
Chapel Hill, North Carolina

HINT:

For the best results, select small sweet potatoes, and cook them whole to keep the sweet potato flesh from getting watery and diluting flavor. Either boil the potatoes in a saucepan of salted water or roast them in a 375° oven until very tender. The mashed potato pulp should have the consistency of canned pumpkin. If the pulp is too wet, spoon it into a wire-mesh strainer lined with a paper towel. Place the strainer over a bowl and refrigerate for at least 1 hour and up to overnight. Discard the collected liquid. Boiled potatoes will have lighter color and delicate flavor. Roasted potatoes will be a little darker and have richer flavor.

THE ART OF THE BISCUIT

Flaky, buttery biscuits are the cornerstone of Southern cuisine.

Perfect hot biscuits can render us speechless. Yet we sure do have a lot to say about them. Each of us has our own definition of perfection when it comes to biscuits. Some of us like thin, crisp biscuits. Others revel in pillow-soft, bouffant biscuits. Some swear that the secret is buttermilk or lard or White Lily flour. And biscuit making can cause some people to just swear. But by any measure, no packaged product can compare to home-made biscuits made with both love and good intentions. Perhaps those emotions are actually the secret ingredients that distinguish stellar biscuits from the so-so. Flour, fat, and liquid no more yield biscuits than canvas, paint, and brushes yield art. Biscuits are handiwork.

Many of us extol the glorious biscuits made by a grandmother, biscuits that were perfect each time despite her never measuring a thing. That's because she baked biscuits regularly, perhaps daily, for years. With that much practice, she didn't need to consult a recipe or measure ingredients. When we've baked that many biscuits, we won't need to either.

So if we want to bake consistently good biscuits, we must be willing to risk baking some bad biscuits at first, until we get the hang of it and own our prowess. Mostly, we must be willing to make biscuits, repeatedly. Practice really does make perfect, or at least points us in that direction.

BUTTERMILK BISCUITS

Makes about 18

3½ cups self-rising soft wheat flour

2 tsp. baking powder

2 tsp. sugar (optional)

¼ cup shortening, cut into small cubes and chilled

¼ cup butter, cut into small cubes and chilled

1½ cups well-shaken buttermilk

All-purpose flour

2 Tbsp. butter, melted

1. Preheat oven to 450°. Line a baking sheet with parchment paper.

2. Whisk together flour, baking powder, and, if desired, sugar in a large bowl.

3. Scatter shortening and chilled butter over flour mixture, and toss lightly to coat. Cut in shortening and chilled butter with a pastry blender until mixture is crumbly.

4. Add buttermilk, stirring just until dry ingredients are moistened.

5. Sprinkle work surface with all-purpose flour. Turn dough out, and sprinkle generously with all-purpose flour. Knead dough 20 to 25 times or until smooth and springy to the touch. Add all-purpose flour as needed to keep dough from sticking to work surface.

6. Pat dough into a ¾-inch-thick rectangle. Stamp out biscuits with a 2-inch round cutter; do not twist cutter. Reshape scraps once. Place biscuits with sides touching on prepared baking sheet.

7. Bake at 450° for 13 to 15 minutes or until lightly browned. Brush tops with melted butter.

From the kitchen of Kregg Owens
Albany, Georgia

WHIPPING CREAM BISCUITS

These light-as-a-feather homemade biscuits are as quick as a mix. The cream provides both the fat and the liquid. These might be the perfect gateway biscuit for novice bakers.

Makes 1 dozen

2 cups self-rising flour
¾ to 1 cup whipping cream, chilled

All-purpose flour
¼ cup butter, melted

1. Preheat oven to 450°. Lightly grease a baking sheet.
2. Pour the flour into a large bowl. Slowly stir in enough cream with a fork to make a soft dough that pulls in the flour.
3. Sprinkle a work surface with all-purpose flour. Turn dough out, and knead lightly 3 or 4 times. Roll or pat dough to ¾-inch thickness. Stamp out biscuits with a 2-inch round cutter; do not twist cutter. Place biscuits on prepared baking sheet. Gather and reroll scraps. (Alternatively, cut dough into squares with a pizza cutter or sharp knife, which eliminates scraps.)
4. Bake at 450° for 10 to 12 minutes or until golden. Brush tops with melted butter.

From the kitchen of Mrs. Martha Giles
Augusta, Georgia

MAKE-AHEAD YEAST ROLLS

Baking with yeast can be tricky in a hot, humid summertime kitchen. Carole says this recipe "turns out the same way, no matter what mood you're in or what the weather is." The baked rolls freeze well.

Makes 32

2 (¼-oz.) envelopes active dry yeast
1¼ cups warm water (100° to 110°), divided
4½ to 5 cups all-purpose flour, divided

3 large eggs, lightly beaten
½ cup shortening, melted
½ cup sugar
2 tsp. salt

1. Stir together yeast and ¼ cup warm water in a small bowl; let stand 5 minutes or until bubbly.
2. Stir together yeast mixture, remaining 1 cup warm water, 2 cups flour, eggs, shortening, sugar, and salt in a large bowl. Beat with a wooden spoon 2 minutes. Gradually stir in enough remaining flour to make a soft dough.
3. Cover and let rise in a warm place (80° to 85°), free from drafts, for 1 hour.
4. Deflate dough, cover, and chill for at least 8 hours.
5. Deflate dough. Turn dough out onto a floured surface, and knead 4 turns. Shape dough into 16 (2-inch) balls. Divide dough balls between 2 lightly greased 9-inch square pans. Cover and let rise in a warm place (80° to 85°), free from drafts, 1½ hours or until doubled in bulk.
6. Preheat oven to 375°. Bake at 375° for 12 minutes or until golden.

From the kitchen of Carole Miller Radford
Lincolnton, Georgia

SPOON ROLLS

These are the fastest and easiest homemade rolls ever. They contain yeast, yet require no rising and kneading—just stir and bake. Because the dough can be made ahead, and the rolls can be baked and frozen, these spoon rolls are home-made convenience food.

Makes 2 dozen

1	(¼-oz.) envelope active dry yeast	¾	cup butter, melted
2	cups warm water (100° to 110°)	¼	cup sugar
4	cups self-rising flour	1	large egg, lightly beaten

1. Preheat oven to 400°. Grease 2 (12-cup) muffin pans.
2. Stir together yeast and warm water in a large bowl; let stand 5 minutes or until mixture bubbles.
3. Stir in flour, melted butter, sugar, and egg.
4. Spoon batter into prepared pans, filling each cup two-thirds full. Bake at 400° for 13 minutes or until golden. Turn out of pans, and serve warm.

NOTE: Dough can be covered and chilled up to 1 week. Baked and cooled rolls can be frozen in zip-top freezer bags. Wrap them loosely in foil to reheat.

MINIATURE SPOON ROLLS:

Spoon batter into 2 greased 24-cup miniature muffin pans or 4 (12-cup) miniature muffin pans. Bake at 400° for 9 minutes or until golden. Makes 4 dozen.

From the kitchen of Lilann Hunter Taylor
Savannah, Georgia

CREAM CHEESE BANANA BREAD with CRISP CINNAMON TOPPING

This might be the most elegant banana bread ever, and perhaps the tastiest as well. We appreciate that banana bread is an excellent way to salvage bananas that have almost—but not quite—gone 'round the bend.

Makes 2 (8-inch) loaves

Topping
½ cup firmly packed light brown sugar
½ cup chopped toasted pecans
1 Tbsp. all-purpose flour
1 Tbsp. butter, melted
⅛ tsp. ground cinnamon

Bread
¾ cup butter, softened
1 (8-oz.) package cream cheese, softened
2 cups granulated sugar
2 large eggs
3 cups all-purpose flour
½ tsp. baking powder
½ tsp. baking soda
½ tsp. salt
1½ cups mashed very ripe bananas (1¼ lb. unpeeled, about 4 medium size)
1 cup chopped toasted pecans
½ tsp. vanilla extract

1. To prepare topping, stir together brown sugar, pecans, flour, melted butter, and cinnamon in a medium bowl.
2. To prepare bread, preheat oven to 350°. Grease and flour 2 (8- x 4-inch) loaf pans.
3. Beat butter and cream cheese in a large bowl at medium speed with an electric mixer until smooth and creamy. Gradually add granulated sugar. Beat for 5 minutes or until light and fluffy.
4. Add eggs, 1 at a time, beating just until yellow yolk disappears after each addition.
5. Whisk together flour, baking powder, baking soda, and salt in a large bowl. Add to butter mixture in thirds, beating at low speed just until blended.
6. Stir in bananas, pecans, and vanilla.
7. Spoon batter into prepared pans. Sprinkle topping mixture evenly over batter.
8. Bake at 350° for 1 hour or until a long wooden pick inserted in center comes out clean and sides pull away from pan, shielding with aluminum foil during the last 15 minutes to prevent excessive browning, if necessary. Cool bread in pans on wire racks for 10 minutes. Remove from pans, and cool at least 30 minutes on wire racks before cutting with a serrated knife.

From the kitchen of Willie Monroe
Homewood, Alabama

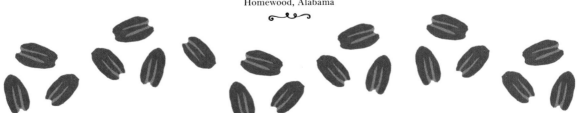

LEMON TEA BREAD

The tangy lemon glaze drizzled over this pleasing cake ratchets up the flavor and keeps it moist. Tea cake doesn't contain tea, but it sure goes well with a nice cuppa.

Makes 1 (8-inch) loaf

Bread
½ cup butter, softened
1 cup granulated sugar
2 large eggs
1½ cups all-purpose flour
1 tsp. baking powder
½ tsp. salt

½ cup milk
1 Tbsp. finely grated lemon zest
Glaze
1 cup powdered sugar
2 Tbsp. fresh lemon juice
1 Tbsp. finely grated lemon zest
1 Tbsp. granulated sugar

1. Preheat oven to 350°. Grease and flour an 8- x 4-inch loaf pan.
2. Beat butter in a large bowl at medium speed with an electric mixer until smooth and creamy. Gradually add granulated sugar. Beat for 5 minutes or until light and fluffy.
3. Add eggs, 1 at a time, beating only until yellow yolk disappears after each addition.
4. Whisk together flour, baking powder, and salt in a medium bowl. Add to butter mixture in thirds, alternately with half of the milk, beginning and ending with flour mixture, beating at low speed only until blended after each addition. Stir in lemon zest. Spoon batter into prepared pan.
5. Bake at 350° for 1 hour or until a long wooden pick inserted in center of bread comes out clean. Let the bread cool in the pan 10 minutes. Remove bread from the pan, and cool on a wire rack.
6. Stir together powdered sugar and lemon juice in a small bowl until smooth. Spoon evenly over top of bread, letting excess drip down sides. Stir together lemon zest and granulated sugar in a small bowl. Sprinkle on top of bread.

LEMON-ALMOND TEA BREAD:

Stir ½ tsp. almond extract into the batter. Proceed as directed.

From the kitchen of Dorsella Utter
Louisville, Kentucky

SAUSAGE and CHEESE MUFFINS

These hearty muffins are impressively moist and tender. They might remind you of the popular and beloved baked sausage balls. They make substantial breakfast bread, but are also great with supper or a bowl of hot soup. For an easy variation, substitute condensed broccoli-cheese soup.

Makes 18 muffins

1 lb. ground pork sausage	1½ cups (6 oz.) shredded Cheddar cheese
3 cups all-purpose baking mix	1 (10¾-oz.) can condensed cheese soup

1. Preheat oven to 375°. Lightly grease 3 (6-cup) muffin pans.

2. Cook sausage in a large skillet, stirring until it crumbles and is no longer pink. Drain and cool.

3. Combine sausage, baking mix, and shredded cheese in a large bowl; make a well in center of mixture.

4. Stir together soup and ¾ cup water; add to sausage mixture, stirring only until dry ingredients are moistened. Spoon into prepared pans, filling each cup three-fourths full.

5. Bake at 375° for 20 minutes or until lightly browned.

From the kitchen of Kathy Poole
Collierville, Tennessee

MORNING GLORY MUFFINS

As their name implies, these muffins make a glorious breakfast. They keep well in the freezer, so you can quickly microwave one or two just before you head out the door.

Makes 2 dozen

3   cups all-purpose flour
1   tsp. salt
1   tsp. baking soda
1   tsp. ground cinnamon
½   tsp. ground nutmeg
2   cups sugar
¾   cup canola oil
3   large eggs
2½ tsp. vanilla extract
1   (8-oz.) can crushed pineapple, undrained
1   cup finely grated carrot (about 2 medium carrots)
1   cup chopped toasted pecans
1   cup golden raisins

1. Preheat oven to 350°. Lightly grease 2 (12-cup) muffin pans.
2. Whisk together the flour, salt, baking soda, cinnamon, and nutmeg in a large bowl; make a well in center of mixture.
3. Whisk together sugar, canola oil, eggs, and vanilla in a large bowl. Fold in crushed pineapple and carrots. Add to flour mixture, stirring just until dry ingredients are moistened. Fold in toasted pecans and raisins.
4. Spoon into prepared pans, filling each cup two-thirds full.
5. Bake at 350° for 23 to 25 minutes or until a wooden pick inserted in center comes out clean. Cool in pans on wire rack 5 minutes. Remove from pans to wire rack, and cool completely (about 30 minutes).

NOTE. Baked and cooled muffins can be frozen in a zip-top plastic freezer bag up to 1 month. Remove from bag, and let thaw at room temperature.

From the kitchen of Geordyth Sullivan
Miami, Florida

HINT:

The secret to good muffins is in the mixing. Combine all the dry ingredients in a bowl, and form a well in the center of the mixture. Add the liquid all at once, and then stir only enough to moisten the dry ingredients. The mixture might be lumpy, but further mixing will make tough muffins with peaked or flat tops.

BEST-OF-THE-BEST

TEXAS TRADITION

Stop and Smell the Rosemary
The Junior League of Houston, Texas, 1997

People who collect cookbooks present a convincing case that *Stop and Smell the Rosemary* was a game changer that redefined Junior League cookbooks. Beyond being an inviting and useful cookbook, this book qualified as a coffee table book, full of professional photography, carefully edited text, and meticulously tested recipes.

Beyond the book's appearance, the 500 recipes in this book announced a shift in what

many people considered to be standard Southern and Southwestern food. In addition to their hometown favorites, these cooks included recipes featuring ingredients discovered during trips abroad and to the big city, ingredients that were considered exotic when this book appeared in 1997. *Stop and Smell the Rosemary* is still a community cookbook in that it reflects a specific time and place and was intended to be both relevant and useful to home cooks.

FRESH ROSEMARY MUFFINS

Makes 1 dozen

¾ cup milk	1½ cups all-purpose flour
¼ cup golden raisins	½ cup sugar
¼ cup raisins	2 tsp. baking powder
¼ cup currants	¼ tsp. salt
1 Tbsp. chopped fresh rosemary	1 large egg, lightly beaten
¼ cup unsalted butter	4 oz. goat cheese

1. Preheat oven to 350°. Lightly grease a 12-cup muffin pan.
2. Cook milk, golden raisins, raisins, currants, and rosemary in a heavy saucepan over medium heat, stirring often, 2 minutes or just until it begins to steam; remove from heat. Add butter; stir until melted. Remove from heat; cool completely (about 30 minutes).
3. Whisk together flour, sugar, baking powder, and salt in a large bowl; make a well in center of mixture. Stir together egg and milk mixture until well blended. Pour into well in flour mixture, and stir only until dry ingredients are moistened.
4. Spoon one-third of batter into cups of prepared muffin pan. Add 2 tsp. goat cheese to each muffin cup. Spoon remaining batter over goat cheese, filling each cup two-thirds full.
5. Bake at 350° for 20 to 24 minutes or until golden brown. Cool in pan on a wire rack 3 minutes. Remove from pan.

Stop and Smell the Rosemary
The Junior League of Houston, Texas

254

MAMA'S MINI CINNIS

These quick little cinnamon rolls will make your kitchen smell wonderful. Smart cooks know that on busy days a favorite shortcut product, such as refrigerated dough, helps us get a home-baked treat on the table in a hurry.

Makes 24 rolls

2	(8-oz.) cans refrigerated crescent rolls	1	tsp. ground cinnamon
6	Tbsp. butter, softened	⅔	cup powdered sugar
⅓	cup firmly packed brown sugar	1	Tbsp. milk or half-and-half
¼	cup chopped pecans	¼	tsp. almond or vanilla extract
1	Tbsp. sugar	⅛	tsp. salt

1. Preheat oven to 375°. Grease 2 (8-inch) cake pans.
2. Unroll crescent dough. Separate each piece along its center perforation to form a total of 4 rectangles. Press diagonal perforations to seal.
3. Stir together butter, brown sugar, pecans, sugar, and cinnamon in a medium bowl. Divide butter mixture evenly among the 4 dough rectangles, and spread evenly to edges. Starting with a long side, roll up each rectangle jelly-roll fashion. To make slicing easier, place logs on a baking sheet, and freeze 10 minutes.
4. Cut each log into 6 even slices, each about 1 inch thick, using a serrated knife. Place slices cut-side down in prepared cake pans, spacing them about ¼ inch apart.
5. Bake at 375° for 15 to 18 minutes or until golden. Cool 5 to 10 minutes.
6. Meanwhile, stir together powdered sugar, milk, almond extract, and salt until smooth. Drizzle over warm rolls.

From the kitchen of Robyn Arnold
Houston, Texas

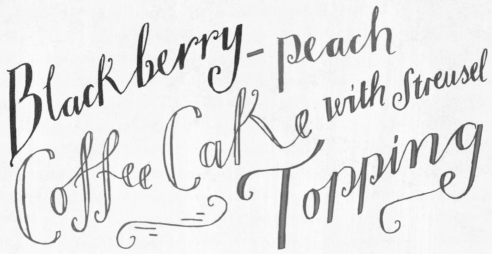

Blackberry-peach Coffee Cake with Streusel Topping

Don't limit your enjoyment of this attractive and delectable cake to your morning cup of coffee. It makes a great dessert, especially at brunch, or an indulgent snack.

STREUSEL TOPPING

1/2 cup butter, softened

1/2 tsp ground nutmeg

1/2 cup granulated sugar

1 tsp ground cinnamon

1/2 cup firmly packed light brown sugar

2/3 cup all-purpose flour

CAKE

1 cup granulated sugar

1/2 cup butter softened

2 cups all-purpose flour

2 large eggs

1 cup fresh blackberries

2 tsp baking powder

2/3 cup milk

2 tsp vanilla extract

2 cups peeled and sliced fresh firm, ripe peaches (about 2 large peaches, 7 oz each)

powdered sugar

1/2 tsp salt

Garnishes: fresh blackberries, sliced peaches

MAKES 8 SERVINGS

From the Kitchen of Aura Leigh Barrett Oregon, Wisconsin

1 Preheat oven to 350°. Grease and flour a 9-inch springform pan. (A shiny or light-colored pan will give the best results. If you have a dark pan, wrap the outside of the pan with heavy-duty aluminum foil to get a similar result.)

2 To prepare streusel topping, beat butter in a medium bowl with an electric mixer at medium speed until smooth and creamy. Gradually add granulated sugar and brown sugar, beating well. Add flour, cinnamon, and nutmeg: beat just until blended. Chill.

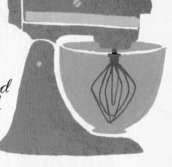

3 To prepare cake, beat butter in a large bowl with an electric mixer at medium speed until smooth and creamy. Gradually add granulated sugar, beating well.

4 Add eggs, 1 at a time, beating only until the yellow yolk disappears after each addition.

5 Whisk together flour, baking powder, and salt in a large bowl; add to butter mixture in thirds, alternating with half of milk, beginning and ending with flour mixture, beating at low speed just until blended after each addition. Stir in vanilla.

6 Pour batter into prepared tin. Top with sliced peaches and blackberries. Drop 1 inch pieces of Streusel Topping over fruit.

7 Bake at 350° for 1 hour 10 minutes to 1 hour 20 minutes or until center of cake is set (A wooden pick inserted in center will be covered in moist crumbs, but not wet batter) Cool completely on a wire rack, about 1½ hours. Dust with powdered sugar.

Peach Coffee Cake: Omit blackberries. Increase peaches to 3 cups sliced (about 3 large peaches, 7 oz each). Proceed with recipe as directed.

MORAVIAN SUGAR CAKE

Makes 12 to 16 servings

1   medium-size russet potato (about 8 oz.), peeled and cut into 1-inch pieces
1   (¼-oz.) envelope active dry yeast
½   tsp. plus 1 cup sugar, divided
¼   cup warm potato water (100° to 110°)
½   cup shortening
¼   cup butter, softened
1   tsp. salt
2   large eggs, beaten
3   cups all-purpose flour
1   cup butter, cut into ⅛-inch slices
1   cup firmly packed light brown sugar
2   tsp. ground cinnamon

1. Place potato in a small saucepan, cover with water to depth of 1 inch, and simmer, covered, for 15 minutes or until tender. Drain well, reserving cooking water. Force potato through a food mill or ricer into a small bowl, or mash as smooth as possible with a fork. Measure out 1 cup of potatoes, and stir in 2 Tbsp. cooking water. Cover and keep warm.

2. Dissolve yeast and ½ tsp. sugar in warm potato water; let stand 5 minutes or until mixture bubbles.

3. Combine potatoes, remaining 1 cup sugar, shortening, ¼ cup butter, and salt in a large mixing bowl; stir until shortening melts. Stir in yeast mixture. Cover and let rise in a warm place (80° to 85°), free from drafts, 1½ hours or until spongy.

4. Stir in eggs and flour to make a soft dough. Shape dough into a ball. Place in a greased bowl, turning to grease top. Cover and let rise in a warm place (80° to 85°), free from drafts, 2 hours or until doubled in bulk.

5. Turn dough out onto a lightly floured surface; knead 5 minutes or until smooth and elastic. Pat dough evenly in a greased 13- x 9-inch baking pan. Cover and let rise in a warm place (80° to 85°), free from drafts, 45 minutes to 1 hour or until doubled in bulk.

6. Preheat oven to 375°. Deeply dimple surface of dough with your thumb or the end of a wooden spoon. Tuck bits of butter into the dimples. Stir together brown sugar and cinnamon in a small bowl; sprinkle evenly over dough and down into dimples.

7. Bake at 375° in center of oven for 20 minutes or until browned and cooked through. Let cool 5 minutes before serving.

From the kitchen of Elizabeth Hedgecock Sparks
Winston-Salem, North Carolina

SIT *and* CHAT

This traditional Moravian recipe has a strong association with Easter, when Old Salem bakers timed the bread to emerge fresh and warm from the oven to serve after the Easter sunrise service. The dough is made with mashed potatoes. Some contemporary recipes use instant mashed potatoes, but this version is closer to the original. The rich yeast dough is topped with puddles of butter and brown sugar.

ITALIAN BREAD

This is a classic crusty loaf with a tender heart. The dough makes equally wonderful focaccia and thick pizza crust.

Makes 1 loaf

1 (¼-oz.) envelope active dry yeast	2 to 3 cups bread flour
1 tsp. sugar	2 Tbsp. olive oil
1 cup warm water (100° to 110°)	1 tsp. salt

1. Combine yeast, sugar, and 1 cup warm water in bowl of a heavy-duty electric stand mixer fitted with the dough hook attachment; let stand 5 minutes or until mixture bubbles. Add 2 cups flour, oil, and salt. Beat at low speed 1 minute. Gradually add additional flour until dough begins to leave the sides of the bowl and pull together. The dough will start to look shaggy as the flour is added. When enough flour has been added, the dough will look supple and smooth, neither wet and sticky nor overly dry with a rough surface.

2. Increase mixer speed to medium, and beat 5 minutes. Cover with plastic wrap, and let stand in a warm place (80° to 85°), free from drafts, for 30 minutes or until doubled in bulk. Deflate dough, and let stand 10 minutes.

3. Preheat oven to 400°. Lightly grease a baking sheet.

4. Turn dough out onto a lightly floured surface. Shape dough into a 12-inch log, and place on prepared baking sheet. Cut 3 (¼-inch-deep) diagonal slashes across top of dough with a sharp paring knife. (The slashes release interior steam and prevent the loaf from blowing apart at the side.) Immediately put bread in oven.

5. Bake at 400° in center of oven for 16 minutes or until golden brown. Cool on a wire rack.

HERBED FOCACCIA:

Prepare recipe as directed, shaping dough into a ball instead of a loaf. Roll dough into an 14- x 11-inch rectangle on a lightly greased baking sheet. Press handle of a wooden spoon into dough to make indentations at 1-inch intervals. Drizzle dough evenly with 1 Tbsp. olive oil; sprinkle evenly with 1 tsp. dried Italian seasoning. Bake at 475° for 12 to 15 minutes or until golden brown.

PIZZA CRUST:

Prepare recipe as directed, shaping dough into a ball instead of a loaf. Roll dough into an 14- x 11-inch rectangle on a lightly greased baking sheet. Drizzle with olive oil, or spread with pesto or pizza sauce, and sprinkle with desired toppings. Bake at 475° for 20 to 25 minutes.

From the kitchen of Gaye Groover Christmus
Columbia, South Carolina

SALLY LUNN BREAD

You won't find a better texture for French toast, bread pudding, or toast with jam than lightly sweetened Sally Lunn bread. (Pictured on page 232)

Makes 12 to 16 servings

2   (¼-oz.) envelopes active dry yeast
½   cup warm water (100° to 110°)
1½ cups milk
¾   cup sugar
½   cup butter
1   tsp. salt
2   large eggs
5   cups all-purpose flour

1. Stir together yeast and ½ cup warm water in a small bowl; let stand 5 minutes or until mixture bubbles.
2. Heat milk, sugar, butter, and salt in a medium saucepan over medium heat, stirring until butter melts. Cool to 100° to 110°.
3. Beat yeast mixture, milk mixture, and eggs in a large bowl at medium speed with an electric mixer until blended. Gradually add flour, beating at lowest speed until blended. The dough will be very soft and sticky.
4. Cover and let rise in a warm place (80° to 85°), free from drafts, 1 hour or until dough doubles in bulk.
5. Deflate the dough; cover and let rise in a warm place (80° to 85°), free from drafts, 30 minutes or until dough doubles in bulk.
6. Preheat oven to 350°.
7. Deflate dough and spoon into a well-greased 10-inch Bundt pan or tube pan. Cover and let rise in a warm place (80° to 85°), free from drafts, 20 to 30 minutes or until dough doubles in bulk.
8. Bake at 350° for 35 to 40 minutes or until golden brown and a wooden pick inserted into center of bread comes out clean. Remove from pan to a wire rack to cool for 10 minutes before slicing.

Tidewater Inn
Irvington, Virginia

SIT and CHAT

The story is told that this buttery brioche-like yeast bread is named for its creator, Sally Lunn, an 18th-century Englishwoman—at least that's one explanation. Another theory is that the name for this round, golden loaf is derived from soleil lune, the French words for sun and moon. The dough rises three times, but requires no kneading. It bakes in a large Bundt pan or tube pan, so the darker the pan, the thicker and darker the crust.

SWEET BEER BREAD

This simple recipe makes it possible for even rookie bakers to make a reliable loaf of tasty bread. Beers with a light color and mild flavor work best, because bitter beer makes bitter bread. Beer bread makes a great grilled cheese sandwich.

Makes 1 (9-inch) loaf

3	cups self-rising flour	1	(12-oz.) bottle beer
¼	cup sugar	¼	cup butter, melted

1. Preheat oven to 350°. Lightly grease a 9- x 5-inch loaf pan.

2. Whisk together flour and sugar in a large bowl. Slowly stir in beer. Pour batter into prepared pan.

3. Bake at 350° for 45 minutes. Drizzle butter over top of loaf, and bake 10 minutes more or until deep golden brown. Remove from pan to wire rack, and cool completely (about 30 minutes).

From the kitchen of Marisa Stone
Jackson, Mississippi

RICE JOURNEY CAKES

Journey cakes—also known as Johnny cakes—are savory griddle cakes that can be served as a bread or as a side dish. They perhaps got their name because they were easy to make by people on the move who cooked each night by a campfire. Most journey cakes are made from cornmeal batter, but these are a great way to use up leftover rice.

Makes 20 cakes

2   large eggs
2   cups milk
2   cups all-purpose flour
2   tsp. salt

2   cups cold, cooked basmati, jasmine, or
    other long-grain rice
1½ Tbsp. butter, melted
    Peanut or vegetable oil

1. Whisk together eggs and milk in a large bowl until well blended. Stir in flour and salt. Stir in rice and melted butter.
2. Pour oil to depth of ¼ inch in a large heavy skillet; heat to 350°.
3. Working in batches, drop batter by ¼ cupfuls into the hot oil. Fry for 2 minutes on each side or until golden, turning once. Drain on wire racks lined with paper towels. Serve hot.

ROSEMARY-GARLIC JOURNEY CAKES:

Add 2 Tbsp. finely chopped fresh rosemary and 1 Tbsp. finely chopped garlic to batter. Proceed as directed.

TOMATO, PARMESAN & KALAMATA OLIVE JOURNEY CAKES:

Add 1 cup seeded and finely chopped tomato; ½ cup (2 oz.) shredded Parmesan cheese; and ¼ cup minced kalamata olives to rice mixture. Proceed as directed.

From the kitchen of Meredith Coxe
Darlington, South Carolina

PICKLES, PRESERVES, and PUT-UPS

MISS KITTY'S CHILI SAUCE

One of the defining characteristics of Southern cuisine is our love of condiments, especially the homemade specialties that good cooks put up during the height of the garden season. Think about a fully laden celebration table. Tucked in between the brimming platters and bowls are jars, bottles, and bowls of jams, jellies, chutneys, relishes, vinegars, and sauces—such as this fantastic chili sauce. The eaters can spoon up dibs and dabs of this and that to doctor their plates to suit their preferences. Ah, that's good eating.

Makes 6 pt.

2   jalapeño peppers, halved and seeded
6   bell peppers, halved and seeded
6   yellow onions, peeled and quartered
2   cups cider vinegar (5% acidity)
4   (28-oz.) cans crushed tomatoes
1   (16-oz.) package brown sugar
¼   cup salt
1½   tsp. freshly ground black pepper
1½   tsp. ground allspice
½   tsp. ground cloves
½   tsp. ground red pepper

1. Working in batches, puree jalapeño peppers, bell peppers, onions, and vinegar in a food processor or blender, stopping to scrape down sides. Pour into a large stockpot.
2. Stir in tomatoes, brown sugar, salt, black pepper, allspice, and cloves over medium-low heat, stirring occasionally, 3 hours or until thickened. Stir in ground red pepper.
3. Pack hot mixture into 6 (1-pt.) hot, sterilized jars, filling to ¼ inch from top. Run a wooden skewer around the inside of the jars to remove any trapped air bubbles. Wipe the jar rims clean. Cover with lids, and screw on bands.
4. Process jars in a boiling water bath for 20 minutes. Let jars stand in hot water for 5 minutes. Remove jars to wire rack to cool undisturbed. Test the seals, and promptly refrigerate any jars that did not seal.

From the kitchen of Kitty Forbes
Fort Valley, Georgia

SIT and CHAT

Chili sauce is a very old-fashioned condiment. It has the gentle heat of mild salsa, the smooth texture and acidity of ketchup, and the sweet spiciness of chutney. Its main use is to perk up simply cooked foods, particularly dried beans, fritters, and meatloaf. Cooks once put up many pints and quarts of this versatile stuff at the end of each summer to ensure that there would be plenty for winter.

RECIPES FROM THE GARDEN

Savory & Sage: Recipes and Gardening Wisdom from the Tallahassee Garden Club
(Copyright 2006; Tallahassee Garden Club)

If you believe that good cooking begins with good growing, then having a well-qualified garden club assemble a community cookbook, especially one filled with month-by-month gardening tips from the collective wisdom of the club's members, sounds like a very good idea.

The accomplished women in a local garden club are often the movers and shakers in town, the ones who get things done and have fun along the way. Thanks to their green thumbs, creativity, and pluck, garden clubs not only make their community a pretty place to see, they make their community a good place to live.

In May 1954, the Tallahassee Garden Club purchased The Rutgers House, the home built in 1840 for Henry Rutgers, a local civic leader. The builder was George Proctor, a free African-American who built many of Tallahassee's finest early homes. The Rutgers House occupies half a city block in the downtown area and is a historic landmark. The TGC uses the home as a location for fund-raisers, workshops, and special events. One of their biggest events is their annual Christmas Tea. Members festoon the house inside and out and fill the antique dining room table with delicious homemade holiday goodies. Most of the recipes, of course, come from *Savory & Sage*.

JEZEBEL SAUCE

Makes 4 cups

1 (18-oz.) jar apple jelly	⅓ cup dry mustard
1 (18-oz.) jar pineapple preserves	1 Tbsp. cracked black pepper
1 (5.25-oz.) jar prepared horseradish	

1. Whisk together apple jelly, pineapple preserves, horseradish, dry mustard, and cracked black pepper in a large bowl. Use soon, or cover and refrigerate for up to 3 days.

Savory & Sage: Recipes and Gardening Wisdom from the Tallahassee Garden Club
Tallahassee, Florida

CORN RELISH

Corn relish looks like summertime in a jar. In addition to your own favorite uses, try it as a condiment or topping for any food that you would serve with fresh corn, such as grilled meat, fish tacos, hot dogs, shrimp burgers, sliced fresh tomatoes, or salads. It even makes a novel salsa for tortilla chips.

Makes about 4 cups

2	Tbsp. cornstarch	3	cups fresh or thawed frozen corn
½	cup white vinegar (5% acidity)		kernels
¼	cup sugar	½	cup chopped onion
½	tsp. ground turmeric	½	cup chopped green bell pepper
½	tsp. celery seed	½	cup chopped red bell pepper
1	tsp. salt		

1. Whisk together cornstarch and ¼ cup water in a medium saucepan until smooth. Whisk in vinegar, sugar, turmeric, celery seed, and salt. Bring to a boil, stirring until sugar dissolves. Boil for 1 minute.

2. Stir in corn, onion, and bell peppers. Return to a boil. Reduce heat, and simmer 5 minutes or until most of the liquid cooks away. Remove from heat, and let cool.

3. Pour into a 1-qt. jar with a tight-fitting lid. Chill overnight before serving. Store refrigerated up to 6 weeks.

From the kitchen of Dorothy L. Driggers
Claxton, Georgia

GREEN TOMATO SANDWICH SPREAD

As the name implies, this is what folks once commonly spread on their sandwiches, hot dogs, and hamburgers. This recipe relies on a food processor to make quick work of the chopping, but old-timey recipes call for running the vegetables through a hand-cranked sausage grinder, which gave them the perfect nubby texture that didn't turn mushy when cooked.

This small-batch recipe will keep in the fridge just fine for a couple of weeks without having to heat-seal the jars. It's just enough to handle a small supply of green tomatoes, not a surfeit.

Makes about 3 cups

1½ lb. green tomatoes, cored and quartered
1   medium onion, coarsely chopped
1   large green bell pepper, coarsely chopped
1½ tsp. salt
¾   cup sugar
½   cup white vinegar
2   Tbsp. all-purpose flour
½   cup salad dressing or mayonnaise
2½ Tbsp. prepared yellow mustard
¼   cup chopped pimiento-stuffed olives

1. Working in batches, pulse tomatoes, onion, and bell pepper in bowl of food processor until finely chopped, stopping to scrape down sides. Do not puree.
2. Pour into a large saucepan, and stir in salt. Cover and let stand for 3 hours. Drain well, and discard the liquid. Return mixture to saucepan, and stir in sugar and vinegar. Bring to a boil, reduce heat, and simmer for 10 minutes, stirring occasionally.
3. Spoon ½ cup of the hot mixture into a small bowl. Whisk in flour until smooth; pour into pan. Simmer, stirring constantly, for 5 minutes or until thickened. Remove from heat.
4. Stir in salad dressing, mustard, and olives.
5. Cool, cover, and chill. Store refrigerated up to 2 weeks.

From the kitchen of Drexel Mills
Pontotoc, Mississippi

From the Kitchen of
Maris Faulkner
Henderson, North Carolina

CHOW-CHOW

For many families, a jar of chowchow is a staple whenever pinto beans and cornbread are served. With its bold flavors and crunchy texture, chowchow sure perks up a humble meal. There are various pickled relishes called chowchow all over the country, but this recipe is for the style that is beloved in the Upper and Mountain South. Chowchow likely started as a great way to use up the ragtag assortment of vegetables from the end-of-season garden. When there wasn't enough of any one thing to put up, resourceful cooks combined them to make batches of chowchow.

INGREDIENTS

5 green & 5 red bell peppers, chopped

2 large onions, chopped

1 tbsp. mustard seeds

2 large green tomatoes, chopped

¼ cup pickling salt

½ small cabbage, chopped

2 large jalapeño peppers, chopped (optional)

5 cups of sugar

2 cups white vinegar (5% acidity)

1½ tsp celery seeds

¾ tsp turmeric, ground

MAKES ABOUT 5 PT.

1 Stir together bell peppers, green tomatoes onions, cabbage, salt, and, if desired, jalapeños in a large dutch oven. Cover and chill 8 hours. Rinse and drain; return mixture to Dutch oven.

2 Stir in sugar, vinegar, 1 cup water, mustard seeds, celery seeds, and turmeric. Bring to a boil; reduce heat and simmer 3 minutes.

3 Quickly pack hot mixture into 5 (1 pt) hot, sterilized jars filling to ½ inch from top.

4 Run a wooden skewer around the inside of the jars to remove any trapped air bubbles. Wipe the jar rims clean. Cover with lids, and screw on bands.

5 Process jars in a boiling water bath for 15 minutes. Let jars stand in hot water for 5 minutes. Remove jars to wire rack to cool undisturbed. Test the seals, and promptly refrigerate any jars that did not seal.

Chow-Chow

KUDZU JELLY

This isn't a stunt. This is really good jelly, akin to all the wild-crafted blossom jellies made in the South. Kudzu blooms during late summer. The attractive bunches of delicate purple blossoms have a fragrance similar to grapes.

We all know that kudzu runs rampant in the South. If you can't beat it, eat it. Make sure your picking area has not been sprayed with chemicals in an attempt to kill or control the kudzu.

Makes 6 cups

4	cups kudzu blossoms	1	(1¾-oz.) package powdered pectin
4	cups boiling water	5	cups sugar
1	Tbsp. lemon juice		

1. Wash blossoms with cold water, and place in a large bowl. Pour 4 cups boiling water over blossoms. Cover and chill at least 8 hours. Strain into a large pot. Discard the solids. (The blossom liquid looks gray until lemon juice is added.)
2. Add lemon juice and pectin, and bring to a full, rolling boil over high heat, stirring constantly. Stir in sugar. Return to a full, rolling boil, stirring constantly. Boil 1 minute, stirring constantly. Remove from heat. Skim off foam with a metal spoon.
3. Quickly pour jelly into 6 (1-cup) hot, sterilized jars, filling to ¼ inch from the top. Wipe the jar rims clean. Cover with lids, and screw on bands.
4. Process jars in a boiling water bath for 5 minutes. Remove jars to a wire rack to cool undisturbed. Test the seals, and promptly refrigerate any jars that did not seal. Some jellies can take up to 2 weeks to fully jell.

From the kitchen of Diane Hoots
Warner Robbins, Georgia

HONEY *and* LEMON JELLY

Makes 4 cups

2½	cups honey	1	(3-oz.) package liquid pectin
¾	cup fresh lemon juice, strained		

1. Stir together honey and lemon juice in a large deep saucepan until well blended. Bring mixture to a full, rolling boil over high heat, stirring constantly.
2. Quickly stir in pectin. Return to a full, rolling boil, stirring constantly. Boil 1 minute, stirring constantly. Remove from heat; skim off foam with a metal spoon.
3. Pour jelly quickly into 4 (1-cup) hot, sterilized jars, filling to ¼ inch from top. Wipe the jar rims clean. Cover with lids, and screw on bands.
4. Process jars in a boiling water bath for 5 minutes. Remove jars to wire rack to cool undisturbed. Test the seals, and promptly refrigerate any jars that did not seal. Some jellies can take up to 2 weeks to fully jell.

From the kitchen of Peggy Fowler Revels
Woodruff, South Carolina

BLACKBERRY MICROWAVE JAM

This homemade jam is so incredibly fast and easy that it could be called spontaneous. Because it cooks quickly and isn't set with pectin, this jam is soft and a little syrupy, so it's quite good spooned over pancakes, waffles, and ice cream.

Makes about 2 cups

½	to 1 cup sugar	1	tsp. fresh lemon juice
4	cups fresh blackberries		

1. Place sugar in a 3-qt.or larger microwave-safe bowl. Microwave at HIGH 2 minutes or until sugar is warm.

2. Stir in blackberries. Cover with plastic wrap, folding back one edge to allow steam to escape. Microwave at HIGH 3 minutes or until sugar dissolves, stirring twice.

3. Uncover and microwave at HIGH 8 to 10 minutes or until berries are very soft and liquid reduces and thickens slightly.

4. Stir in lemon juice. Cool, cover, and chill overnight. Jam continues to thicken as it chills. Store refrigerated up to 1 week.

From the kitchen of Nora Henshaw
Okemah, Oklahoma

PEACH CHUTNEY

Chutney originated in India and spread around the globe with the spice trade. It was a popular condiment for Country Captain and other similar Lowcountry dishes.

Makes about 2 pt.

1	Tbsp. vegetable oil	⅓	cup golden raisins
1	medium-size sweet onion, chopped	½	cup granulated sugar
1	Tbsp. finely chopped fresh ginger	½	cup firmly packed light brown sugar
1	garlic clove, finely chopped	2	Tbsp. fresh lime juice
1	cup white wine vinegar	1	Tbsp. brandy
2	lb. peaches, peeled and cut into chunks	½	tsp. salt
1	Granny Smith apple, chopped	½	cup chopped toasted pecans
½	cup dried cherries		

1. Heat oil in large saucepan over medium-high heat. Add onion, ginger, and garlic; cook 3 minutes. Stir in vinegar, peaches, apple, cherries, raisins, granulated sugar, brown sugar, lime juice, brandy, and salt.

2. Bring to a boil, stirring until sugar dissolves. Reduce heat, and simmer, stirring occasionally, 1 hour or until thickened. (Do not let fruit turn mushy.) Stir in pecans.

3. Pour into 2 (1-pt.) jars. Cool, cover, and store refrigerated up to 2 weeks.

From the kitchen of Rebecca Rather
Fredericksburg, Texas

STRAWBERRY FREEZER JAM

The idea of preserving jam in the freezer popped up in the early 1980s, but as companies continue to offer premeasured, convenient forms of pectin, including one designed especially for freezer jam, the recipe continues to get easier. These days, there are also plastic freezer jars for this type of jam. (Pictured on page 266)

Makes about 5 cups

6 cups whole, capped strawberries
1½ cups sugar

1 (1.6-oz.) envelope no-cook freezer-jam fruit pectin

1. Place strawberries in freezer until partially frozen, about 4 hours. (If starting with frozen berries, place in refrigerator until partially thawed, about 4 hours.)
2. Pulse strawberries in a food processor until chunky, stopping to scrape down sides. Pour mixture into a medium bowl.
3. Stir in sugar, and let stand 15 minutes.
4. Gradually stir in pectin. Stir for 3 minutes. Let stand 30 minutes.
5. Spoon into 1-cup freezer jars, filling to ¾ inch from top. Wipe jar rims clean. Screw on lids. Store frozen up to 6 months or refrigerated up to 2 weeks.

From the kitchen of Susan Erickson
Pocahontas, Arkansas

HINT:

This jam can be made with fresh or frozen berries, but the trick is to start with partially frozen berries, which reduces the wateriness that can plague some freezer jams. If, despite this, your jam turns out juicier than you'd hoped, use it as fruit syrup.

YAM JAM

This cute name is what one clever cook called sweet potato butter. A yam is a completely different vegetable from sweet potatoes, but many of us use the words interchangeably, especially in the Deep South.

Similar to apple butter, this silky fruit butter is heavenly. This is certainly not the only recipe in which a resourceful cook used naturally sweet yams in place of fruit. When boiling sweet potatoes to make puree to use in a recipe, be sure to leave them whole. It takes a few minutes longer, but it keeps the potatoes from getting water-logged with diluted flavor. Compared to the deeply caramelized flavor of roasted sweet potatoes, boiled sweet potatoes are very delicate.

Makes 3 pt.

2	lb. small sweet potatoes, scrubbed but not peeled	2	tsp. ground cinnamon
2	tsp. salt	½	tsp. ground ginger
2	cups sugar	1	Tbsp. fresh lemon juice
¾	cup unsweetened apple cider or water	1	tsp. vanilla extract

1. Place potatoes in a large saucepan. Cover with water, and add salt. Boil 40 minutes or until potatoes are tender. Drain. Peel potatoes, and puree in a food processor or force through a food mill.

2. Pour puree into a large saucepan. Add sugar, cider, cinnamon, and ginger. Cook over medium-high heat, stirring constantly, for 10 to 15 minutes or until mixture thickens. Remove from heat, and stir in lemon juice and vanilla.

3. Pour into 3 (1-pt.) hot, sterilized jars. Run a wooden skewer around the inside of the jars to remove any trapped air bubbles. Wipe jar rims clean. Cover with lids, and screw on bands.

4. Process jars in a boiling water bath for 10 minutes. Remove jars to a wire rack to cool undisturbed. Test the seals, and promptly refrigerate any jars that did not seal.

From the kitchen of Mrs. Natalie Monat
Arlington, Virginia

MUSCADINE SAUCE

The oldest cultivated grapevine in North America grows on the northern tip of Roanoke Island in North Carolina. Affectionately known as The Mother Vine, this single vine once covered nearly a half-acre and has produced fruit for nearly 400 years. Compared to the imported, thin-skinned, seedless grapes found in the grocery stores, our native muscadines might seem like a lot of trouble, but they are worth it for their flavor, perfume, and musky sweetness.

Makes 5 pt.

5   lb. muscadine grapes
9   cups sugar
2   cups cider vinegar (5% acidity)
1   Tbsp. ground cinnamon
1   Tbsp. ground allspice
1   tsp. ground cloves

1. Squeeze pulp from grapes into a bowl, reserving skins.
2. Bring pulp to a boil in a saucepan; reduce heat to medium, and cook 20 minutes or until seeds separate from pulp. Force through a food mill, or push with a spatula through a wire-mesh strainer into a large saucepan, discarding solids.
3. Stir in reserved skins and sugar. Cook, stirring occasionally, over medium heat, 2 hours or until thickened.
4. Stir in vinegar, cinnamon, allspice, and cloves. Cook 10 to 15 minutes or until a candy thermometer registers 225° to 230°.
5. Ladle hot mixture into 5 (1-pt.) hot, sterilized jars, filling to ½ inch from top. Run a wooden skewer around the inside of the jars to remove any trapped air bubbles. Wipe the jar rims clean. Cover with lids, and screw on bands.
6. Process jars in a boiling water bath for 20 minutes. Let jars stand in hot water for 5 minutes. Remove jars to a wire rack to cool undisturbed. Test the seals, and promptly refrigerate any jars that did not seal.

From the kitchen of Jennie Hart Robinson
Fort Valley, Georgia

HINT:

When making this sauce, which can be used as we might use thin cranberry sauce, Jennie Hart Robinson reminds us, "This is a sauce, not a jelly. It will have some run to it. Don't overcook it, or it won't come out of the jar."

HOT and SWEET NO-COOK PICKLES

These pickles are so quick and easy that some people fondly call them "cheater pickles." Each jar gives us three tasty things to eat: pickles, pickled peppers, and brine to use in other recipes, such as vinaigrette, potato salad, or deviled eggs.

Makes 1 qt.

1   (46-oz.) jar dill pickles, drained
18 Thai chile peppers or 2 large sliced
    jalapeño or serrano peppers
2   cups sugar
1   Tbsp. white wine vinegar

1. Cut pickles into ¼-inch-thick slices. Make 4 lengthwise slits in each chile pepper, keeping stem end intact. Layer pickle slices alternately with peppers in pickle jar.
2. Gradually add sugar, tapping bottom of jar gently on a flat surface to allow sugar to settle in jar. Add vinegar.
3. Cover with lid, and let stand at room temperature 1 hour, shaking jar occasionally. Chill 8 hours, shaking jar occasionally to ensure even chile pepper heat distribution. Store refrigerated up to 2 weeks.

SWEET NO-COOK PICKLES:

Omit peppers. Cut pickles as directed in Step 1; return to pickle jar. Proceed with recipe as directed.

From the kitchen of Anita Wilbanks
Canton, Georgia

QUITE A PICKLE

Pickling is a long-standing Southern tradition.

If you are looking to try your hand at pickling something delicious and different, have a go at these gorgeous spicy-tart grapes. The recipe comes together in a minute and the pickling actually happens in the fridge in only a few hours. The results are simply amazing. Pickled grapes are fruity, yet reminiscent of great brine-cured pitted olives.

These curious pickles reveal the oldest traditions and newest practices in home pickling. In the many decades before refrigeration enabled shipping and long storage, home cooks endeavored to make fresh food last as long as possible after the harvest. Pickling was a fundamental preservation method for fresh produce, including fruits and berries. Over time, the availability of imported foods and store-bought supplies has reduced the need for home preservation. Reduced need, however, doesn't always equate to reduced desire. More and more of us are choosing to pickle and preserve because we want to, not because we must. We can pickle what pleases us, in the amounts that are manageable within our schedules and shelf space. Our grandmothers put up gallons of pickles to stash in the cellar, enough to tide us over for months. We are more likely to preserve a couple of pints to stash in the fridge, just enough to tempt us for a couple of weeks.

Pickled grapes sound contemporary, but there is long Southern history of serving pickled grapes from Thanksgiving through New Year's Day as a side dish, condiment, or thoughtful addition to a relish tray. We can also use pickled grapes in salads, on a cheese and charcuterie tray, as a bar snack, or cocktail garnish. Their pleasing sweet-sour flavor, crisp texture, and hint of heat make them addictive. Moreover, the grapes look stunning in the jar. Isn't it nice when a condiment jar can also serve as a centerpiece?

This traditional recipe with a thoroughly modern twist comes to us from Matt Lee and Ted Lee, also known as The Lee Bros., authors of award-winning Southern cookbooks and noted bons vivants.

PICKLED GRAPES *with* ROSEMARY *and* CHILES

Add these gorgeous spicy-tart grapes to an antipasto platter or cheese plate, or stir them into chicken or mixed green salads. Guests will love the complex flavors. But the best part is the astonishingly quick results: Prep time is only 10 minutes, and the "pickling" happens in the fridge in only a few hours.

Makes 3 pt.

3   cups seedless green grapes (about 1 lb.)
3   cups seedless red grapes (about 1 lb.)
5   (4-inch-long) fresh rosemary sprigs, divided
2   cups white wine vinegar

3   garlic cloves, thinly sliced
2   Tbsp. kosher salt
2   tsp. sugar
½   tsp. dried crushed red pepper

1. Pack grapes into 3 (1-pt.) canning jars with lids. Add 1 rosemary sprig to each jar.
2. Bring vinegar, garlic, salt, sugar, crushed red pepper, 1 cup water, and remaining 2 rosemary sprigs to a simmer in a medium saucepan. Remove from heat; discard rosemary sprigs. Pour hot vinegar mixture over grapes.
3. Cover loosely until cool (about 30 minutes).
Cover tightly, and chill 1 hour before serving.
Store refrigerated up to 2 weeks.

From the kitchen of Matt Lee and Ted Lee
Charleston, South Carolina

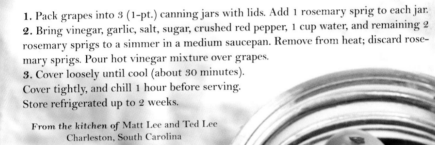

PICKLED OKRA

One could make a convincing argument that this is the most Southern of all pickles. Crisp okra pickles are the only way that some people will eat, perhaps even try, okra. The okra pods stand upright like sentries on guard inside the jars, so if your okra pods are very small, then use half-pint jars instead.

Elizabeth says that her recipe is very forgiving, reassuring us that "You'd have to work to mess it up."

Makes 5 pt.

2¼ lb. small fresh okra pods
5 garlic cloves
5 serrano peppers
5 tsp. dill seeds

5 tsp. mustard seeds
4 cups cider vinegar (5% acidity)
¼ cup pickling salt

1. Brush okra lightly with a piece of nylon net or a brush to remove "fuzz." Trim stems from okra. Pack okra vertically in 5 (1-pt.) hot, sterilized jars, filling to ½ inch from top. Turn half of the pods tips up and half tips down to pack okra tightly.
2. Add 1 garlic clove, 1 serrano pepper, 1 tsp. dill seeds, and 1 tsp. mustard seeds to each jar.
3. Bring vinegar, ½ cup water, and pickling salt to a boil in a large saucepan over medium heat. Ladle vinegar mixture into jars, filling to ½ inch from top. Okra must be submerged. Run a wooden skewer around the inside of the jars to remove any trapped air bubbles. Wipe the jar rims clean. Cover with lids, and screw on bands.
4. Process jars in a boiling water bath for 10 minutes. Let jars stand in hot water for 5 minutes. Remove jars to a wire rack to cool undisturbed. Test the seals, and promptly refrigerate any jars that did not seal. Let stand at least 7 days before serving.

From the kitchen of Elizabeth Gourlay Heiskell
Oxford, Mississippi

HINT:

Yes, it really is this easy. To get started, you'll need a basic canner, a canning rack, and a jar lifter. Look for a 9- or 12-piece canning kit, which will include all of these pieces and more. There are also small-batch canning kits that enable you to process three 1-pt. jars in a Dutch oven or stockpot.

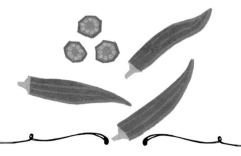

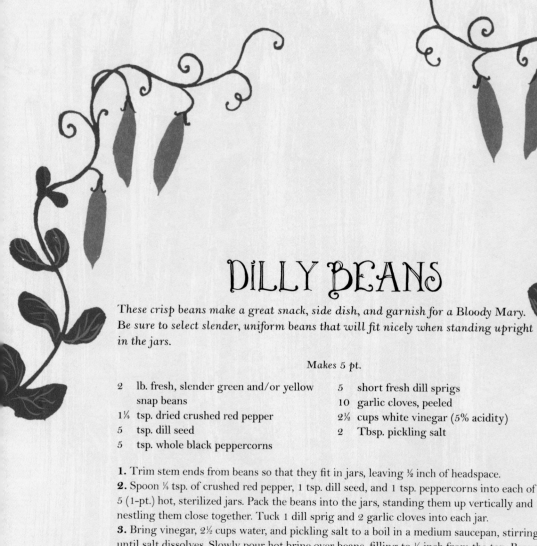

DILLY BEANS

These crisp beans make a great snack, side dish, and garnish for a Bloody Mary. Be sure to select slender, uniform beans that will fit nicely when standing upright in the jars.

Makes 5 pt.

2	lb. fresh, slender green and/or yellow snap beans	5	short fresh dill sprigs
1¼	tsp. dried crushed red pepper	10	garlic cloves, peeled
5	tsp. dill seed	2½	cups white vinegar (5% acidity)
5	tsp. whole black peppercorns	2	Tbsp. pickling salt

1. Trim stem ends from beans so that they fit in jars, leaving ½ inch of headspace.

2. Spoon ¼ tsp. of crushed red pepper, 1 tsp. dill seed, and 1 tsp. peppercorns into each of 5 (1-pt.) hot, sterilized jars. Pack the beans into the jars, standing them up vertically and nestling them close together. Tuck 1 dill sprig and 2 garlic cloves into each jar.

3. Bring vinegar, 2½ cups water, and pickling salt to a boil in a medium saucepan, stirring until salt dissolves. Slowly pour hot brine over beans, filling to ½ inch from the top. Beans must be submerged.

4. Run a wooden skewer around the inside of the jars to remove any trapped air bubbles. Wipe the jar rims clean. Cover with lids, and screw on bands. Process the jars in a boiling water bath for 10 minutes.

5. Remove jars to a wire rack to cool undisturbed. Test the seals, and promptly refrigerate any jars that did not seal. Let stand at least 2 weeks before serving.

From the kitchen of Alice Byers
Mayfield, Kentucky

SQUASH PICKLES

When summer squash season is in high gear, we have so much squash that we cannot eat it all. So, we preserve some of this copious bounty by making pickles. The key to crisp squash pickles is to use small squash and zucchini with thin skins and small, tender seeds.

Makes 7 pt.

6	cups sliced yellow squash	3	cups white vinegar (5% acidity)
6	cups sliced zucchini	4½	cups sugar
2	cups sliced onion	2	tsp. celery seeds
1	Tbsp. pickling salt	2	tsp. mustard seeds
1	green bell pepper, diced		

1. Combine squash, zucchini, and onion. Sprinkle with pickling salt, and let stand 1 hour. Drain. Add bell pepper. Pack into 7 (1-pt.) hot, sterilized jars.
2. Bring vinegar, sugar, celery seed, and mustard seeds to a boil, stirring until sugar dissolves.
3. Pour hot mixture into jars, filling to within ½ inch of the rim. Run a wooden skewer around the inside of the jars to remove any trapped air bubbles. Wipe the jar rims clean. Cover with lids, and screw on bands.
4. Process jars in a boiling water bath for 20 minutes. Let jars stand in hot water for 5 minutes. Remove jars to a wire rack to cool undisturbed. Test the seals, and promptly refrigerate any jars that did not seal.

SQUASH REFRIGERATOR PICKLES:

Fill jars as described in Step 3, but rather than closing jars, leave them open to cool. Cover and chill 3 days before serving. Store refrigerated up to 2 months.

From the kitchen of Patricia Ann Hill
Elizabethton, Tennessee

HINT:

When making pickles, pay close attention to the
type of vinegar and salt specified in the recipe. The 5% acidity
level of the vinegar plays a critical role in safe storage, so double
check the information on the bottle. Likewise, canning
recipes often specify pickling or canning salt because those
types do not contain iodine, which can darken the
fruits and vegetables inside the jars.

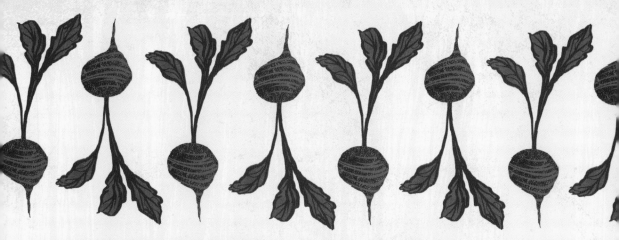

PICKLED BEETS

Many of us love pickled beets, but some of us think that the best part is using the leftover tangy, bright magenta brine to pickle hard-cooked eggs. Be sure to use the smallest and freshest beets available. As beets grow larger and older, they get tougher and lose their wonderful earthy sweetness. You can use beets of any color, but if even one beet is red, all of them will be stained. It's like leaving that one red sock in a load of white laundry.

Makes 8 servings

1¾ lb. small fresh beets
2 small onions, halved and sliced
10 whole cloves
2 (3-inch) cinnamon sticks

2 cups white vinegar (5% acidity)
1 cup sugar
1½ Tbsp. salt

1. Cut tops from beets, leaving a 1-inch stem. Place beets in a large saucepan, and add water to cover. Bring to a boil, reduce heat, and simmer for 30 minutes or until tender. Drain, reserving 3 cups liquid.
2. Pack beets and sliced onion into 5 (1-pt.) hot, sterilized jars.
3. Tie cloves loosely in a cheesecloth bag.
4. Bring reserved 3 cups beet cooking liquid, spice bag, cinnamon sticks, vinegar, sugar, and salt to a boil in a large pot. Remove and discard spice bag and cinnamon sticks. Pour hot mixture into jars, filling to within ½ inch from top. Run a wooden skewer around the inside of the jars to remove any trapped air bubbles. Wipe the jar rims clean. Cover with lids, and screw on bands.
5. Process jars in a boiling water bath for 10 minutes. Let jars stand in hot water for 5 minutes. Remove jars to a wire rack to cool undisturbed. Test the seals, and promptly refrigerate any jars that did not seal.

PINK PICKLED EGGS:

Consider using the gorgeous leftover beet brine to pickle eggs. It's easy. Place 4 whole, peeled, hard-cooked eggs in a heatproof 1-qt. glass jar. Bring the brine to a simmer, and pour over eggs, making sure eggs are submerged in the pickling liquid. Let stand at room temperature for 2 hours. Cover and refrigerate overnight. Store refrigerated up to 1 week.

From the kitchen of Ethel Whalen
Lexington, Kentucky

PICKLED PEACHES

Makes about 3 qt.

4	(2-inch) cinnamon sticks	8	lb. firm, ripe, small peaches
2	Tbsp. whole cloves	6	cups sugar
1	Tbsp. pickling salt	1	Tbsp. ground ginger
1	qt. plus 1 Tbsp. white vinegar (5% acidity), divided		

1. Tie cinnamon and cloves loosely in a cheesecloth bag. Set aside.

2. Make acidulated water by stirring together 2 qt. water, pickling salt, and 1 Tbsp. vinegar in a large glass mixing bowl; stir well.

3. Peel each peach, and immediately drop into acidulated water. Set aside.

4. Combine sugar, ginger, and remaining 1 qt. vinegar in a stainless steel or other nonaluminum stockpot, stirring until sugar dissolves. Bring to a boil; boil 5 minutes. Add spice bag.

5. Drain peaches; rinse in cold water, and drain well. Carefully add to boiling syrup mixture. Boil until peaches are tender, but not soft. Remove from heat; cover and let stand overnight in a cool place, allowing peaches to plump. Discard spice bag.

6. Return peach mixture to a boil; remove from heat. Quickly pack peaches into 3 (1-qt.) hot, sterilized jars.

7. Cover with hot syrup, filling to ½ inch from top. Run a wooden skewer around the inside of the jars to remove any trapped air bubbles. Wipe the jar rims clean. Cover with lids, and screw on bands.

8. Process jars in a boiling water bath for 20 minutes. Let jars stand in hot water for 5 minutes. Remove jars to a wire rack to cool undisturbed. Test the seals, and promptly refrigerate any jars that did not seal.

From the kitchen of Gwen Louer
Roswell, Georgia

Taste of THE SOUTH

peaches

The South is renowned for its excellent peaches, but we all know that peaches are a fleeting treat. In the days before freezing and other handy methods, many cooks preserved their precious peaches in brine or brandy. There is nothing quite like the flavor, aroma, and texture of pickled peaches. They make a lovely accompaniment with roasted meats, particularly a holiday ham, but some of us find them irresistible with vanilla ice cream.

BEVERAGES
and
LIBATIONS

BLOODY MARYS by THE PITCHER

A great Bloody Mary is a must-have at brunch for some of us. Rather than make several cocktails one by one in glasses, why not stir them up by the pitcher? If your guests cannot agree on an amount of vodka, or perhaps want none at all, omit it from the base recipe and serve it on the side.

Makes 1½ qt.

46 oz. low-sodium vegetable juice, chilled
1   Tbsp. freshly ground black pepper
3   Tbsp. fresh lime juice
1   Tbsp. hot sauce

1   Tbsp. Worcestershire sauce
½   tsp. Old Bay seasoning
½   cup vodka, chilled
Garnish: celery sticks (optional)

1. Stir together vegetable juice, pepper, lime juice, hot sauce, Worcestershire, and Old Bay in a large pitcher.
2. Stir in vodka.
3. Serve over ice.

From the kitchen of Regina Hall
Chincoteague Island, Virginia

CAROLINA PEACH SANGRIA

This delicious peach sangria calls for fresh peach slices, fresh raspberries, and peach nectar for its fantastic flavor. Be sure to use rosé, not white Zinfandel, in this cool sangria.

Makes about 9 cups

1   (750-milliliter) bottle rosé wine
¾   cup vodka*
½   cup peach nectar
6   Tbsp. thawed frozen lemonade
    concentrate

2   Tbsp. sugar
1   lb. ripe peaches, peeled and sliced
1   (6-oz.) package fresh raspberries**
2   cups club soda, chilled

1. Combine first 5 ingredients in a pitcher; stir until sugar is dissolved. Stir in peaches and raspberries. Cover and chill 8 hours.
2. Stir in chilled club soda just before serving.
* Peach-flavored vodka may be substituted. Omit peach nectar.
** 1 cup frozen raspberries may be substituted.

From the kitchens of Willson Powell and Karen Brosius
Columbia, South Carolina

JULIAN'S OLD FASHIONED

Many of us associate the Van Winkle family with some of the best bourbon in the world. We can trust Julian's precise advice on making an old-fashioned cocktail.

Makes 1 serving

1	to 2 brown sugar cubes	1	fresh orange slice
2	to 3 drops of orange bitters	1½	to 2 oz. bourbon
2	to 3 drops of Angostura bitters		Ice cubes

1. Place brown sugar cubes on a cocktail napkin. Sprinkle orange bitters and Angostura bitters over sugar cubes. (Napkin will soak up excess bitters.) Transfer cubes to a 10-oz. old-fashioned glass.

2. Add orange slice and a few drops bourbon to glass. Mash sugar cubes and orange slice, using a muddler, until sugar is almost dissolved. (Avoid mashing the rind, which can release a bitter flavor.)

3. Add 1½ to 2 oz. bourbon, and fill glass with ice cubes. Stir until well chilled. Add more bourbon, if desired.

From the kitchen of Julian Van Winkle
Louisville, Kentucky

MILK PUNCH

Not everyone has had a chance to enjoy a delicious milk punch. It is served cold and usually has nutmeg sprinkled on top. It is similar to eggnog, but less rich. At least one batch of Milk Punch is traditional on holidays throughout the Deep South and remains a popular brunch beverage in New Orleans. (Pictured at left)

Makes about 5 cups

2	cups milk	1½	tsp. vanilla extract
2	cups half-and-half		Crushed ice
1	cup brandy or bourbon		Freshly grated nutmeg
½	cup sifted powdered sugar		

1. Whisk together milk, half-and-half, brandy, powdered sugar, and vanilla in a pitcher.

2. Serve over crushed ice. Top each serving with freshly grated nutmeg.

From the kitchen of Natalie Broulette
New York, New York

HINT:

Natalie tells us, "It's unusual to find a cold drink that gives you that sense of holiday coziness, but this one does. Grate the nutmeg fresh. It makes a difference."

BOURBON SLUSH

For a region that shudders at the very mention of slushy precipitation on the roads, we sure do enjoy slushy bourbon drinks.

Makes about 3 qt.

1 (6-oz.) can frozen orange juice concentrate, thawed
1 (6-oz.) can frozen limeade concentrate, thawed
1 (6-oz.) can frozen lemonade concentrate, thawed

2 cups bourbon
1 (1-liter) bottle club soda, chilled
Garnishes: lemon, lime, and orange slices, maraschino cherries

1. Stir together orange juice, limeade, and lemonade concentrates, 4½ cups water, and bourbon. Pour into a 1-gal. zip-top freezer bag. Close tightly; seal. Freeze until solid, at least 8 hours.

2. About 1 hour before serving, remove from freezer, and let stand 1 hour or until beginning to melt. Using hands, squeeze bag until mixture is slushy. Spoon into pitchers or divide among serving glasses.

3. Stir in club soda, and serve immediately.

From the kitchen of Cham and Edie Light
Lynchburg, Virginia

Taste of THE SOUTH

bourbon

Many of us believe that bourbon is one of the dearest gifts that the South has bestowed on the world. Despite what we are often told, bourbon doesn't always have to come from Kentucky, even though the Bluegrass State is home to many of the finest. Bourbon does, however, have to be made in the U.S., aged in new charred white oak barrels, made from a grain mixture that's at least 51% corn, distilled below 160 proof, and placed in the barrels below 125 proof.

UMATILLA SMASH

Makes 1 serving

1   Tbsp. Kumquat Confit
1   to 3 thin fresh jalapeño pepper slices
3   Tbsp. whiskey
    Crushed ice
    Club soda, chilled

Muddle Kumquat Confit and jalapeño pepper slices against sides of an 8-oz. glass to release flavors. Stir in whiskey and enough crushed ice to fill glass halfway; top with chilled club soda.

KUMQUAT CONFIT:

Cut kumquats from 1 (8-oz.) container into thin slices, and place in a medium bowl. Combine 1 cup sugar and ½ cup water in a small saucepan; bring to a boil over medium-high heat, stirring often. Boil, stirring often, 1 minute. Pour mixture over kumquats; let stand at room temperature 30 minutes.

From the kitchen of James Petrakis
Winter Park, Florida

WHISKEY PUNCH

Makes 30 cups

2   liters whiskey or bourbon
½   liter dark rum
1¼ cups sugar
7   cups strong-brewed tea
3½ cups fresh lemon juice
2   qt. orange juice

Stir together all ingredients in a large crock or food-safe container. Cover and chill up to 3 days before serving.

NOTE: For strong-brewed tea, pour 5 cups boiling water over 2 family-size tea bags; cover and steep 5 minutes. Remove tea bags from water, squeezing gently. Add 2 cups cold water.

From the kitchen of Greg McMillan
Glade Spring, Virginia

SIT *and* CHAT

This punch is a communal cocktail. Greg says that he found the original recipe for this potent punch in a local Episcopal church cookbook and later learned that it was included as a joke. He tinkered with the proportions, and the punch has become a staple at his annual holiday social for faculty and staff at Emory & Henry College.

CHAMPAGNE PUNCH with FRUITED ICE RING

A gorgeous punch bowl benefits from a lovely ice ring like a classic dress benefits from the perfect necklace. (Pictured on page 292)

Makes about 2½ qt.

2   cups cranberry juice cocktail
1   (12-oz.) can frozen orange juice concentrate, thawed
1   cup lemon juice
1   cup sugar

1   (375-milliliter) bottle Sauterne or dessert wine
2   (750-milliliter) bottles Champagne, chilled

1. Stir together cranberry juice, orange juice concentrate, lemon juice, and sugar, mixing well. Chill at least 8 hours.
2. Pour juice mixture into a chilled punch bowl. Gently stir in Sauterne and Champagne just before serving. Float Fruited Ice Ring, fruit side up, in punch.

FRUITED ICE RING

Makes 1 ice ring

1½ to 2 cups orange juice
½   cup cranberry juice
6   to 8 seedless red grape clusters

10 to 12 orange slices, seeded
8   to 10 whole strawberries
Mint sprigs

1. Stir together orange juice and cranberry juice in a bowl.
2. Line bottom of a 6-cup ring mold with grape clusters and half of orange slices, using grapes to stand orange slices vertically. Pour a thin layer of orange juice mixture into mold. Freeze until firm, about 2 hours.
3. Arrange remaining orange slices, strawberries, and mint sprigs around grapes. Pour remaining juice mixture around fruit, filling to ½ inch from the top. Freeze 8 hours.
4. Unmold by dipping bottom half of mold in several inches of warm water 5 to 10 seconds to loosen, repeating as necessary to release ring. (Do not immerse entire mold in water.) Invert ring onto plate.

easy ICE RING:

Combine juices. Fill bottom of 6-cup ring mold with 2 cups crushed ice. Lay grape clusters over ice. Arrange orange slices, strawberries, and fresh mint sprigs around grapes. Pour juices around fruit, filling to ½ inch from the top. Freeze 8 hours or until firm.

From the kitchen of Boots Abercrombie
Birmingham, Alabama

MELON AGUA FRESCA

Agua fresca, Spanish for "fresh water," is incredibly refreshing during the hot months. In Mexico and all over Latin America, cups of agua fresca are sold by street vendors during the spring and summer months. This treat is easy to make at home. Juicy fruit, water, and sugar—that's pretty much it. If you like bubbles in your beverage, use soda water.

Makes about 5 cups

4   cups cubed seedless watermelon, cantaloupe, or honeydew melon
2   cups cold water
2   to 4 Tbsp. sugar
Juice of 2 to 3 limes
Garnish: lime slices

1. Process melon in a blender until smooth, stopping to scrape down sides as needed. Pour puree through a fine wire-mesh strainer into a pitcher. Discard solids.
2. Stir in 2 cups cold water. Add sugar and lime juice to taste. Cover and chill until ready to serve. Serve over ice.

From the kitchen of Maria Corbalan
Austin, Texas

Homemade Tomato Juice

3 lb very ripe tomatoes, cored and quartered

1/2 cup chopped celery with leaves

1/3 cup chopped onion

1 large sprig fresh parsley

1/4 tsp paprika

1 bay leaf

1/2 tsp sugar

1/2 tsp salt

MAKES ABOUT 2 QT

1 Bring tomatoes, onion, celery, parsley, and bay leaf to a boil. Reduce heat, and simmer for 30 minutes or until mixture is soft.

2 Remove from heat, and let stand for 30 minutes. Discard parsley and bay leaf.

3 Process mixture in a blender until smooth. Pour through a fine-mesh strainer, and discard solids.

4 Stir in salt, paprika, and sugar. Cover and chill.

From the Kitchen of Peggy Fowler Revels Woodruff, South Carolina

FRESH-SQUEEZED LEMONADE

This is the real deal. Try this old-fashioned fresh-squeezed lemonade recipe, which expertly balances sweet and tart. One sip will confirm why lemonade is a beloved summertime beverage. (Pictured at left)

Makes 8 cups

1½ cups sugar
½ cup boiling water
1 Tbsp. freshly grated lemon zest

1½ cups fresh lemon juice
5 cups cold water

1. Stir together sugar and boiling water in a large pitcher until sugar dissolves.
2. Stir in lemon zest, lemon juice, and 5 cups cold water. Chill. Serve over ice.

From the kitchen of Ginger Gentry
Soddy-Daisy, Tennessee

CALYPSO PRESBYTERIAN CHURCH WOMEN'S LIME PUNCH

This is what some of us call, with great admiration, fellowship hall punch. Who can begin to guess how many gallons have been served at hometown wedding receptions over the years? You can use different flavors of gelatin and sherbet if you prefer the punch to be another color.

Makes 1½ gal.

1 (3-oz.) package lime-flavored gelatin
2 cups sugar
2 cups boiling water
2 cups lemon juice
12 cups pineapple juice

1 (12-oz.) can orange juice concentrate, thawed
1 (2-liter) bottle ginger ale, chilled
1 qt. lime sherbet (optional)

1. Stir together gelatin, sugar, and 2 cups boiling water in a 1½-gal. container, stirring until sugar dissolves.
2. Stir in lemon juice, pineapple juice, and orange juice concentrate. Cover and chill.
3. Pour mixture into a large punch bowl.
4. Just before serving, stir in ginger ale; if desired, drop sherbet by small scoopfuls into punch.

From the kitchen of Carolyn Kornegay
Gray, Tennessee

PARTY PUNCH

Every great gathering needs one.

If there's punch, then it's a party. Punch not only sounds like a happy thing, it is a one-step answer to the question of what beverages to serve our guests. Rather than mixing and matching a bar full of choices, all our efforts can be focused into a single punch bowl or pitcher.

This beautiful, refreshing, slightly effervescent punch combines several favorite Southern summertime beverages and flavors: freshly brewed sweet tea, lemonade, ginger ale, peaches, and mint. The peaches come in the form of nectar, a concentrated fruit juice that delivers the deep flavor of fruit puree that is integral to the recipe. The punch's sweetness comes from a stroke of sugary genius: simple syrup. Making simple syrup is a simple thing, requiring nothing more than dissolving sugar in boiling water to make clear, sweet syrup that mixes easily and completely into any beverage, even ice-cold tea, without us having to stir and stir and stir. Simple syrup keeps well for days at room temperature, ready and waiting to be called into service.

The governor's mansion credited in this recipe title is in Austin, Texas, and this recipe hails from *Austin Entertains,* compiled by the Junior League of Austin. League members report that hundreds, perhaps thousands, of gallons of this punch have been poured at the mansion over the years. Although not always printed along with the recipe, word got around that a tasty way to spike this punch is to add 2 cups of vodka.

GOVERNOR'S MANSION SUMMER PEACH TEA PUNCH

This refreshing, summery peach tea punch is perfect for bridal or baby showers, garden parties, and elegant teas.

Makes about 1 gal.

½   cup sugar
3   family-size tea bags
2   cups loosely packed fresh mint leaves
1   (33.8-oz.) bottle peach nectar
½   (12-oz.) can frozen lemonade concentrate, thawed
1   (1-liter) bottle ginger ale, chilled
1   (1-liter) bottle club soda, chilled
Garnishes: fresh peach wedges, fresh mint

1. Make simple sugar syrup by bringing sugar and ¼ cup water to a boil in a small saucepan over medium-high heat. Boil, stirring occasionally, 2 minutes or until sugar dissolves. Cool to room temperature (about 30 minutes).
2. Bring 4 cups water to a boil in a medium saucepan. Add tea bags and mint leaves. Boil 1 minute, remove from heat, cover, and steep 10 minutes. Discard tea bags and mint. Pour into a 1-gal. container.
3. Add peach nectar, lemonade concentrate, and simple sugar syrup. Cover and chill 8 to 24 hours.
4. Pour chilled tea mixture into a punch bowl or pitcher. Stir in ginger ale and club soda just before serving.

Austin Entertains
Junior League of Austin, Texas

CAJUN COOKING

Talk About Good!
(Copyright 1967; The Junior League of Lafayette, Louisiana)

We have to appreciate a cookbook that is unequivocal about the appeal of its recipes, and says so right on the cover. When the very title of a cookbook is an endorsement, how can we resist opening it up and heading to the kitchen? With over 1,200 recipes, this one could keep us busy for a while. This time-honored book has many fans, having sold upwards of 800,000 copies.

This is the cookbook that many people regard as an essential Cajun collection. The first chapter is "Mardi Gras," and gumbo warrants its own section, so there's no mistaking the food and recipes as coming from anywhere other than the heart (and soul) of Southern Louisiana Cajun country. The foreword gives us an overview of the influences, traditions and origins that converge in the wonderful cuisine shared on the pages: "Few locales have such a beautiful blend of heritage from the Indian encampments, the first Spanish explorers, the French whose influence still dominates today, to the German, Scots, Irish, English, and West Indian flavor....From the Attakapas Indians to its present 'pot pourri' [sic], Lafayette's pots, kettles, and pans reflect this mélange."

At the top of the Table of Contents page, a poem lists some of the recipes and ingredients that evoke the diversity of what we collectively call Cajun cooking, an ode to their bounty: "Sugar cane, syrup (cane), saffron, dill and 'roux'. Etouffee, café au lait, flan and bisque and stew. Sabayon and courtbouillion, corn bread, jambalayas, Enchiladas and tostadas, peppery jelly and papayas. Creme glacé, sweet parfait, batter breads and mustard, Chocolate mousse, duck and goose, caramel cup custard!"

SANGRITA

Makes 1¼ cups

⅓ cup fresh orange juice
⅔ cup tomato juice
½ tsp. salt
¼ tsp. freshly ground black pepper
3 Tbsp. fresh lime juice

¼ tsp. Worcestershire sauce
½ tsp. hot sauce
1 Tbsp. minced onion
Serve with: tequila, lime wedges

Stir together all ingredients, and mix well. Chill. Serve in individual shot glasses alongside shot glasses of tequila. Sip alternately.

Talk About Good! Le Livre de la Cuisine de Lafayette
Junior League of Lafayette, Louisiana

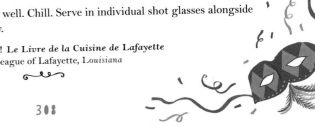

308

FIVE DECADES of READER RECIPES

"We are looking for recipes using peaches and will pay readers $3 for each one we use in *Southern Living*. In submitting your recipe, tell us something of its origin and other foods you would serve with it for a complete meal."

And with those two lines, it began. *Southern Living* called and the readers responded. Since March 1966, hundreds, sometimes thousands, of recipes arrive in the office mailboxes and inboxes each month. Other than the first, every issue of *Southern Living* has included recipes from readers. It's a hallmark of our pages.

Over time, the readers revealed the repertoire of our region. Five decades of published reader recipes covers a lot of territory, both geographically and conceptually. The collection includes recipes so common and popular that they seem universal across the South. It also contains equally Southern recipes that are intensely important to a very specific community, those that capture the very essence of local flavor, but are virtually unknown elsewhere. Finding expected recipes reassures us. Discovering new recipes that exceed our imagination inspires us. We get to say both "Oh my, yes!" and "Who knew?"

Southern Living is savvy enough to know that a great recipe is a great recipe, no matter who created it. Cooks from all walks of life and skill levels can have something worthwhile to share. Any given issue features recipes from amateurs, enthusiasts, home cooks, restaurateurs, trained chefs, bloggers, and cookbook authors. All submissions merit the same consideration, respect, and appreciation. Every recipe is read and the best move on to the Test Kitchen for further evaluation and consideration.

Readers share recipes they are willing to put their name on. That's no small thing. It means the recipe is taste-tested in a home kitchen and approved by those sitting around the family table. In the magazine's professional kitchen, the process is similar: Each workday at 2, the testing team gathers around a Test Kitchen table to give that day's recipes thoughtful and thorough consideration. Each recipe—whether from a reader, freelance recipe developer, or staff member—is evaluated on taste, appearance, practicality, and ease of preparation. Each recipe is tried, tested, tasted, and tweaked until *Southern Living* enthusiastically puts their name on it as well.

At one time the test team was comprised of home economists, mostly women. These days, the test team is made up of women and men who are culinary experts and professionally trained chefs. Their credentials are impressive, but each team member is also a home cook who understands the real-world challenges and opportunities that come with feeding family and friends. When a *Southern Living* reader generously shares a recipe, the team gratefully receives it. They work hard to put the selected recipes on the page in the best way possible.

Each issue aims to present the best recipes the South has to offer. That's how and why the magazine earned the reputation as "The South's Most Trusted Kitchen."

Reader recipes confirm the magazine's belief that each of us is a cook. Some cook daily, some weekly, and some only on special occasions, but we do cook, and we can be really good at it. Readers can brilliantly apply new techniques and ingredients—even new ways of thinking—to our collective recipe box. The goals of readers and the staff are united: We strive to put good food on our tables, prepared in the most efficient and effective way possible. The magazine's food stories wouldn't be nearly as successful, or as much fun, without the tremendous response and cooperation of the readers.

So why did, and do, readers send recipes to *Southern Living*? A hundred cooks would give a hundred valid answers, but all are rooted in generosity. Sharing a recipe is an eminently hospitable thing to do. It also gives readers a chance to be writers, a way to say a little something about themselves and to convey their take on things. A recipe is a snapshot that captures a moment, a family tradition, a hometown quirk, or a holiday ritual. A recipe can reveal the ways we approach an ordinary day and the ways we esteem once-in-a-lifetime events. For many cooks, writing a recipe was the only time they expressed their ways in words.

In the decades before the internet, *Southern Living* was the social media of the time. Handwriting or typing a recipe and mailing it to Birmingham was a home cook's equivalent of posting, pinning, blogging, and tweeting. It was an outlet through which they could share their culinary prowess. These days, the magazine looks to social media as a source for great recipes and food writing. And, in turn, readers post excerpts from the magazine online. Things have a way of coming full circle.

No matter the motivation for submitting a recipe, every person who shares a recipe hopes to see it in the magazine. That prospect is exciting. *Southern Living* enjoys legendary status and clout in home kitchens. To have his or her name and recipe appear in an issue is high praise for a home cook. (To be sure, the pros appreciate such kudos as well.) It can garner bragging rights for generations. It can also make the cook a little bit famous. Published readers tell of becoming local celebrities and hometown heroes, receiving invitations for radio and newspaper interviews. Published recipes are clipped, framed, and displayed proudly for all to see. When cooks see their names on those pages, they feel gratified and validated.

As with any community cookbook, the reader recipes and food stories in *Southern Living* are both a self-portrait and a landscape. We recognize ourselves and have the opportunity to appreciate the scope of what it means to be Southern. Just as there is no single South, there is no single definition for Southern food or single profile for Southern cooks. Reader recipes give us a taste, both literally and figuratively, of the many dishes and cooks who, regardless of where they live or where they come from, claim Southern food as their own, whether for a lifetime or a meal time. So let's fix a plate and raise a glass. There is much to celebrate.

ACKNOWLEDGMENTS

Sheri Castle is an award-winning cookbook author, food writer, and recipe developer who is known for melding storytelling, humor, and culinary expertise. As an experienced cooking teacher, Sheri has taught thousands of people to approach home cooking with confidence. Originally from the Blue Ridge Mountains, she lives in Chapel Hill, North Carolina, with her husband Doug Tidwell, daughter Lily Castle Tidwell, and beloved dog, Domino.

It takes a huge team to bring a cookbook to fruition. I can't thank each talented person individually because I never got to meet them all, but they deserve my heartfelt gratitude nonetheless. Others I can call by name, namely:

Susan Hernandez Ray, my editor at Oxmoor House. Editors navigate the perilous path between the author's wildest dreams and the realities of modern publishing. Susan does that with aplomb.

Hunter Lewis, Executive Editor of *Southern Living,* fellow Tar Heel, and my friend. Hunter appreciates the gems to be found in community cookbooks, especially the hidden food stories. Thank you entrusting this fantastic topic to me.

Melissa Clark of Oxmoor House, whose stunning design made this book a real head turner.

Sara Mulvanny for her charming illustrations. Everyone just loves the chickens.

Becky Luigart-Stayner and her talented styling team for the gorgeous photographs. You didn't just take pictures of food, you created portraits of these recipes.

David Larabell, my agent, for your wise counsel and steadfast support. You help me believe that my pursuit of telling good stories and cooking good food is more than folly.

Doug Tidwell, my well-read husband who is always my first reader. He knows me well and loves me anyhow. Thank you for making me laugh until bourbon squirts out my nose and for your ability to unjam that confounded printer.

Lily Castle Tidwell (my daughter) and Madge Marie Reece Castle (my mama). Through Mama, I got to know how it feels to eat food cooked by someone who adored me. Through Lily, I get to know how it feels to cook for someone I adore. Thank for you being the finest women I will ever know.

Domino, my beloved dog, for being my beloved dog.

No Southern food writer worth her salt can fail to thank John Egerton for his legacy. I considered John to be my good friend, as did every person lucky enough to meet him and benefit from one of his close talks. We miss you. I hope you are now feasting at the ultimate welcome table, saving our seats until we catch up to you.

As preparation for this book, I read every single recipe printed in *Southern Living* from February 1966 through February 2014. I offer my deep respect and gratitude to the talented and devoted professionals at *Southern Living,* past and present, for taking their readers to heart and striving to ensure they remain "the South's most trusted kitchen."

A good cookbook is a found poem. This one wouldn't be possible without the thousands of cooks who took the time to jot down a recipe to share with a family member, a neighbor, a community cookbook, or *Southern Living.* I doubt all of you loved to cook, but all of you seem to have cooked with love.

The recipes that appear in this cookbook use the standard U.S. method for measuring liquid and dry or solid ingredients (teaspoons, tablespoons, and cups). The information in the following charts is provided to help cooks outside the United States successfully use these recipes. All equivalents are approximate.

METRIC EQUIVALENTS FOR DIFFERENT TYPES of INGREDIENTS

A standard cup measure of a dry or solid ingredient will vary in weight depending on the type of ingredient. A standard cup of liquid is the same volume for any type of liquid. Use the following chart when converting standard cup measures to grams (weight) or milliliters (volume).

Standard Cup	Fine Powder (ex. flour)	Grain (ex. rice)	Granular (ex. sugar)	Liquid Solids (ex. butter)	Liquid (ex. milk)
1	140 g	150 g	190 g	200 g	240 ml
¾	105 g	113 g	143 g	150 g	180 ml
⅔	93 g	100 g	125 g	133 g	160 ml
½	70 g	75 g	95 g	100 g	120 ml
⅓	47 g	50 g	63 g	67 g	80 ml
¼	35 g	38 g	48 g	50 g	60 ml
⅛	18 g	19 g	24 g	25 g	30 ml

USEFUL EQUIVALENTS FOR LIQUID INGREDIENTS by VOLUME

¼ tsp					=	1 ml
½ tsp					=	2 ml
1 tsp					=	5 ml
3 tsp	=	1 Tbsp		=	½ fl oz	=	15 ml
		2 Tbsp	=	⅛ cup	1 fl oz	=	30 ml
		4 Tbsp	=	¼ cup	2 fl oz	=	60 ml
		5⅓ Tbsp	=	⅓ cup	3 fl oz	=	80 ml
		8 Tbsp	=	½ cup	4 fl oz	=	120 ml
		10⅔ Tbsp	=	⅔ cup	5 fl oz	=	160 ml
		12 Tbsp	=	¾ cup	6 fl oz	=	180 ml
		16 Tbsp	=	1 cup	8 fl oz	=	240 ml
		1 pt	=	2 cups	16 fl oz	=	480 ml
		1 qt	=	4 cups	32 fl oz	=	960 ml
					33 fl oz	=	1000 ml = 1 l

USEFUL EQUIVALENTS FOR DRY INGREDIENTS by WEIGHT

(To convert ounces to grams, multiply the number of ounces by 30.)

1 oz	=	¹⁄₁₆ lb	=	30 g
4 oz	=	¼ lb	=	120 g
8 oz	=	½ lb	=	240 g
12 oz	=	¾ lb	=	360 g
16 oz	=	1 lb	=	480 g

USEFUL EQUIVALENTS FOR LENGTH

(To convert inches to centimeters, multiply the number of inches by 2.5.)

1 in				=	2.5 cm		
6 in	=	½ ft		=	15 cm		
12 in	=	1 ft		=	30 cm		
36 in	=	3 ft	=	1 yd	=	90 cm		
40 in				=	100 cm	=	1 m

USEFUL EQUIVALENTS FOR COOKING/OVEN TEMPERATURES

	Fahrenheit	Celsius	Gas Mark
Freeze water	32° F	0° C	
Room temperature	68° F	20° C	
Boil water	212° F	100° C	
Bake	325° F	160° C	3
	350° F	180° C	4
	375° F	190° C	5
	400° F	200° C	6
	425° F	220° C	7
	450° F	230° C	8
Broil			Grill

INDEX

ISBN-13: 978-0-8487-4354-3
ISBN-10: 0-8487-4354-7
Library of Congress Control Number: 2014944831

Printed in the United States of America
First Printing 2014

Oxmoor House
Editorial Director: Leah McLaughlin
Creative Director: Felicity Keane
Art Director: Christopher Rhoads
Executive Photo Director: Iain Bagwell
Executive Food Director: Grace Parisi
Senior Editor: Rebecca Brennan
Managing Editor: Elizabeth Tyler Austin
Assistant Managing Editor: Jeanne de Lathouder

Southern Living® **Community Cookbook**
Editor: Susan Hernandez Ray
Project Editor: Emily Chappell Connolly
Senior Designer: Melissa Clark
Editorial Assistant: April Smitherman
Assistant Test Kitchen Manager:
    Alyson Moreland Haynes
Recipe Developers and Testers: Tamara Goldis,
    Stefanie Maloney, Callie Nash, Karen Rankin,
    Leah Van Deren
Food Stylists: Victoria E. Cox, Margaret Monroe Dickey,
    Catherine Crowell Steele
Senior Photographer: Hélène Dujardin
Senior Photo Stylists: Kay E. Clarke,
    Mindi Shapiro Levine
Senior Production Manager: Sue Chodakiewicz
Production Manager: Theresa Beste-Farley

CONTRIBUTORS:
Author: Sheri Castle
Copy Editors: Julie Bosche, Barry Wise Smith
Proofreader: Donna Baldone
Illustrator: Sara Mulvanny
Indexer: Marrathon Production Services
Photo Stylists: Cindy Manning Barr,
    Mary Clayton Carl
Photographers: Jim Bathie, Becky Stayner
Food Stylist: Ana Kelly
Fellows: Ali Carruba, Kylie Dazzo, Elizabeth Laseter,
    Anna Ramia, Deanna Sakal, Megan Thompson

Southern Living®
Editor-in-Chief: Sid Evans
Creative Director: Robert Perino
Managing Editor: Candace Higginbotham
Executive Editors: Hunter Lewis, Jessica S. Thuston
Deputy Food Director: Whitney Wright
Test Kitchen Director: Robby Melvin
Test Kitchen Specialist/Food Styling:
    Vanessa McNeil Rocchio
Test Kitchen Professional: Pam Lolley
Recipe Editor: JoAnn Weatherly
Style Director: Heather Chadduck Hillegas
Director of Photography: Jeanne Dozier Clayton
Photographers: Robbie Caponetto,
    Laurey W. Glenn, Hector Sanchez
Assistant Photo Editor: Kate Phillips Robertson
Photo Coordinator: Chris Ellenbogen
Senior Photo Stylist: Buffy Hargett Miller
Assistant Photo Stylist: Caroline Murphey Cunningham
Photo Administrative Assistant: Courtney Authement
Editorial Assistant: Pat York

Time Home Entertainment Inc.
President and Publisher: Jim Childs
Vice President and Associate Publisher: Margot Schupf
Vice President, Finance: Vandana Patel
Executive Director, Marketing Services:
    Carol Pittard
Publishing Director: Megan Pearlman
Assistant General Counsel:
    Simone Procas